W9-DBT-470

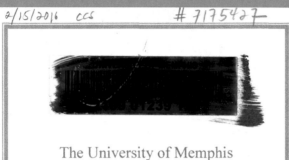

Politics Is My Parish

AN
AUTOBIOGRAPHY
BROOKS
HAYS
Foreword by
Arthur Schlesinger, Jr.

Politics Is My Parish

Louisiana State University Press
Baton Rouge and London

Copyright © 1981 by Louisiana State University Press
All rights reserved
Manufactured in the United States of America

Design: Patricia Douglas Crowder
Typeface: Linotype Sabon
Typesetter: G&S Typesetters, Inc.
Printing: Thomson-Shore, Inc.·
Binding: John Dekker & Sons, Inc.

LIBRARY OF CONGRESS CATALOGING IN PUBLICATION DATA

Hays, Brooks.
   Politics is my parish.

   Includes index.
   1. Hays, Brooks. 2. United States. Congress.
House—Biography. 3. Legislators—United States—
Biography. I. Title.
E748.H3878A33   973.9′092′4 [B]   80-29144
ISBN 0-8071-0798-0

CONTENTS

FOREWORD

THESE are bad times in America, yet Brooks Hays's memoir is an affirmation of hope. Its force derives from the fact that his is hope rooted not in sentimentalism but in experience. He has lived a long life, not without its share of setbacks and disappointments, and he has seen America, and especially the South, change in many ways. *Politics Is My Parish* is, among other things, a notable record of these changes. It describes the transformation of the Old South of segregation and poverty into the booming New South of today. It recalls significant episodes in the struggle, still sadly unfinished, for racial justice. It also illuminates a perennial question: the relationship between religion and politics in a democratic society. And it provides a self-portrait, moving in its very diffidence, of a man of gentle courage, unquenchable humor, and serene faith.

Brooks Hays was born in Arkansas during the administration of William McKinley. As a small boy, he heard William Jennings Bryan in full oratorical flood. He was a fascinated youth in the Senate gallery during the final debate on the Versailles Treaty. He fought the Ku Klux Klan in the 1920s and stood in the anxious crowd at Franklin Roosevelt's first inauguration. He was a front-line soldier in the New Deal's fight against rural poverty and thereafter served eight terms in Congress, until he was defeated because he believed black children should be permitted to exercise their constitutional rights to attend public school in Little Rock.

President Eisenhower made him a director of the Tennessee Valley Authority, and President Kennedy made him first an assistant secretary of state and then a special assistant in the White House. He has been president of the Southern Baptist Convention, an office rarely yielded to a layman; when one Baptist minister objected, "We don't want a politician for president, do we?" another replied, "Well, Brooks ain't enough of a one to count" (or so Brooks likes to tell the story). He is a founder of that useful organization Former Members of Congress, visiting professor in fortunate colleges across the land, unparalleled raconteur, philosopher at large, and one of the best-loved men in America. He loves nearly everyone back, including, on the testimony of this book, such unpromising objects as Orval Faubus and Richard M. Nixon. But his love, like his hope, is realistic, not sentimental.

His sweetness of temper, his realism, his calm courage spring in part from the early years in the hill country of western Arkansas so vividly evoked in this book. These years gave him an appreciation for the strength of character that enabled rural people, for all their limited opportunities, to endure poverty, disease, drought, and storm. At the same time, his parents supplied intimations of larger horizons. He went on to college and law school, met Marion Prather and was blessed with a marriage of singular felicity.

His personal development was shaped too by a profound religious commitment. For a time he considered entering the ministry. Finally he was persuaded that public life, if accompanied by dedication, could be as significant in a religious sense as pastoral service. The Southern Baptist church of his youth seemed to him preoccupied with sterile theological quibbles. The human plight of poor whites and poor blacks did not trouble the white Christian conscience. But for Brooks Hays, as for Walter Rauschenbusch and Reinhold Niebuhr, Christianity was a call to duty; it was judgment as well as consolation. His life has been a quest to find ways of relating religion and politics without violating the constitutional separation of church and state.

The determination to apply Christian ideals to the human environment intensified when the Great Depression brought already destitute tenant farmers and sharecroppers to the edge of despair. And the quest drew him into the problem of racial justice. With characteristic modesty his memoir understates the risks run, the courage required, and the obloquy incurred a generation ago when a southern politician spoke and acted for the rights of black Americans. For a more detailed account of his crucial role in the resolution of the Little Rock crisis, the reader should turn to his book of 1959, *A Southern Moderate Speaks* (University of North Carolina Press).

Though Little Rock ended Brooks Hays's legislative career, it did not affect either his devotion to or effectiveness in the cause of racial justice. He remained, as they had called him in Arkansas in the 1920s, "the Cheerful Crusader." Humor came unbidden to him but turned out to be one of his most potent weapons. *Politics Is My Parish* supplies many examples of the way his stories became a technique of subversion, confounding opposition by stating points in a manner that made those about to thunder against him suddenly feel a little ridiculous. In doing this, he drew on the tradition of southwestern folk humor with its resources of parody and hyperbole and its skill in deadpan turning of the tables. For a generous presentation of the Hays repertoire, the reader is advised to consult his delectable book *Hotbed of Tranquility* (Macmillan, 1968).

For Brooks Hays both religion and politics enjoin a mission to the poor and powerless in society. As he told the Southern Baptist Historical Society in 1976, "From the glib way in which some of the zealous ones speak of Jesus in current discussions, without evidencing an interest in the application of his teachings to social evils, doubt is cast on their understanding of His place in history." He joins Christian determination with Christian gentleness, detests the sin but embraces the sinner, and moves us all because he has, as Senator Sam Ervin noted, "an understanding heart." Or as Martin Luther King, Jr., once said on introducing Brooks Hays to a friend: "This is Mr. Hays. He has suffered with us."

ARTHUR SCHLESINGER, JR.

ACKNOWLEDGMENTS

I wish it were possible in this account of my public service to provide an adequate picture of the vital part played by the staffs of my various assignments. I am aware of the burdens that my staff members bore and the concern they had for the success of our joint undertakings. I am deeply grateful for the help I received from this grand group of associates:

In the Congress, John S. McLees, Paul L. Barnard, Lurlene Wilbert, Claude Curlin, H. A. (Dick) Emerson, Kitty Johnson, Warren I. Cikins, Ann Lyon Shub, Grace Crane Stokes, Imogene Dunlap, Annette Grace, Ruth Murphree, and Jason Rouby. Under the boundless exertions of John McLees, whose title in military terms would have been "chief of staff," the administrative performance of our office was unexcelled.

In the TVA, Dorothy Morgan.

In the White House, Stephanie Floyd, Paula Roberts, Martha Creed, Norma Tema, and Mary Ferro.

In the Ecumenical Institute, Wake Forest University, Mrs. Sadie Hendrix and Mrs. Bertie Slate.

In the Capitol Hill United Methodist Church special ministry, Mrs. Eleanor Jensen.

I hope that my staff in the State Department during my brief service as assistant secretary in 1961 will not feel overlooked. I could never forget their exceptional service, but the considerable size of that operation makes it impossible to name all of them.

Also unnamed are those who worked for me before 1942 and the countless number of loved friends who have participated in various ways in my life struggles. They too will always be remembered by me and my family.

Chapter 1 A HOUSE DIVIDED
1898–1903

*A person who forgets his ancestors is like a brook
without a source, or a tree without roots.*
Chinese proverb

MY grandfather was a Republican.
To some this may not sound like
an arresting statement, but to one
born in 1898 in the impregnable Democratic South, and destined to spend
a lifetime in politics, the fact was of profound significance.

I made my first race for governor of Arkansas in 1928, when Civil
War memories were still emotion-charged factors in politics. I had not
realized what a handicap I was under until I arrived at Mammoth Spring
for a speaking engagement one hot August afternoon, and was greeted
by a worried chairman: "Brooks, our opposition is claiming that your
grandfather was a Republican! It's not true, is it?" I admitted it was true,
and in my speech I met the difficulty head-on: "My friends, I hear there
is a rumor going around that my grandfather was a Republican and a
carpetbagger. He was indeed a Republican. And it is unfortunately a fact
that he and Grandmother Hays did not get to Arkansas till 1879. They
came here seeking a better opportunity in life; and I am sure that when
they packed their few belongings to journey halfway across the continent
in response to the warm welcome that Arkansas promised to those who
would come here to settle and help build the state, they never dreamed
that fifty years later it would be said that their grandson should not hold
public office because his grandfather did not reach the state till 1879!"
Thereafter the Hays family's Pennsylvania background was no issue.

My mother's father, Dr. William Butler, a native of west Tennessee,

1

was so opposed to slavery and secession that he took the hard and un-popular course of changing his party. And I am no prouder of my great-great-grandfather, who apparently fought in Washington's army, than I am of this simple country doctor and Baptist preacher who acted in ac-cordance with the dictates of his conscience. In 1873 Dr. Butler moved into Arkansas with his wife, my grandmother, and settled in Logan County. Some ten years later he unsuccessfully ran for the Arkansas state senate.

Grandfather David Hays, the studious member of his farm-loving family, was a surveyor and bookkeeper. Employed for a while by a rail-road company, he admired one of the officials, Hiram Adelbert Steele, and when my father was born in 1872 in Titusville, he was named Hiram Adelbert Steele Hays.

My grandmother had been my grandfather's pupil and was only eigh-teen when they married. Soon after the marriage, the young couple went to Lawrence, Kansas, where Grandfather taught one year in an institution that I am told grew into the state university. But Grandmother became homesick, and they returned to Tionesta. There, all the children, except Maud, the youngest, were born. Finally, in 1879, Grandfather, thinking that a warmer climate would mean improved health, accepted temporary employment as bookkeeper for a friend in Van Buren, Arkansas, where he would remain for ten years. A few months later, Grandmother, then thirty, followed with her little tribe: John, eleven; William, nine; Steele, seven; Fred, five; and Mae, three.

Less than a year after Grandfather Hays moved to Van Buren he re-ceived a letter signed by William H. Butler, informing him that he had been chosen by the school board at Ellsworth, fifty miles to the east, to teach and to preside over an expanded school program. The Butlers were well established after seven years' residence in Arkansas, and the doctor was enjoying an excellent practice. His own family was growing and he led the movement for improved school facilities. My mother, born in 1874, was his eldest child. She was given a biblical name, Sarah Tabitha, but she was always called Sallie.

There was a stability and attractiveness in Arkansas' cultural life that had not been possible before the violence and irresponsibility of the early settlements were put under control. The frontier churches, Meth-odist, Baptist, Presbyterian, and later the Catholics, did their part. Then came the wave of enthusiasm for education. The Hayses and Butlers were greatly influenced by these movements. All became church members, and all were school enthusiasts. The Hays men got their start by teaching, and my mother, after a term at Ouachita Baptist College and a year on a scholarship in George Peabody College at Nashville, taught two or three years before her marriage.

My father taught at Atkins, London, and Russellville, all in the same county, as well as in single-room village schools. Not until 1901, when he made the break to secure a brief instruction in law at Washington and Lee University, did he rely upon any other vocation for his livelihood.

He was teaching a short summer term at London when I was born on August 9, 1898, in a three-room house, rented furnished. A month later we were in Atkins where we remained until the summer of 1903, when we three, with Grandmother and Aunt Maud, moved to Russellville, destined to be home for my parents until Mother's sudden death while I was serving as a delegate to the United Nations in 1955, and Father's passing in 1959.

The fact that I was born in London but taken to Atkins by my parents when a few weeks old and later when five years old moved again with them to Russellville caused some confusion in my first race for governor in 1928, which I was not above exploiting. Atkins neighbors knew me as a preschool child and assumed I was born there. Russellville saw me enter the first grade there, and assumed I was born in Russellville, so one really might sympathize with a campaign speaker who toured Pope County for my opponent, reporting to his headquarters that "Brooks will take the county—can't beat a guy who was born in three different towns." And when my mother, who was quietly touring the territory alone, stopped at the post office in London, thinking she was recognized, said, "How's the governor's race going?" she received this reply from an old timer: "We're all for Brooks—he wuz born right over there in thet little green house." Mother's reply was something like, "You're telling me!"

The Ellsworth period, 1880–1888, were halcyon years for the Butlers and the Hayses. Dr. Butler was busy riding up and down the Old Military Road, which was the main artery between Little Rock and Ft. Smith, paralleling the river, "administering herbs, roots, and bitters to suffering humanity," as one neighbor expressed it, to say nothing of a vast amount of calomel and probably a discreet number of drops of paregoric for the babies. He prospered. He owned a farm and a big two-story white house where he provided well for his daughters, his sister Tabitha (Mother's beloved "Aunt 'Bitha") and his devoted "Miss Lou," his name for my grand-mother, who was sixteen years younger than he. "Miss Lou's" brothers fought with the Confederacy, and her stories of that tragic period revealed sympathies quite different from Grandfather's.

During the period of my grandfather's moderate political activity in the 1880s, when he ran for the state senate, there was not much interest in politics. People were occupied with routine tasks and political decisions did not appear important. There was no serious challenge to the state Democratic party, partly because the opposition had bungled its chance to produce an attractive alternative to Democratic rule. Still, that Republican opposition did not deserve the imprecations heaped upon it. The outstanding Reconstruction governor Isaac Murphy had, as a representative from Madison County, opposed secession, and was responsible for some splendid progressive measures, some of which were beneficial to both the white and black races. (Madison County produced another governor, Orval E. Faubus, nearly a hundred years later.) Public schools received the first serious attention of state political leaders and, if race feeling had not obstructed progress, the Republicans might have laid the basis for a long political tenure. But power brought a form of intoxication. Their excesses in expenditures and the downright corruption of some officials, coupled with failure to plan a constructive participation by the emancipated Negroes in political life, led to disfavor and a long political drought.

There is no sadder chapter in the history of southern politics than the cruel and highly effective measures adopted by the white majority around the turn of the century to close the door to the Negro's political participation. The principal mechanisms adopted for this purpose were the poll tax, a complicated ballot, and the white primary. The Republican and Populist opposition to these measures was feeble or altogether lacking, so the Democrats were gleeful. They were not to atone for this mistreatment of the black community for another half century. True, there were sensitive white leaders who knew that what was happening was wrong, but there were not enough of them to provide resistance.

Having failed in his try for a state senate post, my grandfather in later years demonstrated only a slight interest in state politics. Capable but unimaginative governors were being elected in the twenty-year economic expansion period ending the early nineties, when the "panic" began, and the agrarian movement struck fire due to the misery of the farm population. Grandfather probably attended Grange meetings and used such help as he could get from official government bulletins. The only federal legislation of substance was the Morril Act, initiated in the Lincoln administration, and under its beneficent aegis the state university, then called "The Arkansas Industrial University," had been given an auspicious start at Fayetteville. The later programs which produced such a revolutionary impact upon agriculture under the Smith-Lever Act, the Smith-Hughes Act, and others, ushering in the county agents service and many practical aids, had not come into existence.

State government under the Democrats, like the federal government under the Republicans, was a sort of noblesse oblige—mild aids to farm production, but never bearing the impress of radical change in marketing, credit, or land tenure policies that were essential to any substantial improvement of conditions.

And organized religion, as I have intimated, was too absorbed in unrelated and irrelevant questions to help the distraught lower classes—small farmer and town laborer. The plight of the black people did not appear to trouble the white Christian conscience very much. "The panic" (mid-nineties word for depression) therefore caused much suffering. Radical Populists offered nostrums of a questionable kind. The historic social ethics of the churches could have helped, but, again, their intellectual energies were being dissipated in meaningless dissertations. A debate between the favorite orators of the Baptist and Methodist churches and those of the new and burgeoning Disciples of Christ would always draw a crowd. The subjects most often adopted were: "Is baptism essential to salvation?"; "Is foot-washing a biblically required ordinance of the Church?" "Is security of the saints taught in the New Testament?"; "Can a saved person fall from grace?" The "doctrine of hell" was a common subject of discussions, and grave decisions were known to rest on individual beliefs on the subjects. The following somewhat familiar story originated in this period. An engaged daughter said, "But, Mother, I can't marry George; he doesn't believe there's a hell."

'Well," said Mama, "You go ahead and marry him, and between the two of us, we'll show him that there is."

Came the late nineties and politics took on new meaning. Men who had never had occasion to study monetary policy began to explore its relationship to the lives of people who had, prior to that time, gotten along well in ignorance of money and commerce. My grandfather rode just as many miles as in prosperity—wore out as many horses—but his patients had no money with which to pay him, and when he died in September of 1896, during the first McKinley-Bryan campaign, I doubt that he had given much thought to the issue upon which the Populists and Democrats were assailing his party. Washington and Little Rock still seemed far away. In their simple rural society they just hadn't needed much money or credit.

Ellsworth's general mercantile store didn't sell much meat—everyone raised his own. But scarcity of money hurt the school children who ordinarily would receive a few coins for farm and household chores and thus be able to have occasional sacks of candy—though the choice was limited. Candy bars were not to be displayed for many a year, so the choices lay between stick candy, gum drops, jaw breakers (or suckers), and licorice (we grew up pronouncing it "lickwish").

The general store, the Foster Store, had such a variety of articles that the lack of the sophisticated things city people were used to proved a fascination for the strangers. It was this aspect of store life that accounts for the establishment of the replicas—the signs that the American tourists see: "Visit the Country Store Ahead." In the Foster Store were iron pots and kettles, pans and tubs galore, stacks of white tableware, and of course, the harness in the leather corner—horse collars and saddles and plow paraphernalia.

But life went on. And economic developments, such as opening of new fields in the West for gold mining, fortified to some extent by more progressive national policies, deadened the impact of depression, and reversed the economic movements.

The Ellsworth community straddled the Old Military Road that led to Fort Smith on the border of the Indian Territory. Its scattered homes graced the peaks of small attractive hills that huddled around Rich Mountain like little chickens around a hen, and Rich Mountain in turn linked her western rim by a ridge to Magazine Mountain, highest peak between the Rockies and the Appalachians.

The Old Military Road was not an ordinary road. It was once a vital line from Little Rock to the border defense at Ft. Smith and had been maintained not only to move troops and supplies but to give the swelling tides of settlers access to new land for cultivation. It was not, however, an artery to the West. The East's corridor to Kansas lay to the north, and the corridor to Texas was to the south—both historic highways. But Arkansas was isolated for nearly a hundred years largely because her western border was a wall between the white men and the Indian tribes which had been pushed out of the East.

Still the farmers and artisans and tradesmen around Ellsworth found plenty to do without worrying about outlets. There was the sound of hammer and saw in the woods. Even the simple cultural needs of their families were being met by "Professor" Hays's new school and the competing religious services thrust into western Arkansas by the Baptists, Methodists, Presbyterians, and finally by the Disciples (or, if one preferred, "the Campbellites," but the persons sensitive to their feelings didn't say it in their presence).

The ecumenical idea had not been heard of. Rivalry was keen. The story of the Baptist evangelist may be apocryphal, but it reflects a point of view entertained, I fear, by many people in that period. The preacher was asked, "How was your meeting at Boiling Springs?" only to get this reply: "Didn't do a bit of good. Spiritual tone of that community is awful low. Didn't have a single convert. But I'll tell you one thing: I sure fixed it so nobody else'll get 'em." And thirty years later I saw an advertisement in a Baptist journal carrying a minister's announcement to this effect: "If the Methodists in your community are giving you trouble, send twenty-five cents for my new pamphlet, 'Sixty-seven Hotshot on the Methodists.' It has all the answers."

Not all of the local theological debates were in the great Ellsworth shed, an open tabernacle-type structure with a sturdy frame of hand-hewn beams and pillars, with a roof of homemade shingles calculated to protect the crowds from cloudbursts and a hostile summer sun. Some of the fiercest discussions were around the iron stove in the rear of Mr. Foster's store, or in warm weather on the front porch of his establishment.

I once related this story to Dr. Tom Staples, the Hendrix College professor of history: The unscheduled subject being argued was the doctrine of "total depravity." The differences were profound. Suddenly Uncle Johnnie Smithers joined them, and they informed him of the impasse. "Uncle Johnnie," the unofficial chairman said, "do you believe in total depravity?" He received this answer: 'Believe it? Hell, I've *seen* it!" Dr. Staples smiled, "Yes, I know that story originated in Randolph County, Alabama, in 1878."

The word *welfare* was not in the political vocabulary of the 1880s. Family responsibility was, however, a basic virtue among the frontiersmen, and neighborliness was often expressed in volunteer nursing for the sick or needy and in providing food for them. Quilting and barn raisings were not only a part of the community's sense of concern for its members but provided outlets for the festive spirit that craved a temporary escape from individual labors in favor of group assemblying.

Only the poor families had to have outside help when serious misfortunes struck. There were simple patterns of social security that the bread winners were expected to follow. The maiden aunts, for example, never secure in the modern sense, rarely lacked a place to live. My Grandfather Butler doubtless gave his sister Tabitha every evidence that she was as much a part of the family circle as when he and she were growing up together in Tennessee. And Aunt Bitha carried her part of the routine work of the household.

The new opportunities for women in our century are certainly a vast improvement over this type of security, but the affection which the Aunt Bithas received in the earlier period was a compensating factor. In turn she exuded a love and devotion for the family that adopted her. That love has made the memory of my Aunt Bitha a cherished one during the seventy years that have intervened since her death. I rather believe my father was thinking of Aunt Bitha, when, on one Mother's Day, he was called on by our minister to pray. He was thankful "for all mothers," and he linked motherhood to divine influences, but the moving part of his prayer was the reference to "the women who, having no children of their own, possess the impulse of a mother's heart, and are propelled in devoted service by it to care for the children of other women."

There is an obscure passage in Albert Beveridge's volume on Abraham Lincoln's youth that celebrates this aspect of pioneer life. Tom Lincoln was able to provide only a crude shelter for his family in the Indiana wilderness, and when Nancy Hanks was stricken, Abe and his sister nursed her with only the help that their nearest neighbor, a kind-hearted woman, could give them. She trudged through the snow two miles daily on her missions of mercy. It was frontier life at its best.

Today, such sacrifices are not required, but it seems to me that society has yet to extol properly the compassion that is reflected in the elaborate and professional aids which every level of government provides for ailing people. The Indiana wilderness has vanished, but doubtless there are people in trouble today in the same spot where Abe Lincoln tried to make his mother comfortable in her last illness. Today the visiting nurses and welfare workers have become symbols of a corporate compassion, just as the Lincoln neighbor symbolized an individual kindness upon which the nineteenth-century society had to depend.

Sorrow had often struck the Ellsworth community, the well-to-do and the poor alike. Eight of my mother's sisters and brothers died in infancy or early childhood, most of them victims of epidemics. Diphtheria was the chief enemy. Mother's story of the passing of her younger brother and of her twin sisters when they were just six years old strongly affected my feelings about the desperate health needs of rural Arkansas. It also gave me an insight into the power of religious comfort in the presence of death. The Bible may be, for some, a mere talisman, but its truths became a buttress for me. I was old enough to appreciate the comforting elements in these truths long before I discovered that the Bible is also a prod to give comfort as well as receive it. The Old Testament was as comforting as the New. The poetry and philosophic depths of both buoyed me in the sorrow which my mother's story of her family's suffering induced. I warmed to the orators of that era whose occasional high passages touched this theme. An example was the matchless speech of Robert Ingersoll, the skeptic, who nevertheless was capable of saying at his brother's funeral, "In the hour of death, hope sees a star, and listening love can hear the rustle of an angel's wing."

My father's family did not suffer the vast casualties of Mother's family, but the story of his brother William's death as related by Dad also affected me. (The papers of the Ellsworth generation are scarce. I have looked in vain for the help that old letters provide. There was simply no occasion to write to the family—people didn't travel far or for long—so I have grasped at the few missives I have found for insights.) This older brother William wrote a letter to his parents while on a trip to sell nursery stock for Grandfather Hays. He was working north of that sprawling river, the Arkansas, conveniently using the train, which probably fascinated him, as it did all who had had to depend largely upon the conventional horse plodding along the Old Military Road. Willie wrote, "All is quiet along the railroad tonight except now and then a stray order . . ." indicating his familiarity with Civil War literature. But my Uncle Willie died of pneumonia shortly after that at the age of eighteen.

Enlarged portraits of deceased members often hung on family walls, and Grandmother Hays, who lived with us nearly twenty years, placed his picture in a favored spot. He was always "Uncle Willie" in my conversations until suddenly, when I was in my forties, I realized that I was twice his age at the time of his death; so in my later conversations with Dad I called him "Willie," but always with a bit of self-consciousness. Dr. George Truett, our Baptist hero, was right, "The generations are bound together in unbroken solidarity."

Thus the forming of a matrix of my political, social, and religious philosophy began in western Arkansas nearly a century ago. An observer of the Washington political scene during my service there viewed with mild criticism some provincial aspects of my philosophy, but he credited "Mr. Hays" with advancing far beyond the culture of the rural South "which nurtured him." This was in the context of early civil rights struggles, and my part in those struggles did not obscure the deep sentiments that I feel for the people and the places which are identified with my life and career. It was obvious that my opinions on the Little Rock school desegregation crisis of 1957–1958 were "an advance" over the conventional views of my constituents, but just as obvious, I hope, is my appreciation of the genuinely admirable things about the ways of life of Arkansas village and farm people.

However, I must concede that the rural South has lagged in erecting adequate educational standards, that the rural South has held on to a dubious theology, and that the rural South has a paucity of practices calculated to improve the total society; in short, that there is in certain areas a shocking mediocrity. My hope for the South is based not on blindness to these facts, but on an underlying faith in the South's actual and potential goodness—in its aspirations, as distinguished from its achievements, and in the toughness of mind as well as of body of the sons of the soil and their women folks.

I trust that my story reflects an authentic hope for triumph by them over adversity; also that their respect for moral and legal authority, entertained in the face of many affronts by political establishments to their human dignity and pride, will be maintained. Consequently, what I have done, what I have experienced in suffering and success, what I have thought about events, what I have felt, and what I still hope for in the relating of southern life to the nation's and to the world's is recorded here in joy and in satisfaction.

Chapter 2 THE NURTURING SOUTH 1904–1914

Mr. Hays loves the rural South which
nurtured him.
Robert Allen, *The Washington Merry-Go-Round*

IT was in Atkins, a little town of about two thousand, that I became aware of life as a series of exciting adventures. My days were full of little events that seemed to follow each other with kaleidoscopic abandon.

There was the memorable day, for instance, when our uncooked roast fell into the cistern. In 1901, the standard way of keeping meat and butter cool was to lower them by ropes to a place just above the cool waters of the cistern. I loved to watch my mother perform this minor miracle, and I always held my breath as I watched the plate of butter, sitting precariously on two crossed ropes, or the next day's meat, going down toward what seemed a certain watery grave. But my satisfaction and complaisance when the rope trick was successfully negotiated was as nothing to my excitement when the fine four-pound roast slipped and plunged with a big splash into the water below. I realized that that was what I had half fearfully, half hopefully, awaited all along. My father was away and so my mother had to call on a neighbor to get it out for us.

Another early experience left an equally vivid image. To celebrate their sales day, the enterprising Board of Trade had brought a balloonist of sorts to Atkins. He was to ascend in a primitive hot-air balloon, then parachute to the ground. Volunteers held the swelling bag by ropes until the performer gave the signal to let go. As the balloon rose, a gasp went up from the crowd. An awe-struck teenager, Joe Cosley, had been stand-

11

ing too close to the basket as he watched, and a rope had formed a noose around his leg. By the time the balloonist knew he had an unwanted passenger, the dangling boy was fifty feet in the air. The performer did the only thing possible—he cut the bag loose, and he and Joe descended to the earth.

I faintly remember a trip with my parents to Little Rock when I was about three. We stayed at the Gleason Hotel—"The Gadsby Tavern of Arkansas" and center of political activity. We stepped into the elevator, which appeared to me to be a little room, and the door quickly closed. I was not aware of any movement, and when we emerged three or four floors above, I was shocked at the quick change of surroundings. But later in the day, Mother and I alone started to our room from the lobby, and this time the elevator started upward before the operator closed the door. I leaned over to see what was happening, and my head struck the top of the first floor, and I was propelled to the bottom of the shaft, unhurt, but it took thirty minutes, and a full bottle of smelling salts, to revive Mother.

But I survived all the hazards of childhood, including the enmity of our cow, "Old Bess." She had a violent disposition, and my father had neglected to trim her horns, leaving her well equipped to intimidate all who crossed her path. One day, to prove that she didn't like me a bit more than I liked her, she went after me with those lethal horns, and only the intervention of a passerby saved me from serious injury. That incident may have had something to do with my father's selling her. I never knew whether the buyer was someone wanting a good Jersey milch cow, or the butcher. I didn't want to know, for, with all of my distaste for Old Bess, I would have been saddened by the sight of her carcass in Doc Barton's butcher shop.

Our other animals, Dolly, the faithful mare, and Jackie, my dog, who lived to be fifteen, were on good—very good—terms with me. Dolly's broad back provided pleasant transportation for me in delivering the daily newspaper to scattered customers on the edge of town, beginning in 1909. She also carried me as I rounded up the cows of our neighborhood and drove them back and forth to pasture in summer months, for which I earned one dollar a month per cow. I think that the affection I had for Dolly and Jackie was an incipient feeling for living things that gave me a warm responsiveness in later years to Albert Schweitzer's philosophy and produced a personal gratification in the passage of the humane slaughtering bill during my service in the Congress.

By 1903 my father had cut loose from a teacher's salary and gave full time to the law practice. We moved twelve miles west to Russellville, the county seat, where Dad bought a little frame house for one thousand dollars and mortgaged it for half the price. It was our home till after my graduation from college. Life in Russellville during the next twelve years was in a quadrangle, marked by a line from that home to the public school, to the courthouse, to the little Baptist church, and back to the home. I did not find a life so circumscribed as dull and prosaic. Each corner of that quadrangle represented a major interest of my young life, and the great world seemed to be compressed within it. Russellville was at the western end of a prairie, surrounded by mountains that lay on each side like huge fingers attached to a giant hand, which was the Ozark plateau. Erosion of the edges of the plateau had produced those mountains.

The years sped by. In March of 1908 when I was not yet ten years old, I attended my first Democratic convention. I went with my father, who was always expected to help with the clerical duties, and having admonished me to sit quietly beside him, he seemed oblivious to my presence. The following account may not be entirely accurate; hence I am using fictitious names, but I trust it will convey the flavor of such conventions in that period.

It was the biennial meeting of our county convention and its only function was to canvass and certify the results of the primary election that had only a few days before determined the party choices. It was generally a routine affair, but always a time for handshaking and backslapping in the hallways, congratulations for the victors and commiserations for the vanquished. This time, however, when the venerated circuit judge, who was traditionally the unanimous choice for chairman, was raising the gavel for adjournment, a powerful voice was heard from the rear of the courtroom, and a delegate strode toward the rostrum. "Mr. Chairman," he roared. It was Colonel Hollins. The chairman gently lowered the gavel and with a soft voice inquired, "For what purpose does the delegate from Potts Township seek recognition?"

"A point of high personal privilege, sir." Again in a muted tone, "Please state it."

"I wish to claim the privilege of speaking for a Democratic victory in this year of our Lord 1908, something no one has yet done."

The judge was still patient, "But I will say with great respect for my friend that that is not a point of personal privilege."

"Then," said the persistent delegate, "I move to amend the order of business by permitting this presentation."

A less tolerant person might have banged the gavel for adjournment, but with the gentleness and patience that made him a beloved figure in that area he replied, "No, Colonel, I'm sorry, but there is no business before the body; it has been concluded The time for your motion was when the Committee on Order of Business reported. However," the chairman added, "it is always in order to submit a unanimous consent request and I shall submit it myself. Gentlemen of the convention, I ask unanimous consent that the delegate, Obadiah Hollins, may speak for five minutes on a subject of his own choosing." After a very short pause, "Hearing no objection, it is so ordered."

The colonel had reached the front of the room, and whirling around he was already into his speech before the delegates saw his countenance. "Thank you, Mr. Chairman. I salute the captains of commerce, the local potentates of industry, and most important of all, my fellow commoners, the honest yeomanry of this throbbing county for, my fellow delegates, our glorious party covers the spectrum of human activity. We are concerned with the welfare of all strata of economic and social life."

A voice: "Hurrah for the spectrum."

The colonel recognized the voice of his neighbor, Joseph Webb, whose piquant comments in the country-store circle had given him a reputation as a political sage and gadfly. When one of his listeners said that his barbs were "poisonous" the nickname "Spider" seemed appropriate. But Spider Webb was a favorite in any gathering. "Thank you, Brother Webb," replied the colonel, concealing irritation that the rhythm of his speech had been broken. Continuing, "I shall not carry owls to Athens, I wish only to grasp a shining shaft from the panorama of political history."

"Hurrah for the panorama."

"Thank you, Brother Webb." Colonel Hollins was frowning. He continued, "I have a major premise, a minor premise, and an irresistible and irrefutable conclusion."

"Leave the premises"—a voice from the rear and not as friendly as Spider's. A quizzical expression spread over the speaker's face. Spider called out, "He means, Colonel, leave *out your* premises and proceed."

The colonel's face brightened, "Thank you very much, Brother Webb. I shall do so." He continued: "Gazing backward down our country's long corridors of time we should exult over the careers of the great Democrats of earlier centuries. Ours is the party of Thomas Jefferson, Andrew Jackson, and Grover Cleveland; finally, the incomparable William Jennings Bryan. His words so eloquently uttered fell like silver dew drops around him." A Republican who had secretly infiltrated the gathering was heard to mutter, "Foaming at the mouth, sounds like to me." The colonel didn't hear this affront.

"Not since the Galilean walked the Judean hills has a greater friend of the poor comforted the children of men." Spider was silent. He, like the other delegates, was feeling the hypnotic effect of the uninhibited oratory.

"Though twice defeated he is the logical one to lead the militant hosts of Democracy once more against the entrenched powers of corrupt and irresponsible wealth represented by the Republican party. I love the Republicans, my friends, I love them as neighbors, but as a party they are ignominious." Drawing in a deep breath he found fresh strength for his appeal. The chairmen looked at his watch, said nothing. Fifteen minutes had elapsed. But the verbal torrent was far from terminated. The delegates had succumbed to the spell of his eloquence. Stamping feet and cheers were a fillip to the colonel and he plunged ahead.

"Providence has given its blessing to this great adventure in proving the practicality of the federal system, resting as it does upon the indestructible union of the indestructible states. Altogether the states, shining like stars in the sky form a single constellation in the canopy of heaven. William Jennings Bryan will preserve the states."

"Hurrah for the constellation."

"Thank you, Brother Webb."

"Mr. Chairman, when I prepared to leave Kentucky to make a new home in this happy land, I said good-bye to my boyhood friend, the governor of my native state, and he said, 'Obe, you will be dwelling with a great people. Streams of rugged pioneers migrating from every southeastern state will converge in Arkansas to brighten and to strengthen it.' The names of our villages confirm his prediction. We have New Bern to remind us that North Carolinians are here. Our own community, Due West, signifies that the Palmetto State is here. Chesterton reminds us of Maryland, Middletown of Kentucky, and Tupelo of Mississippi, to mention only a few of the noble sister states who tried to save the Confederacy. We are legatees of great forebears, Mr. Chairman, and there wasn't a Republican among them."

Colonel Hollins decided upon one more thrust for the ticket that he felt sure would be headed by Mr. Bryan. "He will save us against the greedy monsters of Wall Street. He will make sure they will not press down a crown of thorns upon the brow of labor nor crucify mankind upon a cross of gold."

"Hurrah for mankind."

"Thank you, Brother Webb."

The colonel was grateful for Spider's interruptions now. It provided the pauses that he needed for deep breath.

"Let us, the sons of toil and sons of the soil rally to him in this final struggle for democracy and justice. So, Mr. Chairman, may my tongue cleave to the roof of my mouth and my right hand lose its cunning if I should ever weaken in my loyalty to the Democratic party."

Turning toward the chairman he said with a trace of exhaustion, "Have I used up my five minutes, Mr. Chairman?" With his usual patience the judge replied, "I'm afraid so." He knew, of course, that the colonel had talked for more than thirty minutes.

The judge benevolently paused again seeing that the colonel was ready to conclude. He did it with these words. "And so my friends, as you continue on this earthly pilgrimage may your stream of life unruffled run and may every day be a blessed one. I thank you all." Spider Webb arose and the chairman permitted him to offer this brief addendum after which the gavel sounded final adjournment.

"I wish to say that when my time comes to die and the doctor tells me that I have but one hour to live I want Colonel Obadiah Hollins to hold the watch." This began my absorption in the political procedures of the South.

Father's law practice grew. He was appointed county examiner for the county schools, having as his single duty the examining of applicants for license to teach, and as a collateral service, to conduct an institute for a few days each year for the improvement in teaching methods for a hundred or more teachers serving independent school districts.

His closest friends were two young lawyers, Bob Lawrence and Tom Brooks. All three became active in politics. Mr. Brooks was elected to the house of representatives, Mr. Lawrence to the state senate. They sponsored Dad for chief clerk of the house, and he served in that capacity for several biennial sessions. The best proof of my father's devotion to these two friends was his giving me the name (with Mother's consent) Lawrence Brooks Hays. Sometimes Mother called me Larry (and my wife's pet name for me at the university was Laurie), but Dad called me Brooks. In college, it was L. Brooks, but I dropped the hanging initial when I got into politics. (Hadn't Stephen Grover Cleveland and Thomas Woodrow Wilson found it advisable to use only one given name—and weren't they pretty successful in politics?)

My father was strong-willed, but very convivial and his regular evening sojourns with members of the legislature to Garibaldi's saloon in Little Rock were accompanied by his own daily indulgences. The visit of legislators to Garibaldi's saloon was such a constant practice that one of their number introduced a resolution to relocate the capitol's cannon— "It's pointed toward Garibaldi's, and if it ever went off accidentally it would kill half the legislature," he warned his colleagues.

My father's habit persisted, and I believe that his family griefs and his problems of family finance encouraged escapism, fastening a grip upon him that threatened to plunge him into an incurable illness. But it was cured. There was a happy ending. If the ending had been otherwise, I doubt that I would record this chapter of my father's life, but his triumph over the habit is one of the most convincing elements in my claim that he was a strong and admirable person. My mother was also strong and admirable. She suffered greatly, but insisted to me that this was a burden that love of a good man required us to carry. It caused her to take an interest in temperance organizations (she became a state officer in the WCTU) and to become inflexible on the prohibition question. Dad also became an ardent prohibitionist, and in the last thirty years of his life he never touched a drop.

An Arkansas judge, W. L. Moose, who appreciated my father's potentialities, convinced Dad that he should seek a cure and begin a new course in life. This he did. The decision took us to Mineral Wells, Texas, a health resort, in January, 1915, and when we returned to Russellville three months later, Dad was on the road to recovery. I give the greatest credit to Dad's firmness and his decision not to let us suffer any longer. God had already done his part in endowing my father with a moral competence, and the battleground was inside the structure of this moral nature, as it is in most of the human struggles against weaknesses and wrongs.

A newsman once said in an article, published when I entered politics, "Mr. Hays neither smokes nor drinks nor swears." I protested mildly that he had hurt me considerably with the voters, for he left me only the snuff dippers, and there weren't many of them. Furthermore, I asked him, "Why didn't you add, 'nor dances nor gambles, nor goes to Sunday movies or ballgames'?"

My father's religion was wholesome. He was never fanatical, but he was certainly more conventional in his attitudes and utterances than I. The Baptist Church and the Democratic party were his great institutional interests. My father's generosity, though limited by his modest income, was expended upon his own and Mother's families and upon indigent friends, but never seemed to draw him into any profound conclusions regarding a political program dealing with poverty. Perhaps he was too busy earning money to support his family and his personal charities to expend mental energies in this direction. The ravages of ill health and poverty fell no more heavily upon our families than on many other residents of rural Arkansas, and perhaps the identification with them helped supply what my father and mother needed for calmness of spirit. Neither of them ever seemed to succumb, even momentarily, to cynicism or bitterness.

After Grandmother Butler lost the fine Butler home to the mortgagees a few years after Grandfather's death, she moved with her youngest daughter and family to a little one-story farmhouse nearby on a lateral road to enter a new kind of life on a hillside forty-acre farm. She married the father of her son-in-law, a kind and good man whom I called "Grandpapa." My parents called him "Mr. Lile."

We went every summer to visit them, thirty miles away. Mr. Lile's four sons lived in the neighborhood, and our coming seemed to give them and their families great enjoyment. I was not spared by reason of being "a guest" from some of the toil. I helped Mr. Lile worm his tobacco plants. I helped the women shell peas and string beans and churn milk, and helped the men round up the horses when they were needed, and other chores.

And when at night the weather was clement, as it nearly always was, I slept on one of the pallets provided for my cousins and me on the front porch. I loved the sounds of nighttime—still do—the crickets—and night birds—and early in the morning the crowing of a score of roosters on the ridge who waited their turn to tell us that Old Sol was on his way. All those things softened my feelings of gloom that life had to be so grim for my mother's people.

The work was not a hardship, for I had been exposed to many household duties in our own home—cleaning lamp chimneys, drawing water, stacking stove wood, picking bugs off the potato plants, and putting poles in the ground for the bean vines to climb—these are a few of the things my parents found for me to do. Some chores are, in reality, rather pleasant. Churning, for example, can get irksome, but to see the little flecks of butter show up around the hole in the lid of the crock, signaling that butter may shortly be lifted, is a minor pleasure that should not go unacknowledged.

When we returned to the ridge the following summer (I was thirteen) my aunt met us at the gate, and we saw anxiety on her countenance. "Sally, I wrote you," she said to Mother, "about the boils that Ma had—well, they haven't gone away, and there's more of them. I'm worried." The doctor came from the village every two or three days, but he could not help. It was not an easy illness to treat or nurse. The carbuncles had spread. But mother and my aunt understood that it was the last opportunity for the ministrations of filial love, and they did little else that summer but care of her.

I tried to stay awake with the grown-ups on the night that she died. I was affected by the mystery of death and the pall of sorrow that filled the cabin. This was "the suffering of destiny" that unites families. But shortly after midnight I lay down in heavy sleep. Toward morning my father shook me gently and asked if I didn't want to see Grandmother again before she died. I knew he felt that she should not slip away without all of her children and grandchildren around her bedside. It happened that way. Just before dawn she died, and I was glad her suffering was over. I watched the elders prepare for the funeral. There was no undertaker near, and the only preparation for burial was given by the women. My father sent for an inexpensive coffin at the village, and she was laid in it. At noon the coffin was placed in a wagon and taken to the family burying ground three miles away.

The road to the cemetery was a little-used lateral with deep ruts and big rocks to make the going hard. Most of the family went in wagons, but I rode with my parents in the buggy that brought us to the ridge, our big mare pulling us patiently and steadily. Over the mare's head I could see the coffin in the open wagon under a hot September sun, and the men in the wagon had to hold it when the wheels struck the deep ruts. Mother said nothing, but she was probably thinking of the hardships in her mother's life. Grandmother's goodness shone through in simple toil and devotion to her family. It was the kind that Jesus must have had in mind when he said, "The earth of itself bringeth forth fruit." The deprivations of her later years contrasted sharply with her life as Dr. Butler's wife in the big house. The prosperous years had been but an interlude. She had grown up like most of the Tennesseans, not in plantation ease and luxury, but in the poverty of the nonslaveholding classes. I have since wondered how much of her frailty was due to the malnutrition of an inadequate living standard of the girlhood days, and the accentuation of that condition resulting from the war. She might have lived twenty years longer without the world feeling that she was overstaying.

Less than one-tenth of white southerners of the prewar period had lived in the great houses. Most of them had lived as she did in relative poverty. Her patent medicine shelf was a more authentic symbol of southern life than the white-columned mansions, and her family's struggle against the elements and economic adversities were of the kind that led Will Alexander to say that, "no flood or famine or tornado has ever produced the suffering caused in a single season by poverty and malnutrition and disease." It has been a drab, hard fight for our people to come through this. None of the South's struggles for survival were done in technicolor.

The little service at the grave was consoling to the group of mourners. Such services generally are. No preacher of her own faith was available, and a "Campbellite" was asked to preside. These country preachers are at their best in the graveyard ceremonials. In the pulpits they are controversial and stern. They are generally loud exhorters, and often fearful mouthpieces of a wrathful God. But here in the cemetery they can see the inappropriateness of sternness and abuse being associated with religion, so death becomes the mediator and the great adventure. The picturing of God as a father who sorrows with his children becomes a favorite theme. I have seldom witnessed a burial service by a country preacher of any denomination that did not reveal a tenderness and understanding that drew his listeners close to him and to his religion.

The country preacher has been a great influence in the past, but adverse forces have been depriving the rural church of its place among the social forces of the region and the chief responsibility is now upon the country preachers to capitalize their power of personal influence and abandon the agitation for fine-spun doctrines that cannot interest people any longer. This service for Grandmother did not offend in that regard. One of the favorite old Baptist hymns, "In the Sweet Bye and Bye," was sung without accompaniment, and the preacher gave a comforting talk. So my grandmother's life ended when she was only sixty-five, a life of the rural South's struggle with want, and bearing for a half century some of the sorrows of the most cruel war in our history.

The following year (1912) my father ran for prosecuting attorney for our four-county district. I wanted to campaign for him, so he had some campaign cards printed with my picture on the back, and help for Dad in that crucial race was limited to passing out the cards. The Democratic primary, tantamount to election, was in August. Dad came home at midnight, when fewer than a half dozen boxes were out, and his opponent's margin was too big to overcome. Mother cried a little, and I threatened to—we needed the money so badly. But adversity was not a stranger in our home, so we went to bed at midnight, feeling sure that we would not be downcast the next day. Dad went to town the next morning ready to concede defeat, but at noon he came in the front door for the midday meal (dinner), exclaiming, "Wonder of wonders! I'm *in*. There's been a recount and I've got it by fifty-one votes." A glorious feeling, but it was the last victory that Dad or I would win for thirty years, almost to the day until I was elected to the Congress in 1942, not counting my election to the Democratic National Committee in 1932 or reelection in 1936.

My father's personal problem was aggravated by the tensions growing out of his new work as a prosecutor. Consequently, the office was both an advantage and a handicap. His civil practice suffered. Mother, who had a good business head, something Dad was never blessed with, tried to help in various ways, such as handling his fee collections and managing the small rental properties he had accumulated. She assigned to me the monthly errand of collecting the rents on three small houses. The tenants were poor people, so poor that I hated to take the $8.00 for the month's occupancy. An illness or a spell of unemployment would always put a family in the arrears column. This contact helped to develop my concern for social conditions. Social security, unemployment insurance, and, at the state level, workman's compensation, all came twenty years too late for them.

My parents encouraged my natural impulse to make my own spending money. I purchased the franchise for the *Saturday Evening Post* from a schoolmate and systematically built up the circulation of the weekly magazine to a hundred a week, which was about saturation for a town of three thousand in those days. For several years I delivered the town's afternoon newspaper and that produced $1.10 for me every Friday. In the summer I mowed lawns. And one Fourth of July one of my cousins and I set up a hamburger and cold-drink stand at the Russellville annual picnic. We borrowed my mother's oil stove and some pans and bought a big five-gallon can of vanilla ice cream with a supply of cones and the usual assortment of soda pop. Our stand was a crude arrangement of stakes and boards, with a little bunting for decoration. We had hardly hung out our sign when a wind and rainstorm came up. We managed to anchor everything but we could not protect all our perishables against the deluge. At noon the sky cleared, and a bright summer sun soon changed the outlook. We bought a new supply of bread and cones and made some quick calculations of our financial structure. We concluded it was worth the struggle to stay in business for the half day. The crowd swelled, and the humidity and heat sent them to the stands for drinks and ice cream. We worked furiously through the long afternoon, screaming our wares and dispensing them without a pause. We had estimated our needs well—we had only a few leftovers and little demand that we could not meet. By hard work and with some lucky breaks we broke even! This childhood venture gave me an insight into the meaning of "business risks," and its impression remained with me through my service in the Congress, particularly when we got around to considering rain insurance.

There were chores for us around the farm (and in the Russellville neighborhood when the town was scarcely more than a farm service center) that were not always pleasant. I remember my discomfort when we boys were asked to catch and hold the pigs for the surgery of castration and to round up the cattle for dehorning. Later on I was eager enough to make money to try nearly any available job, but two undertakings did not last long. I worked only one half of one Saturday at a canning factory, cleaning rust stains off of the tin cans for five cents an hour. At noon, I collected my fifteen cents and quit without notice. This job made a believer in collective bargaining.

The other job I couldn't adjust to was picking cotton. The fifty cents a hundred pounds did not interest me, although I did give it a try on Mr. Cal Hall's farm. There was some compensation in the festive spirit of the band of pickers moving along the rows of cotton, but the fun was not great enough to make up for the drudgery. It was this festivity, however, that sustained unnumbered southerners through the backbreaking hours of the autumn work. After more than fifty years, I recall the discomfort of a cotton field, and I have a feeling of deep regret that in Congress I did little more to help provide an adequate wage for farm labor than an occasional reference in legislative discussions to its neglect and a plea for solutions.

One or two questions regarding my boyhood might occur to one interested in my evolving political philosophy. What of our entertainment in the small town life of sixty years ago? Well, we did have the Friday night concerts of the Russellville Band, and the open-air movies at twenty-five cents for an adult and ten cents for a child. In the fall, we had the Saturday afternoon high school football games, and they were pretty rugged! Even if we knew that on the days we played Little Rock or Ft. Smith our boys had to hold them to 75–0 to feel any satisfaction at all, no one could ever complain about support in the stands. We would yell ourselves hoarse: "Hold that line, hold that line" over the difference between 70–0 and 76–0.

My interests were not in athletics so much as in debating, declaiming, and journalism. Summer brought the tent Chautauquas, which gave us a week of intensive intellectual diet that sufficed for another year. My father was usually chosen to introduce the distinguished lecturers, and I remember three of them: Richmond Pearson Hobson, Eugene V. Debs, and William Jennings Bryan. Mr. Bryan was given the best room in the town's leading hotel, The White House, a rambling frame hostelry just fifty yards from the railroad, and I recall that the man whom all Democrats rejoiced to call "the Great Commoner" laid his hand on my head in a sort of papal blessing.

Both of my parents loved books. My father probably spent more on "sets" than was wise, but bookstores in towns the size of Russellville were unheard of in my boyhood, so a glib traveling salesman had little difficulty in getting Dad to part with his extra change for new books when the samples were laid before him. On the few shelves in our home were a half dozen big volumes of Shakespeare, Mark Twain (entire writings), a collection of southern writings, a quantity of poetry books, and some odds and ends that Dad could not resist buying. Rounding out our home reading were *Uncle Remus*, Louisa May Alcott's books—*Little Women* and the rest—and the complete set of McGuffey's readers, much loved by my parents.

When electricity was brought into the town my daily reading time was extended. Always we had the daily *Arkansas Gazette*—oldest newspaper west of the Mississippi River—which came from Little Rock on the noon train, the St. Louis *Post Dispatch* on Sunday, and a few magazines. I read the *Youth's Companion* and the Baptist weekly, *Kind Words*, and occasionally the product which I peddled, the *Saturday Evening Post*. I should add two single volumes of biographical sketches—one, a collection of the adventures and achievements of America's great men, and the other devoted to Bible heroes, which was bought for me. Both of them undoubtedly contributed to my enthusiasm for history and conceivably fanned the flame of ambition.

That flame would have burned rather brightly, I think, even without such stimuli. Perhaps there is no accounting in terms of such influences for the urge I felt to make more than an ordinary contribution to my circle and my times. There was an element of mysticism in my reflections on the kind of professional course I would pursue. The impress of formal religious instruction, though inadequate and sometimes unscientific, was reflected in my hopes for a political career. It was a pathetically adolescent feeling, but a potent one, and this feeling carried over into the maturing college period when its validity could be tested by larger reasoning powers. Its relevancy to this story is that I probably would not, in the absence of such incentives, have endured the austerity of my college schedule, much of it devoted to self-imposed extra duties. These I regarded as a necessary part of my discipline for growth and competence. By the time I had discarded the overweening ambition for distinction, I had become conditioned to a rigorous schedule.

Unresolved when I finished high school was the persistent question, "Would I be a lawyer or a minister?" Perhaps more of my fellow Baptists were aware of my dilemma than I realized. This was revealed in the introduction I received when I spoke in Kansas City during my service in Congress. The chairman had stopped at a Russellville filling station one day and learned from the old gentleman who was filling the gas tank that this was where Brooks Hays lived. The conversation went like this:

"Did you know him?"

"Why sure. Ever'body knowed the boy."

"What kind of boy was he?"

"Ordinary normal boy."

"Can't you tell me anything at all special about him?"

"Well, I recollect that he loved that little Baptist Church. They jes' didn't open the door without him a-being there, but it didn't keep him from being a ordinary normal boy. Folks thought he'd be a preacher. One fellar even took bets—would politics or the church get him. When Brooks decided not to be a preacher, the stakes holder said, 'Well, the church won.' "

So, I grew up, nurtured by the rural South, carrying into late adolescence the influences of a family held together by the cement of love and forbearance, and in a town somewhat inhospitable to liberal ideas. I did not carry the word *liberal* in my meager lexicon, but I believe I was aware that neither church nor school environments had provided me with some of the things I hungered for. Nevertheless, I was proud of my identification with a rural society, even though it was distinguished by limited opportunities and traditional ways, and I loved the people who, while victimized by it, were still its hope and strength. I had suffered with them sufficiently to cling to the determination to work *with* them and *for* them as long as I should live.

Chapter 3 CAMPUS YEARS 1915–1919

The romance land of yesterday,
It sometimes almost seems
As if our outstretched fingers may
Half grasp its vanished dreams.
Margaret Sangster

ON a fine September morning in 1915, I boarded the seven o'clock westbound Missouri-Pacific train to enter the University of Arkansas at Fayetteville. The distance between Russellville and Fayetteville was only 140 miles, but Arkansas trains gave you your money's worth in at least one respect in those days—they were very generous about the amount of time you could spend on them! At Fort Smith, where I had a three-hour wait, I changed to the Frisco station, where I spent a quarter for lunch, and then boarded a train for the remaining sixty-five miles. We rolled into Fayetteville about four o'clock.

There was little activity on the station platform, and only a few students to greet the train, a fact that disappointed me unreasonably since I knew I was ahead of the crowd. I had hoped to make an entrance! I felt better when I found I was being met by a professor, Dr. J. R. Grant, a long-time friend of my family. As a first grader, he had gone to school one summer to my father, and an enduring friendship had resulted.

We walked together to the university campus, a block from the station, and up the long elliptical walk, lined with maples, past the main building to the dormitory. "Old Main," as the great old structure has been affectionately called by many generations of students, is an exact copy of the original University of Illinois main building. It was erected in the early seventies with brick from native clay, kilned on the site. I didn't know all this as I approached it for the first time, but I knew it was beautiful, and I fell in love with it on sight. The walk of old pink brick led us around Old Main to "Buck Hall," named for a former president, Dr. Buchanan. It was the dormitory where I was to spend a good part of the next four years.

I was stunned to find the rooms of Buck Hall not only unpopulated but unfurnished. I knew that I was to pay $16.00 a month for board, room, and laundry, and for that munificent sum I was expecting something resembling hotel accommodations! I soon learned that it was not the policy of the university to supply furniture for the boys (they did for the girls); and so on the first day or two of school a lively commerce in second-hand beds, tables, and chairs took place in all three dormitories. I was more fortunate than most freshmen, for my roommate, Bill Wooten, another Russellville boy, was a junior, and while he had not yet arrived, his worldly goods were in the room and awaiting us. He was the owner of a bed, two chairs, two small tables, and a washstand with a tin pitcher and basin. These had been bought from some senior who was happy to see the last of them. I could enter without strain into the outgoing senior's sentiments regarding them, for while they might accurately be termed antiquated, they lacked either the beauty or value that might have made them antiques. However, I was too vibrant with anticipation to let the decor of my college home depress me.

From the window, I could look down on Jeff Hall, the bath house, which provided showers and toilet facilities for the three dormitories. This arrangement was another shock, for I had never had to go outside and cross a stretch of some fifteen yards to take a bath. But I soon grew accustomed to seeing students running from dorm to bathhouse wrapped in nothing but a bath towel! This humble structure—the bathhouse—was named for a former student who became governor and United States senator, Jeff Davis. He had transferred from the university to Vanderbilt before his senior year because his fondness for high jinks diverted his attention from his class work, and created tension with the faculty.

The first days at the university were more exhilarating than any I had ever experienced. Intellectual adventures lay ahead. The campus was a microcosm, and I was part of its throbbing life. I studied every new face. I was fascinated by every new acquaintance. I forget how I learned that the upperclassmen were planning a Saturday night affair that was not exactly a tea party in the freshmen's honor. Something about the invitation gave me a clear impression that it would not be in my interest to plead that I had another engagement! Also that it would be the part of wisdom not to wear my new seventeen-dollar suit. I overheard a sophomore mention "running the gauntlet" and my imagination supplied the rest. I assumed from the length of the line that every upperclassman was there, and suspected that they had imported some Indians from Oklahoma to join them. Every one of them had a strap or a belt. I was among the first to run. "Good prospect for the track team," I heard somebody say—"ran like a colt with a bee in his ear."

It was my introduction to hazing. I didn't like it, not because there was much pain in the contact of leather, but because it was an affront to my dignity and a slight dilution of my earlier impression that I was welcome around that place. But what followed was worse. We were made to march down dark and unfamiliar streets and roads to the county fairgrounds, and on arrival told to take off our shoes and throw them into a big pile. Suddenly our tormentors were gone and the scramble to locate matched shoes began. I was next to the last one to leave. A few feet up the road I looked back to see a fellow freshman sitting on the ground trying to tie a shoe in the dark. I went back. We introduced ourselves and it was the beginning of a lifelong friendship with Beloit Taylor, who was to figure prominently in my campaigns for governor and Congress and to achieve a career of his own as lawyer, businessman, and political leader.

We were far behind the other victims and we were lost! Fairly sure of the general direction, we started east along a dirt road. We found plenty to talk about. We had walked a few hundred yards when we came to a railroad overpass. We climbed the embankment and followed the rails. But we had turned south *away* from the university instead of toward it. We were utterly without landmarks. Our only tie to civilization was the occasional sound of the courthouse clock. We went on, and on, and on. Finally, just after the clock's friendly notes had struck, Beloit said, "The last time we heard it, the sound was louder, we're walking away from it." We reversed our movements and finally arrived at the Frisco station, each able under the street light to determine what his companion looked like. It was twenty minutes of four when I piled into bed.

On the first Sunday morning of my new life, an upperclassman rounded up the Baptist freshmen who wanted to go to Sunday school and church. There was also a brief YMCA service on a week-day evening, and thus we had a sufficiency of religious instruction. The "Y" met in drab surroundings in a little Buck Hall corner room, the only adornments being a few folding chairs and an upright piano. The songbooks contained the familiar ones, but I noticed that the favored songs were based on military themes, "The Son of God Goes Forth to War" and "Onward Christian Soldiers," signifying that college men of that period had not been affected by the incipient pacifist movements.

On Monday I was formally enrolled in the class of 1919. There was some latitude of choice for freshman courses, and I lost no time in making an error of judgment that I lived to regret: I decided to elect "math," not because I liked the subject, I didn't, or because my grades in high school had been outstanding, they weren't, but in order to demonstrate that I could master it. It was a mistake. To keep it from mastering me, keep up in my other subjects, and indulge in all the extracurricular activities I had in mind, I had to work harder than a growing boy should have had to work. I use the phrase "growing boy" advisedly—between the summer of 1915 and the Christmas holidays my height increased by several inches. I enjoyed the gasps and stares when I went home for the holidays. To find me only one inch short of a six footer was something no one had expected.

Analytical geometry was not the only difficult and uncongenial course I elected to pursue. I enrolled in one that only engineers were expected to take, Foundry Instruction, which consisted of practical training in iron molding by the shop foreman. I wish the dean, or somebody, had said, "Crazy, man, crazy!"—because it was. But it was all a part of satisfying my enormous curiosity about everything.

Another of the fringe courses I elected to take was one in basic art. This one I enjoyed. In high school I had been a compulsive doodler, the doodles usually taking the form of cartoons, and in college I managed to do some sketches that secured a place in the various publications. In later years it gave me the preparation for some amateur creativeness in drawing and painting—the nearest thing to a hobby I had during my congressional years.

My university curriculum, therefore, became a hodgepodge. If I were starting again I would concentrate on fewer subjects. About the only courses I had passed up entirely were music and physical education. I got enough exercise from the military drills (required during the first two years), and I even elected the junior and senior military science courses, but chiefly because we were paid $8.00 a month for drilling. But in my junior year I loved to hitch my ceremonial sword to my belt and hear myself called "Lieutenant Hays," as I helped command Company C. Another appeal for me was eligibility to Scabbard & Blade, a prestigious campus organization. Why this should be true is hard to understand as I reflect upon it now, for I never had military aspirations and I already belonged to three honorary societies—Skull and Torch (which became Phi Beta Kappa). Tau Kappa Alpha (debating), and Pi Delta Epsilon (journalism).

One of my dormitory neighbors was a very popular junior, Jim Trimble, who was editor-in-chief of the university weekly, and destined to serve in the Congress from 1944 to 1966. He gave a warm response to my request to serve as a freshman reporter and immediately assigned me to the coveted job of covering the president's office. Our friendship, which began at that time, ripened in our association in the House of Representatives.

I gave priority to everything that would enable me to be skilled in communications. The old literary and debating societies still flourished and I chose the Periclean. Saturday night was sacredly reserved for its rites, and the training I received in the weekly meetings was invaluable. I was able, largely as a result of this experience and that supplied by the Baptist Young People's meetings, to win a place on the varsity debating team in my sophomore year, which was a source of some pride. I was one of the three-man team which defeated the University of Mississippi in a confrontation on the Monroe Doctrine—Arkansas upholding its importance and efficacy. The following year I was one of a two-man team which won the debate with the University of Texas.

My excitement over being selected for the debating team was boundless. I resolved to concentrate on the preparation of material and to practice hard on the delivery. Occasionally I would go off to the woods just west of the campus to give my memory test, with only the trees as audience. Sixty years later I was guest speaker at a meeting of history teachers in a building erected over the very spot where I practiced for the debates, and I told them that "my hyperboles, apostrophes, and similes reverberated from hill to hill."

In the preliminary trial debates in some surrounding towns, I had the sad fact impressed upon me that chance remarks may turn out to be loaded, and the fall-out everlasting. We staged a "model" debate at Rogers, near the Missouri line, and as we entered the high school building I innocently said, "This is the furtherest north I have ever been." My colleagues doubled up, and one wit immediately termed our trip "the Hays Expedition to the North." I was never permitted to forget it. It took commencement day, like the Judgment, to erase it finally from my colleagues' memories.

The first university football game was a thriller. I had never seen college teams perform, and I had never seen anything like the corporate expression of enthusiasm from the stands. In retrospect, it appears rather pitiful—there was no stadium—only a baseball field converted into a football gridiron, and the only seats were those in the small wooden grandstand and on a few bleachers. Much of the crowd of three thousand stood along the sidelines, posing a problem for the officials. An alumni Razorback star of 1903 told me that the players in his day bought their own uniforms. Even in 1915 there were no athletic scholarships or subsidies. But the game had the same crowd-pleasing qualities as today.

One slight discomfort marked the first Saturday's game. I observed bits of ribbon placed on the lapels of some of my fellow freshmen. I overheard enough conversations to understand that it was fraternity pledge day. I recognized on some of them the colors of Sigma Chi, the only fraternity that had taken notice of me. I felt a momentary disappointment but quickly pulled out of it. I had not been interested enough in fraternities to be sure that I wanted to join one. I had a faint suspicion that the democratic spirit suffered a bit from their practices, so I gave it no further thought until just before Christmas when the Sigma Chi's offered me a bid—inspired to act sooner than they intended, because Beloit Taylor's Kappa Alpha brothers and two other chapters got interested in me. When Sigma Chi pledged me the feeling "maybe I want to be a barb" dissolved, and I soon became very fond of my fraternity brothers.

Two practices of the Arkansas chapter disturbed me. One was the hazing of pledges, or "house initiation," preceding the formal initiation, which left emotional scars that lessened the effect of what I am sure is one of the Greek world's most inspiring rituals. The other was the annual "chicken stew," climaxing a rite of pure larceny during which the chicken roosts of the community were raided.

Both of these atrocious traditions were out of harmony with our cultural standards. During one house initiation, I was so repelled by the indignities imposed upon some sensitive freshmen that I shouted my objections and walked out of the house. No one confronted me with any criticism of my little drama, either privately or in chapter meetings.

Doubtless some of the tougher brothers attributed it to a hypersensitive point of view—something that produced my nickname "Deacon"—but its use was apparently not accompanied by disdain. The brothers sensed my fondness for the "tough members," and I never made congeniality a test for fraternal feelings. After these fifty years I think I can say, therefore, that I was a fairly good fraternity man.

I was only mildly interested in the co-eds that brightened the campus and classrooms, although every boy I knew was interested in one or more of them. Life was a rather serious matter to me in those days, and education to fit me for negotiating it successfully was my primary concern. If I had any plans for singling out any girl for a possible friendship, they were nebulous and consigned to the future.

And then Cross Dudney, president of the freshman class, got in difficulties and appealed to me for help. I suppose he knew I would not be likely to have a date, since we had been in school three months and I had never taken such a drastic step. He had two girls on his hands, and wanted me to take one of them. Although he had been so attentive to one girl that she would be confidently expecting to go with him to the freshman class dance on Friday night, December 3, he had been attracted to a second girl and had impulsively asked her to be his date for that occasion. Now, the consequences of yielding to a sudden whim were facing him, and he was finding the situation pretty uncomfortable. Would I, he pled, please get him off the hook by taking one of the girls?

I agreed willingly. I wasn't at all afraid of girls, and having this *fait accompli* presented to me in a way that relieved me of all the preliminary arrangements was a pleasant prospect. I liked what I knew of Una Simmons, though that wasn't much, and I enjoyed the thought of how I could now join in the usual bragging of Bill Wooten and the other boys I knew best who were in the habit of discussing the attractiveness of their "dates" after an evening's campus party. I had begun to feel myself, at these post-mortem sessions, just a little out of the mainstream.

I had never learned to dance, as neither the curriculum of the Russellville High School nor the programs of the First Baptist Church had provided for that exercise. I would have to limit my attentions to getting partners for Una, or talking to her when or if she was obliged to sit one out.

Everything worked out as planned. Following the dance, I walked with my date to Carnall Hall, and then went to Nolan Irby's room where some of the fellows often congregated, and there I proceeded to give a glowing but fictional account of what a fine time I had had and what a great girl I had been out with. I got more than my share of their attention, which included laughter and teasing comments, because I had finally taken the plunge into what was considered the normal way of campus life.

The next night, Saturday, December 4—a date that proved to be of supreme importance in the Hays family annals—I went to a meeting of the Periclean Debating Society. It was a special occasion because girls had been invited, and a program planned which might be presumed to be of interest to them. I climbed the stairs to the fourth floor of Old Main and there I had a soul-shattering experience. I met a small girl, only five feet high and weighing no more than ninety-two pounds, of no particular attainments, but who somehow knocked me for a loop. When the evening was over, I rushed back to my room in Buck Hall, flushed with what I believed was my success in capturing the interest of the little Fort Smith girl. I could hardly wait to tell Bill about it. I had forgotten all about my enthusiastic account of my Friday night date until Bill interrupted my transports by exclaiming, "Good lord! Another one!" All I could do was to protest, "But this time I mean it!"

The next day I had the doubtful felicity of seeing her again, doubtful because she was with another boy. Sunday noon was a popular time for both boys and girls to have dinner guests at the dormitories, and I saw her come into the dining room with John Carroll, a friend of mine. I had mixed emotions, even after she saw me and smiled.

On the strength of this brief encounter, and one other contact where she saw me at the train window as I was starting home for Christmas and reached up to shake hands and wish me a merry Christmas (she was leaving on a later train), I gave my surprised relatives the impression that I would shortly be on my way to the altar. To my grandmother, aunt, and assorted cousins, who were Methodists, I called her "my little Methodist girl," which delighted them as there was always a faint hint of rivalry in the family, my parents being such fervent Baptists. Of course, there were only two of them to a whole passel in the other denomination, but three Baptists can outweigh and out-do any number of other adherents!

One might wonder why, if I was so impressed, I had not made an effort to be with her during the next three weeks before Christmas. The reason I held back was that she had been elected secretary of the fresh-man class, and no distinction could have so appealed to me and have ele-vated her as a political honor. As I learned later, though, she had no po-litical ambitions whatever, and felt only a mild pleasure at being chosen. When we came back to school after Christmas vacation, I didn't let any more grass grow under my feet, and because she responded satisfactorily to my overtures, I realized that life began for me on December the fourth, 1915.

At the end of my freshman year I learned that my father had procured for me a three-month summer teaching job at Sunny Point, two miles south of our home. It was a typical one-room frame building, on a hill with a southern slope. I was to be paid fifty dollars a month. In 1916 the school system of Arkansas, as in most other rural sections, was completely decentralized, and the one-room school house was the hub of the system. In our county, for example, there were more than one hundred districts, and not over five of them provided instruction beyond the eighth grade.

Few pupils were interested in more than a grammar school education. In my high school graduating class, in 1915, there were only fifteen mem-bers, and only two of us completed college. But the basis for an adequate education had been laid, and the idea was catching on rapidly. When I was invited back to give the commencement speech at my high school twenty-five years later, I addressed a class of three hundred and fifty grad-uates, though Russellville's population had not grown appreciably. The explanation was in the burgeoning interest in education. The breakdown of the little red school house pattern, so familiar to northerners, had begun. By 1926, a candidate for governor with the slogan "Better roads to better schools" was chosen to lead the state to a brighter era.

It would be an understatement to say I started my summer-school teaching without enthusiasm. Shakespeare's school boy "creeping like a snail unwillingly to school" had nothing on me! I usually walked the two miles from home to school, but occasionally my mother would drive out in the afternoon to get me. That was welcomed, since it was an extremely hot summer, and by four o'clock I was physically and mentally exhausted.

It seems to me now that it was the most miserable summer of my life, and I don't know who suffered more, my pupils or I. There were eighty-two enrolled, but fortunately for me not all of them came every day. I was only seventeen when the term began, and I had several pupils who were in their teens. This was rather disquieting, as the school had a reputation for being poorly disciplined. However, I was almost as frightened of the first graders, since I knew almost nothing about teaching methods. Some of these were only five years old and shouldn't have been there. I knew the harassed mothers were making a baby sitter out of me; but instead of sending them home I just sent them outside to play, and added to my duties the responsibility of keeping one eye on them.

As the term wore on, and the heat did its malevolent work, and tension made its impact on my nerves, discipline problems showed up. I had to use a switch, finally, on one of the larger boys to establish my authority. Since it was for an open insult in the presence of the others, I decided quickly not to wait for the end of the day, but to administer justice promptly. I had barely begun when an eraser, not the soft modern kind but one of those with a heavy wooden handle, thrown by the boy's brother, whizzed by, just missing my ear, and struck the wall. At that point, judging discretion to be the better part of valor, I ordered both boys to gather up their books and go home, and not to come back until they could show me "proper respect."

They were sons of one of the three school directors, and I was not surprised when he returned with them. While he did not say he approved my actions (I am not sure I did either), he was reasonable, and the incident caused no crisis. I was greatly relieved when the cotton bolls opened early and the directors decided, since most of the children could be helpful in picking the cotton, that the school should close two weeks early. So the terrible summer ended, and I prepared to return to the university and to Marion.

There were some plus quantities in the experience. If I did not impart much knowledge, I did try hard enough to develop a desire on their part for mental growth to enjoy partial success on the inspiration side. One of the patrons was reported to have said as much. Also, partly to make up for my pedagogical deficiencies, I took an interest in the little community. In response to the pathetic suggestion of some of the parents that they needed help in dealing with the moral problems of their young people, I even organized a church for them. I became attached to many of my pupils and often wished in later years that I could see some of them again, so I was quite pleased a few years ago, when an elderly little lady came up to me in the waiting room of a Russellville clinic and asked, "Didn't you teach school at Sunny Point?" When I said yes, she exclaimed, "I told my grand-daughter you did!"

"Oh," I said, "your grand-daughter went to school to me?"

"No," she replied. "*I* did." My reaction was shock, until I reminded myself that several of those pupils were my own age.

When asked at a press conference at Rutgers if I had had previous teaching experience, I said, "Oh, yes. I was the 1916 summer session teacher at Sunny Point, District number seven, Illinois Township, Pope County, Arkansas. I was seventeen years old and had eighty-two pupils enrolled, so you know I learned 'em a lot." I never used that quip again, for I heard a newsman say to his friend, "I reckon the educational standards of Arkansas are not as high as we thought."

My first disillusionment with politics came in my sophomore year. Campus politics is a mild form of the genuine thing, and this first frustration was a poignant one, partly because it happened with surprising suddenness, and partly because it revealed that many personal friendships have only a surface quality. The college annual publication, *The Razorback*, was sponsored by the junior class, which designated the editor-in-chief and the business manager, and then traditionally left the job and the profit (or the deficit) to them. The election always took place at the spring meeting of the sophomores.

My candidacy for editor was not overt, but it was human that I wanted the honor (and one half of the profit), and there was surprisingly no open contest for it. It seemed that a quiet general agreement had been reached that I would be tapped and that my friend Jim Bradley would be the business manager. Not until the events of the class meeting did I have any warning that one of Sigma Chi's rival fraternities wanted one of its junior members to be assistant manager, and they were interested enough in him to make a deal with some nonfraternity men whereby I would be dropped in favor of a dormitory man, with Bradley unopposed for manager. The coup worked. I was edged out by a narrow vote—the first of many defeats I was to experience during the next twenty years. I swallowed hard and moved to make the vote unanimous.

The college defeat was good conditioning for what was to be a common experience years later. That really was its only significance, since the student who defeated me did not return for his junior year. I was quickly elected without opposition to take his place. Jim Bradley did come back, and the two of us put in a busy year at this extracurricular activity, winding up, however, not with a profit but with a deficit which took us three years to dispose of. The deficit was obviously attributable to the higher prices and lower sales resulting from the war.

By early spring of my sophomore year the war clouds had become ominous. Few people on the university campus were surprised when President Wilson summoned the Congress in April of 1917 to declare that a state of war with Germany existed. Overnight everything was changed.

In my junior and senior years, partly due to the decimation of student ranks by the war, I accepted more responsibilities for extracurricular activities than I should have undertaken. I undertook the presidency of the YMCA, and this became one of my major interests. The feebleness of our organization was probably typical of the college YMCAs in that period, but I had a deep concern about it. I thought there should be better religious nourishment during the college years than the conventional church life of the community afforded, and that the YMCA was the logical focus of interest.

I learned that my unquenchable and perhaps irritating zeal for religious activity was not shared by all of the fellows. One of them later revealed that he got tired of my pressuring him to participate in the weekly YMCA service, and came up with a scheme "to get Brooks off his back." His plan worked. When called on by me to give the routine devotional, he announced, "I am an Episcopalian, and it is our practice to kneel for the prayers and the readings, so will you all please kneel." The small group complied, but with great discomfort, for the floor was of rough timber with no carpeting. The knees, even of the most rugged, were soon aching. Shifting posture did not bring relief. But our brother diabolically droned on. Gleefully he later related, "I could see Brooks grimacing as I continued. I knew most of the men were not only in physical pain—they were annoyed by the delay in winding up that service so they could be on time for their dates. Finally, I decided that they and Brooks had suffered enough. So I wound up what was probably the longest reading of sacred literature ever imposed on a college group. Brooks never invited me to conduct a service again!"

The YM and YWCA Boards attempted in my junior year to establish a mission Sunday school in a Fayetteville slum, Rose Hill, located in an attractive scenic area near the university campus. It revealed a considerable sense of idealism for those of us who were interested in it, because it took our Sunday afternoons. All of us had pretty strenuous schedules, but we did attempt it. I taught a class of intermediate boys, and even made visits to some of their homes in an effort to understand their basic problems.

The little building where we met was an old church, abandoned by a congregation that had probably disintegrated under the impact of adversity. The boys were rather unruly, and I had trouble even keeping them in their seats. The section of the church where my class met was in terribly bad repair, and there was a hole in the floor big enough for a boy to escape. Some of them did! This was my introduction to social work, which became subsequently one of my major interests.

In the fall of 1917, Senator Joe T. Robinson, who had achieved considerable prestige in the Senate, came to Fayetteville to address the student body. In the course of his speech he castigated the German ambassador in a manner I thought excessive. It was the only part of his speech which was interrupted by applause. Since there were constructive passages in his speech which were heard in silence, I wrote an editorial for the university weekly (of which I was assistant editor) deploring the tendency in war times to exalt the elements of bitterness and hatred. This, in turn, drew criticism from some students, the implication being that the editors were not wholly patriotic. It was in this period that some American towns with German names were being changed. An Arkansas town changed its name from Germantown to Kenwood, and it has been Kenwood ever since. (In contrast, William Howard Taft, speaking in Fayetteville during the war, pleaded for a tolerant attitude toward the German people, "the poetry-loving, musical people who have contributed much to our own culture.")

At the end of my junior year, I was selected as one of the uninducted trainees in the Fort Sheridan, Illinois, summer officer candidate school. It was my first serious study of miltiary tactics, as the R.O.T.C. course at the university had been very casual. The glamor of military service, which never captivated the public in later wars to quite the same degree, was strong enough to sustain my excitement in spite of my aversion to the rather blood-thirsty type of training which some of my instructors adopted, especially in simulated bayonet combat. In spite of my slight frame, I developed some skill in the art. I was shocked, however, to hear the instructor say, as he pictured imaginary enemies in front of us, that we should delight in driving the bayonet into "the abdomen" of a German. "Hate him and kill him!" he said. Naturally, nobody in the platoon argued with the officer, but I wondered if others didn't feel as I did—that we needed no appeal to hatred in order to learn how to perform well. However, I learned that summer that in spite of American traditions, the war spirit tends to weaken the finer instincts, and discourages the expressions of sympathy and compassion which fighting men are capable of entertaining for the enemy.

The one month's training at Fort Sheridan contributed little to my conditioning for war service. It was exciting to be a part of the Army-Navy complex in Chicago, but I was not impressive enough to be picked for the regular officer candidate school which followed the June training. I was nineteen and age may have had something to do with it. At the end of the month, I headed for Arkansas, stopping a night in Chicago to enjoy the sights, something I could manage at low cost. A narrow room at the YMCA cost me only fifty cents. After I bade good-bye to the other trainees, anonymity overwhelmed me. The only person who noticed me was a little boy on State Street who said, "Mister, are you in the army or the navy?" I identified myself as an army man, and got this reply, "Then I guess you don't know my brother Walter. He's in the navy."

My return from Fort Sheridan was by the way of St. Louis, and I took the night train to Little Rock. I decided to go by coach and save the $3.50 pullman fare so that I could respond, as people were being urged to do, to the appeal to buy war savings stamps. This was a very small sacrifice but I was proud of myself for assuming the discomfort of a night coach trip so that I could do what Uncle Sam was asking. I fear that my patriotism produced a bit of self-righteousness, though it may have been part of a pattern, particularly among college students, who, it seems, from one generation to another, exhibit a degree of idealism.

In September, after two months at home, I enrolled at the university's new Student Army Training Corps, and early in October was sent to the Camp Pike Infantry Officers' School near Little Rock. My transfer from a quiet and sheltered camp to the vast spaces of Camp Pike for the final conditioning of a "shave-tail" deserves more than one short sentence. I was one of about fifty picked for the officers' school, and we were very suddenly advised of the fact. A night trip on the train from Fayetteville to Little Rock, with a change of stations at Van Buren in the middle of the night, was necessary. I sent an indirect message to my parents that their only son would be glad to see them at the Russellville station about 3 A.M. before being swallowed up in the mighty army. But they were not there to greet me. Later I learned that they had indeed gotten the message, but my Father didn't trust it, was sure it was a mistake, so he talked Mother out of going to the station at that inconvenient hour.

The next morning when a neighbor, the mother of one of the others being transferred, phoned to ask why my parents hadn't been there, the balloon went up. The station platform had been crowded with people, the neighbor said, drawing a pathetic picture of me asking everyone if they had seen my dad and mother! Mother wept, thinking I would be on the front line shortly, and my father was deeply penitent. He promised to go with her to Camp Pike on the first day the commanders would let us have company. And mother reported that he was "an angel" for weeks.

Train trips for the members of the armed services during World War I were generally in coaches, and not very attractive ones at that. The trip from Fayetteville to Little Rock was under real hardship conditions. A sergeant was in charge, and shortly after midnight he distributed sandwiches and coffee. When we arrived in Little Rock about dawn, he said that his allowance had been consumed except for five cents apiece, so he smilingly handed us each a nickel, but added that he hoped that we all had a little money of our own to supplement the government's allowance and could go upstairs to the railroad lunchroom for breakfast.

I sat down by a civilian but, as it turned out, he was on his way, in response to the draft notice, to San Antonio to enter the service. His allowance for each meal was one dollar, and without knowing that I had only a nickel for my breakfast he said, "Could you help me eat up the dollar's worth of food?" I cheerfully agreed, but told him that I thought, however, he should enjoy the dollar meal himself, because, once in uniform, it would be closer to a nickel!

The Sergeant arranged for our busing to Camp Pike, and before sundown we were duly enrolled as "officer candidates." Most of the men in my platoon were fresh from Arkansas and Tennessee campuses. The intensive routine began early the next morning, and the strenuous schedule continued even after the armistice. On November 11 we were on a hike on country roads when word reached the camp of the German surrender, but we were not brought into the camp for the celebrations. The regular training schedule continued, so the later discussions of people's ecstasy over the news had a strange sound to us.

Late in October my father and mother came out to the camp for a few hours for the promised visit. I did not know of their arrival. Our company had experienced the usual intensive maneuvers that day, and we were a mile from the barracks when the field assignment ended. The captain called out, "Corporal Hays, take the platoon in and dismiss them." That called for route step and a few songs on the way. Maybe "Tipperary" and "Beautiful Katie," and always "Over There." It was the first time I was given the command.

About a hundred yards from the barracks I looked up and there were my father and mother standing near the barracks! I don't know how soon they realized that their son was in command, but Dad insists that Mother said, when she heard me giving orders, "I knew he would advance in a hurry." The men wondered, though, not knowing the identity of the couple, why there was such an extended final exercise in the manual of arms under the loud commands of the rookie who had just been granted his moment of glory!

I seldom had the blues, but at one stage during the army experience I suffered a mild mental depression. I recall going to the army chapel service one Sunday morning in that mood, hoping that the chaplain would be able to lift me out of it. I wish I knew that chaplain's name and address, because he really knew how to lift! But like ships that pass in the night it was not repeated; he never preached to us again and I never got to thank him. His text was taken from one of the moving passages in the book of Job. "The Lord knoweth the way that I take, and when I have been tried I shall come forth as gold" (Job 23:10).

While in Congress I sometimes heard World War II stories that resembled the stories we were familiar with in the first World War. I recall, for example, the story of the rookie, son of a wealthy New York businessman, who was sent to Camp Robinson, Camp Pike's later name, for his basic training. With disdain for my state's salubrious climate, the young man wrote to his father:

Dear Dad:
Here I am in Arkansas where it's summer all winter and hell all summer. I have to tell you that I am not able to wear that beautiful suit you purchased for me. They put me in a drab khaki outfit that doesn't fit in any particular. And Dad, I am also sorry to relate that I no longer bear your proud name. I am just a number. They gave me a number, "97," I am always "97." They take me out on the drill grounds and into the training areas working me until sundown when we come shuffling back to the barracks. Last Sunday I went to a chapel service for what I thought would be spiritual nourishment and I had hardly sat down

until a cheerful little chaplain jumped up with a song book in his hand and said, "We will now turn to number 97, Art Thou Foot Sore, Art Thou Weary," and Dad, I'm doing five days in the guard house just because I hollored, "hell, yes."

That yarn was one of many that were circulated for our delectation, and no one cared whether they were true or not.

Following the armistice, I was discharged in time to pick up my senior studies at Fayetteville in January. This was a happy time, marred only by an uprising of the students, sparked by those who considered the penalty rule for absences from class known as "sticks" was unfair; but some of President John C. Futrall's practices in fiscal affairs and faculty relationships also came under fire.

I became involved when I found that President Futrall had required the beloved college nurse, "Ma" Hardin, to turn in to the university treasury eighty dollars paid to her by the United States Government for extra-time service to soldier patients. His theory was that her full time belonged to the university, and that she should not have the extra compensation. This appeared to be a harsh and unjust attitude, and I said so in a speech to the students in a protest meeting. It was an emotion-charged speech and probably had a good deal to do with the overwhelming vote in favor of a resolution introduced by another student, asking the president to resign. "Ma" Hardin's case replaced "the sticks" as a rallying cry, for she was known to have been on duty around the clock during the terrible influenza epidemic in the fall of 1918.

However, the students went too far in suggesting the president's resignation, and even though I did not advocate resignation I should bear some responsibility for passage of the resolution. I centered my opposition on the action of denying the nurse her payment from the army. I was the lone senior in the leadership of the protest. The others were juniors, all prominent student leaders. They sensed the logic of my strong appeal not to quit classes, but to submit our grievances to the Board of Trustees. They fell in line with this idea, although we knew the only hope of any adjustment lay not in any positive board action but rather in a gradual yielding by the authorities.

None of us was prepared for the board's drastic action in expelling most of the juniors who took part in the protest. I was suspended for three days for my speech. I would probably have been expelled with the others, had it not been apparent that my position on the eighty-dollar item was essentially correct, and that my influence had been cast against the extreme course of a student strike. Dr. Futrall never told me so, but I suspected that he felt that he had not properly evaluated Ma Hardin's claim to the money. In any event, he was always thereafter exceedingly gracious to me, and I assume that he perceived in me in later years a genuine friendliness and an appreciation of his great contribution to the university. In the early years of his distinguished service he exhibited an inordinate concern for finances which at times overshadowed a sense of human values.

We students were too severe in our attack upon his handling of the nurse's check and other incidents. However, the board's summary disposition of the student protests was likewise too severe. I think I suffered more over the punishment administered to Professor J. Roger Williams than to any of the students. He was summarily dismissed from the faculty on the charge that he had conspired with the students to secure the president's resignation. It seemed a travesty. Roger Williams had been open in his criticism, and there was no dishonorable conduct attributed to him that I was aware of. However, Dr. Robert Lefler, a junior during the year of the disturbance, states in his history of the university that the board's dismissal of Roger Williams was his violation of a state law forbidding a faculty member to join a fraternity.

He was a splendid instructor in the English department, with a gentle manner, a soft voice, a fine sense of aesthetic values and a poetic temperament. When he was brusquely brought into the trustees' meeting to defend himself, one of the board hammered the desk and glared at the kindly little professor. It had been correctly reported to him that Mr. Williams had said that Dr. Futrall should ponder the words of Thomas Carlyle: "If a man hath but two pence, he should buy with one a roll as food for his body, and with the other a hyacinth as food for the soul." The trustee jumped on that like a hungry frog on a fly. "Perfessor," he said, "Fust thing I wanta ast you is jes whut was it you said about a hy-a-ceenth?" The board's mishandling of the entire episode could well be included in an account of the modern universities' handling of student problems. Fifty years after that incident the United States was being shaken by complaints regarding the inadequacy of plans for the governance of institutions of higher learning. It is to be hoped that the ferment of discussion eventually will produce improved methods of adjusting student grievances.

A footnote of interest to Arkansas alumni is the fact that some forty years after the 1919 board's crude handling of the student unrest, a motion was unanimously adopted to the effect that "the offenders" were absolved and their records cleared of the penalties that had been applied. The list of those reinstated included such distinguished men as Judge Bolon B. Turner of the Tax Court of the United States, my law partner in Little Rock from 1929 to 1934; and William J. Knight, a prominent Houston attorney who had gone on to an instructor's position at The University of the South and a Harvard law degree after the expulsion.

Chapter 4 QUEST FOR A VOCATION 1920–1922

What is the city but the people?
Coriolanus, Act III, Sc. i.

IN July after my graduation, my father, sensing the fact that at twenty-one I was ready to cast off the paternal restraints which he was noted for applying, decided that I should proceed to Washington to accept the Treasury Department job that his friend, Congressman H. M. Jacoway, had procured for me. I preferred to wait until September, wanting to stay close to Marion (she was in Fort Smith) as long as I could. We were both of a mind to get married then, but economic considerations fortified parental insistence that we wait, so I reluctantly departed for Washington.

I reached the capital at four o'clock on the afternoon of July 19, 1919, and registered at the Metropolitan Hotel at Sixth and Pennsylvania Avenue, Northwest. When told that the room would be three dollars, I gasped and resolved to lose no time in moving to a rooming house. In those days room and board (two meals) were available at thirty dollars a month, and I found a very acceptable place at 324 Maryland Avenue, Northeast. One can still see on a brick wall near Seventh and E Streets, Northwest the words "Tiogo Hotel—Board and Lodging—$1.00 a day."

By October first I was rooming with Bolon Turner, later my law partner, and still later judge of the Tax Court of the United States, at 1744 Riggs Place, Northwest. I was pleased to write home that we had good neighbors. Victor Murdock, prominent Kansas congressman, lived next door, and Colonel Robert E. Lee, grandson of the general, lived across the street. The fascination of being in proximity to notables did not rub off during my three years in law school.

But in the midst of crowds I was lonesome. For three and a half years I had never been far from Marion and I missed her terribly. There could be no Christmas visit with her—it would have taken a month's salary—and telephone calls were too novel and expensive. In my junior year I did try to talk to her one Sunday evening (the toll was three dollars and seventy-five cents), but I could hear only a few words. Loneliness in the midst of people is a common experience, but my problem was compounded by the rigid schedule, a forty-eight-hour work week (uninteresting and uncreative work at that), and twelve hours classwork every week at George Washington Law School. I have met no test of personal determination during my lifetime that was any more painful than this one.

There were many respites, of course. I enjoyed sermon tasting for the first time. I would occasionally sit in the back row of the balcony of the old Covenant Presbyterian Church at 18th and N Streets and listen to an excellent sermon by Dr. Charles Wood. During that first winter I rotated the visits to First Baptist (I heard William Jennings Bryan preach there one Sunday), Foundry Methodist, Calvary Baptist, First Congregational, New York Avenue Presbyterian, Mount Vernon Place Methodist—and almost invariably benefited by pulpit excellence. It was the outcropping of an interest in ecumenism that was climaxed forty-eight years later in my acceptance of the appointment as the first director of the Ecumenical Institute of Wake Forest University in 1968.

I became more interested in politics and church life than in the law studies. The rational course seemed to be to graduate as a lawyer, return to Arkansas to practice with my father, and perhaps get into politics right away. But the law school routine requirements were irksome, and in contrast with my record at the University of Arkansas, I had trouble making good grades. I can recall only one A during the three years.

I mistook dissatisfaction with the law course for a pull toward the ministry—it hovered over me for months—and there was no one to help me! That is, not until I met a Lutheran minister named John G. Fleck of Baltimore. And this was accomplished by a classmate named Sarah Tilghman, who became a federal judge in Dallas, Judge Sarah T. Hughes. My law school stay would not be complete without a reference to Sarah. We were on the debating team in our junior year and became congenial friends. Sarah sensed my unhappiness over the vocational problems. She admired Dr. Fleck, the young Lutheran minister in her home city of Baltimore, and was concerned enough to ask him to come over to Washington to advise and help me.

We spent an evening together and he did help me. Not by reaching any categorical judgment about what I ought to do with my life, but by interpreting the spiritual and moral aspects of a political course, if I should finally be drawn in that direction. As a professional churchman, he convinced me that there are many parishes for one who wants to utilize his talents in useful and gratifying ways, and that politics may be on a par with the Christian ministry, depending, of course, on how it is pursued. He was quite sure that if I chose a political career I could view it as a parish. A few weeks later he wrote me from Baltimore, and I am heavily in his debt for counsel and encouragement in a difficult and crucial stage of life.

After many years of neglect, I suddenly remembered that I had not seen Dr. Fleck again and had never really impressed upon him the depth of my gratitude. In the meantime Sarah had become a distinguished federal judge, and was widely known for administering the oath of office to Lyndon Johnson at the end of the tragic day of John Kennedy's assassination in 1963. I asked her for Dr. Fleck's address and wrote him. He sent a moving reply with evidence that he recalled the details and indicated that he had followed my political activities.

My acquaintance with Sarah Tilghman Hughes brought illumination on the feminine mind. I carried to Washington the assumption of most westerners that law is the exclusive domain of men—that women are too delicate for that profession. But George Washington Law School, even sixty years ago, was enrolling women in numbers. Sarah was endowed with a tough mind and a sensitive social conscience. I was not surprised at her rise to prominence as a member of the Texas legislature, and finally as a federal judge. In law school days she was a member of the Washington Women's Police Force, though she was just a little more than five feet tall and tipped the scales at a hundred pounds.

Women were not voting in 1919 but neither was I. So I was pleased that in my first experience of voting (in 1920, having reached twenty-one) the suffrage amendment had been adopted, and I stood in line with women to exercise the right to participate in "government by consent of the governed." In later years I enjoyed relating something told me by an election clerk (I don't vouch for it) that one of the new lady voters told the election officials, "All the candidates were such lovely men I didn't want to vote against any of them. I just wrote at the bottom of the ballot, 'God bless you all.' "

Later, while I was in Congress, Marion and I were at a reception in Washington, where a lady said, "I want to introduce my daughter Sarah." I said, "It's one of my favorite names. My mother's name was Sarah, my youngest granddaughter is named Sarah, and one of my very favorite judges is named Sarah." I then identified the judge, and mother and daughter looked quizzically at my wife. She gave them a quick and sincere answer, "She is one of my favorites too." Sarah and I were members of the university debating team which met two Pennsylvania teams, losing to both, defeated first by Swarthmore College and then by the University of Pennsylvania. Another member of the six-man team was Michael Mussman, who, upon graduation, restored the Italian spelling of his family's name, Musmanno. He too became a judge, a colorful member of the Pennsylvania Supreme Court, after a career as a trial lawyer, achieving prominence as a defender of Sacco and Vanzetti.

In the later afternoon of March 19, 1920, I went out to the Capitol, alone, to hear the final debate on the Versailles Treaty. I knew that the roll calls on the treaty with the reservations on the powers of the League of Nations that Henry Cabot Lodge had managed to attach to it, would be completed that evening. I waited in line awhile for a gallery seat and remained until the bitter end. When the clerk announced the vote and the chair declared that the treaty was not approved, Senator Joe Robinon was on his feet with a motion substantially as follows: "I move that the Senate now reconsider the vote by which its consent thereto was withheld." Senator Lodge immediately made a point of order that the Senate, having declined to approve the treaty, had no power over it, since it was automatically returned to the president and was no longer subject to Senate action. Senator Robinson then stated that if the point of order should be sustained he would move to request the president to return the treaty to the clerk's desk "where it is now lying." After considerable parliamentary skirmishing the Robinson motion for reconsideration was defeated. Finally, about 7:35 P.M. the Senate adjourned.

The tragic chapter was thus closed. President Wilson, holding that the reservations had emasculated the treaty, had asked friends of the League to vote against ratification. The moderates were defeated then by the combination of the die-hard isolationists and the partisans of the

League. William Howard Taft, having agreed generally with the president that the League would increase the chances for peace, urged the Senate to approve. He too was disappointed. I walked out of the Capitol into the night, convinced that American participation in the League of Nations was a lost cause. I was heavy hearted, knowing that without the United States, the League would perhaps be impotent.

Who knows what the League might have done with us as a member. I resolved to do what I could as a lawyer to help increase public understanding of the League. Events helped friends to lead us out of isolationism, although my eight-year service on the House Foreign Affairs Committee, and a brief service as delegate to the United Nations General Assembly in 1955, gave me outlets for an avid interest in the United States assuming our rightful place in world leadership. Henry Cabot Lodge's grandson and namesake was our ambassador at the time of my tour at the United Nations, and I recall that he once introduced the subject of his grandfather's ideas about world cooperation in a conversation with me. I think his twofold aim was to assure me that his own commitments were not diluted by the events of 1919–1921 to which I have alluded, and also to bring out some extenuating circumstances which a grandson's pride would naturally induce.

There were distinguished men on the floor of the Senate on that fateful March day. On the Democratic side, in addition to Robinson, there were John Sharp Williams of Mississippi, and the famous J. Hamilton Lewis of Illinois with pink whiskers and a brightly colored vest. He also wore a toupee, and some of his colleagues suspected that he put a little artificial dandruff on his shoulders to add to the deception. On the Republican side, in addition to Lodge, there were Robert LaFollette of Wisconsin, William Borah of Idaho, and Hiram Johnson of California.

Not a member of the Senate as then constituted is now living. Carl Vinson of Georgia was a House member having been elected in 1914 and is the only living member of the World War I Congress. He served until 1965 and thus established an unequaled record of service in the Congress. It was Joe Robinson's performance in the League of Nations' fight that won a glowing accolade from President Wilson, who called Robinson "the moral leader of the Senate." On that issue the senator was certainly on high moral ground.

My mother came from Arkansas for a visit with me in the spring of 1920. I had a vicarious pleasure in her fascination with Washington. It was her first trip to the capital and one of her few trips outside Arkansas. Our congressman and his wife did what Marion and I had an opportunity to do for constituents twenty years later—provided a tea at the Congressional Club, introductions to important people, and visits to Senate and House galleries. Blasé Washingtonians do not realize how the hinterlanders feel swept up into another world by such courtesies. Back in Russellville, Mother talked for years about hearing Galli-Curci sing, and meeting the daughter of U. S. Grant. There had been periods when, in deference to the South's feelings, she would have refrained from mentioning U. S. Grant to her southern associates in the women's clubs in Russellville, but in her later years that had vanished. She even enjoyed telling them in 1953, when Marion and I bought a Washington home, that our windows had shutters retrieved from the Grant home on K Street, and dining room paneling from the John Sherman home. If this raised southern eyebrows, she quoted me, "just some of the loot we recovered."

Mother was unhappy, I think, because I showed little interest in her claim that her paternal grandmother, Frances Webb, had descended from a signer of the Declaration of Independence. "Stephen Hopkins, it was" she would say. However, someone in the Library of Congress had told me that Stephen Hopkins of Rhode Island had no children. But I later learned that indeed he had four sons and I was happy to discover that some of them had settled in southeast Virginia in the county where our Webb ancestors originated, so my great-grandmother Webb was probably right. In any event, there were in the eighteenth century, in addition to that Webb ancestor, sixty-three other persons who contributed just as much to my biological heritage as the Webbs. Each family flows in and out of the great human family.

The extracurricular interests, the intercollegiate debates, and my activities as president of the junior class helped speed the time that separated me from Marion. I was chosen to speak at the law school's centennial banquet, sharing the podium with none other than the famous Roscoe Pound, dean of Harvard Law School. Elmer Lewis Kayser, our university historian, reminded me of this event fifty years later, having run across an account of it in the records he was studying in preparation for the university's sesqui-centennial.

Living and studying in proximity to the White House brought some interesting experiences. In June, 1921, for example, members of our law fraternity, Phi Alpha Delta, were invited to attend a reception on the

White House lawn for the newly initiated honorary member "the president of the United States." Bolon Turner, Joe Barrett, and I were among those who grabbed the chance to see and be seen by President Harding. Luck was with us. When the picture of the distinguished group was to be made with student members in the background, the photographer beckoned a half dozen of us to come around in front of the president, Chief Justice Taft, and General Pershing and sit on the grass.

We then heard the two highest officials in the land in light conversation. With his unique and engaging chuckle Chief Justice Taft said, "Mr. President, did you read what Abe Martin said about me yesterday?" The president said, "No, please tell us." We perked up because Bolon and I had read it just hours before and wondered if Mr. Taft had seen it. Now our curiosity was being relieved. The chief justice continued, "Well, Abe said, 'I thought when Mr. Taft got to be chief justice he'd put on a little dignity but he always looks like a fellow who has looked in an old vest and found a dime!' " After the pictures were taken we shook the president's bulky hand and for a moment looked into his handsome countenance.

In 1943, in my first year in Congress, Marion and I became active in the Calvary Baptist Church in Washington, which Harding had attended. Many members of the congregation remembered his occupying a place, with Mrs. Harding, in a center section pew, and he was known to have admired the pastor, Dr. W. S. Abernethy. It was not known, however, until Francis Russell's biography, *The Shadow of Blooming Grove*, appeared in 1970 that Nan Britton sat in the gallery in at least one service looking down at her inamorato. The author relates that Nan, knowing that Mrs. Harding was away, came one Sunday to the White House, just before the church hour. The president was in a formal outfit, but removed his frock coat and went into a locked room with Nan for a brief enjoyment of her company before going alone in the presidential car to hear Dr. Abernethy preach. But he asked one of his aides to drive Nan to the church for a gallery seat.

It was noted by others on Communion Sundays that he always passed the bread and wine trays on to others without partaking. He told the pastor that he regarded himself as "unworthy" of participation in the sacrament. My judgment regarding the tragedy of this handsome man, so favored by nature but with great limitations, is that he was without venality while making little effort to control carnality. Just as he sincerely disclaimed a sense of adequacy as president so he was evidencing humility in his profession of Baptist faith. He was not hypocritical in seeking the comfort of religion and the forgiveness of God, one of whose commandments he had violated.

One of my favorite professors was Judge Wendell Phillips Stafford, who was also a poet. Like myself, he did not dance, and his fiancée, like Marion, did. One of his verses went like this:

> My lady goes to the dance tonight.
> Her feet glide free, and her eyes glance bright,
> But her heart, sighs she, is away with me
> While we sit and dream in the candle light.

When I learned what was happening in Fort Smith, Arkansas, that year I wanted to say to the Judge, "That's what *you* think." Marion was being rushed by a handsome fellow teacher whose room adjoined hers. I nearly lost her. During my short vacation trip to Arkansas she was honest enough to tell me so, and I returned for my senior year in despondency. Early in the fall, however, a letter came saying she had thought it through and had decided that our original dreams should guide her; in short, that I was for her. It produced a new tranquillity. I determined not to let any further postponements take place. Plans for the wedding early in February were quickly completed. Her resignation from her position as English teacher in the Fort Smith High School at mid-term was accepted.

Before picking up the thread of my happy new prospects, let me refer to a couple of Judge Stafford's fellow professors who were not poets and one who almost was. The near poet was our dean, Merton Ferson, whose lectures in the prosaic course on contracts sounded like the *Odyssey*. Even his name rhymed. Almost forty years after I told him good-bye he wrote me, expressing sorrow over my defeat for a ninth term in Congress.

Another favorite was Dr. Charles Collier, instructor in constitutional law, a familiar law school figure. His lectures and conversations abounded in quips, some of which were bizarre, but always revealing imagination. He had difficulty in pronouncing some words, notably *applicable* and *efficacy*. He grinned at his difficulty with the latter in class one day, having called it "effie casey" and said, "It would be a nice name for a little Irish girl."

Then, there was Professor Hector Spaulding, a brilliant theorist. His hypothetical cases were marvelous, and kept us alert while their intricacies involving *A, B, C, D, E,* and even more characters unfolded. He laughed with us when, pausing after a long statement, he asked, "What should *D* do?", only to have a front-row student say, "*D* died in the early stages of your hypothesis."

I returned to Arkansas for my wedding between semesters. It is easy to remember the date, January 28, 1922, for it was on the Saturday night of the Knickerbocker Theater catastrophe when the weight of snow (Washington's "great snow") collapsed the roof, and more than a hundred people were killed. By the time I was leaving street cars could not operate, so I walked, carrying a heavy bag through the snow, to the Union Station for a midnight departure. I did not learn of the full extent of the tragedy until my bride and I arrived in Washington on the following Sunday, after our wedding on Thursday. Then I learned that one of the young ladies I had supervised in the Treasury Department had been severely injured, and her father, sitting in the next seat, had been killed.

Snow was still piled up in places when our train rolled up to the station. Just as I feared, my Sigma Chi brothers were there to meet us. Poor Marion! She knew only one of them, Bolon Turner, but he was swallowed up in the crowd of strangers throwing confetti and rice. The presence of Bolon's future wife, Essie Lee Pearson, and other Pi Phi sisters did not help very much, as they were strangers to her. We were forced to head a parade through the crowded station with the tallest one of our welcomers going in front ringing a loud cow bell. Ordinarily I would have enjoyed the prominence, but I had a timid wife, and her embarrassment dissipated the fun for me.

Our inexpensive two-room apartment was in a row house owned by my close friend Jack Harlan, a married student with two sons, six and four, and a further increase due in the spring. He and his wife Anne had married before he had completed his undergraduate work. We felt the pinch of the monthly rental of thirty-five dollars but we knew that the pinch on the Harlans was just as great, and therefore we got some satisfaction out of having them as "landlords." The house was located in northeast Washington near the Capitol.

Marion's natural frugality, augmented by her experience in helping her widowed mother make ends meet, was a great help in getting us through our four months in Washington. I had accepted a job as salesman for a new filing system, "The Findex," first of the punch cards, and was given an advance of thirty-five dollars a week. I didn't sell any filing systems during the four months—they were new and expensive and com-plex–but I wore out a lot of shoe leather, and before I finished, a great many Washington executives had a thorough working knowledge of what was happening in the card index world!

Out of my income of approximately $115 a month after paying the apartment rent, $18 went for the tuition. Then I had car fare two ways each day, and I spent twenty-five cents a day for lunch. Marion's allow-ance for groceries and personal needs was only $7.50 a week. She would walk blocks to save two or three cents on meat, or other items.

With neither the time nor the money for full enjoyment of Washing-ton we found our diversions chiefly in the free attractions such as the zoo, art galleries, and the national memorials, with an occasional picture show. We kept up our church attendance habits. One Sunday morning as we went into the National Memorial Baptist Church, we nearly got mixed in with President Harding's party. In fact, the usher tried to seat us with him and his entourage, consisting of Mrs. Harding, Postmaster General Will Hays, and two aides; but while the usher was still bowing to us and indi-cating the last two places in the pew, we firmly declined and seated our-selves across the aisle, two pews in front of the president. We really got a better place from which to view the presidential party, and as that was my first glimpse of our democratic "royalty," I availed myself of the opportunity. This incident illustrates how much simpler the security ar-rangements were in the twenties.

I could not help noticing that the president often glanced at my bride. Later when I saw the picture of Miss Britton I concluded that my wife's looks had a special attraction for him. There was an unmistakable resem-blance between Nan Britton and Marion Hays.

As the end of our Washington "honeymoon" approached I felt sure that in spite of my tight law school schedules, limited finances, and the usual newlyweds' problems, Marion had found excitement in having a home to manage and in exploring her new environment, what I consider the world's most exciting city. My boost in morale was best reflected in the fact that my grades in the final semester were the best of my three years in law school. In June, 1922, I received my law degree in a typical ceremony. And now Arkansas beckoned.

Chapter 5 LIFE IN A QUADRANGLE 1922–1925

The little things of living
*   are dearer than the large,*
The scallop shell of poets
*   than Cleopatra's barge,*
Singing words of kindness than
*   tomes by sages wise,*
A smile from one who loves us
*   than promised paradise.*
Anon.

FOLLOWING graduation, with me clutching my diploma, we headed quickly for Arkansas, riding in a soot and smoke infested Pullman car to St. Louis, and then to Little Rock. Air conditioning was not even a gleam in the engineering eye in 1922, so everyone suffered without the pleasure of foreseeing the day when traveling in comfort would be possible, even in one-hundred-degree outside temperature.

I knew it would be a new life for Marion. Fort Smith, where she had grown up, was Arkansas' second city in size, and Russellville, which was to be our home for the next three years, had scarcely six thousand people. Only the downtown business section had pavement, and she was to be exposed to dusty streets and other discomforts. But she bore it without complaint, and she was able to find a fairly congenial atmosphere at the church and in the simple social and cultural activities of the town.

The July before we returned, my father had announced his candidacy for the congressional seat being vacated by our friend Mr. Jacoway and I plunged into his unsuccessful campaign, helping to direct his headquarters in Little Rock. I was never sure that his heart was in the race. He knew that Mother and I were ambitious for him, and in deciding to run he may have been unduly influenced by our wish to see his remarkable talents utilized in the Congress. He was just fifty.

55

The outcome was determined largely by the Ku Klux Klan, which was at the height of its political power. It was a three-man race, so my father was splitting the anti-Klan strength with a strong candidate from Little Rock. The Klan candidate won. My father was third, though he showed considerable strength outside the Klan centers and ran a respectable race. I was in Russellville receiving returns on election night, and after midnight had a phone call from a friend of the other anti-Klan candidate.

"Brooks, obviously your father can't win," he said. "I know you would rather our man would win than see a Klansman take the office. You can throw enough votes to us to win. Won't you touch base with your people in the townships that haven't reported, and tell them to do some switching?" I could hardly believe my ears. I had heard of such irregularities and was destined later on to be a victim of the practices, but I was not prepared for that kind of shocking manipulation in our district. I promptly told him that we would not consider doing such a thing.

After the primary I was informed by the state Democratic organization that I had been designated as secretary of the state convention to meet in the fall. I was scarcely twenty-four, and at that age was probably the youngest person ever to hold the job. It was a nice honor and put me in a position of advantage in getting acquainted with party leaders around the state.

During the summer I took the examination for admission to the Arkansas Bar. As a boy, I had heard circuit judges in open court announce the application of someone for license to practice, and at the same time appoint a small committee to examine the applicant. They would retire to interrogate him, and return shortly with the recommendation that he be admitted. Few were ever refused admission, though, occasionally, there was a postponement for further study. I understood that the questions put to the budding barristers were uncomplicated.

By 1922 the procedure had been changed to require written examinations at the district level, the papers to be graded by lawyers appointed by a state board. But the methods adopted by our district committee were just as ludicrous as the oral examinations had been. Members of the bar walked at will in and out of the room where we applicants were preparing our answers. They enjoyed reading the questions aloud and engaging in prolonged arguments about the answers. There was seldom agreement among them, but the examining committee members were just as eager as others to express their opinions, and their opinions obviously helped us with the answers. Under these circumstances, I did not feel proud of my certificate of admission. Fortunately, the weaknesses in the system were evident, and changes were made in the procedure so that there is now a central examining committee for the whole state, with the identity of the authors of the papers undisclosed to the committee.

The next step in the process of my initiation into the legal profession was getting my place in my father's firm prescribed. I had hoped that we could have a father and son partnership, but Dad wanted another senior member, and since I was a fledgling, I could understand that. He chose A. B. Priddy, who was stepping down from the circuit judgeship, so very shortly the words "Hays, Priddy, and Hays" were emblazoned above the entrance to our second-floor suite across the street from the courthouse. Judge Priddy was able and colorful, also patient with my lack of maturity. He was accustomed to emitting cheerful little quips during the day or breaking into a religious song. One of his favorites went "How tedious and tasteless the hours when Jesus no longer I see ..."

One morning he greeted me like this, "Brother Brooks, do you know any schemes and stratagems whereby we may fall upon the unwary and gather in a little coin of the realm?" The rhetorical question intrigued me, for my share of the firm income was only 20 percent, and during the first year was under two thousand dollars. I certainly needed more coin of the realm! However, I probably produced little business for the firm, and most of the "heavy" work during my two and a half years in the Russellville firm was by my father and Judge Priddy. Clients preferred "the old heads." It was perfectly natural that I would drift into a sort of public relations representative of the firm. My interests in rural problems mounted, and it meshed with the political, economic, sociological, and theological complex which filled my quadrangle.

My father's reputation as a trial lawyer was equaled by few men in Arkansas. He was even employed to try criminal cases in eastern Oklahoma, where his name was something to conjure with. His most famous trial involved one of my schoolmates, Arthur Tillman. We were shocked one morning to read in the *Arkansas Gazette* of the disappearance of Amanda Stevens, a young lady living in a rural community near Father's boyhood home in Logan County, which adjoined our county. There were no clues and no suggestions of foul play. We had another shock a few days later when the same newspaper announced the discovery of Amanda's body and the arrest of Arthur Tillman on a charge of murdering her.

The Tillmans had lived in Russellville a few years prior to moving to Logan County, and I had been in the same classes with Arthur. He was a member of the high school football team. Under modern conditions with grade standards prescribed for team members, Arthur probably could not have made the team, but one of the other players told me that if Arthur once got the football it was good for a touchdown. Nothing could stop him.

The circumstances surrounding Arthur's arrest were very unusual. The families, Stevens and Tillman, had lived in a sparsely settled area. Arthur had been courting Amanda, and testimony at the trial established that they had been intimate. Speculation was rife when Arthur also disappeared about the time of Amanda's disappearance, but there was no evidence of anything of a criminal nature until an amazing event took place.

Near the Tillman farm was a rental dwelling that had recently been occupied, but the couple had moved away. It was located near the top of a hill which had been cleared of timber so that one standing on the porch of the little house could have a view extending several hundred yards. One day the former occupants returned to get some things they had left. At a pause in their work of gathering the items together, the husband walked out on the porch and was just preparing to light his pipe when he looked across the open space at an old well, no longer in use, covered with boards after its abandonment. He saw a figure approach the well, kneel down, and remove the boards. He called to his wife to join him, saying, "There's Arthur Tillman looking in that old well. I'll bet Amanda Stevens' body is in there." The person disappeared into the woods. Help was summoned. The water was bailed out, and the body of the unfortunate girl was discovered weighted down with rocks.

Arthur was immediately arrested. He did not deny looking in the well, but insisted that he was looking for one of his father's calves which had disappeared, and he thought perhaps the calf had fallen into the well. The girl was found to have been pregnant and it was assumed that this supplied the motive for her murder. At the trial Arthur's defense was an alibi. The case against him was circumstantial. His best witness was his father, who gave a recital of Arthur's movements during the period, and if his statements on the witness stand were true, someone other than Arthur committed the crime.

The trial commanded statewide attention. Strong legal talent appeared for both the state and the defense. My father was employed by local friends of the dead girl to assist the state's attorney. Being older and better known, he overshadowed the prosecuting attorney.

I attended the trial on the closing day to hear the arguments to the jury and the judge's final instructions to them. I saw Arthur escorted into the courtroom by the sheriff, looking very pale from a long incarceration, but smiling faintly. I hoped that he would not see me and I am confident that he did not. I listened intently to what the judge had to say about circumstantial evidence. Generally, such evidence is likened to a chain with the argument that it is no stronger than the weakest link. The judge told the jury, however, that it is more like a rope, the strands being supplied by different witnesses, and altogether, if believed and meeting the legal requirements, constituting strength. Some testimony might be discarded without weakening the rope.

My father in his argument conceded that if Arthur's father spoke truthfully the verdict should be "not guilty." His most eloquent passages had to do with the incidents connected with the discovery of the body and the nature of the father's testimony. Since I figured in the latter reference, I can hardly forget it. Father said, "If you believe him, you should clear the son, set him free, and if not, then do not think harshly of this father for perjuring himself. His son's life is at stake. I have a son, gentlemen of the jury, and if that lad were in this dire condition, threatened with execution, the night would not be so dark nor the elements so forbidding as to prevent my going to his rescue to perjure myself! Yes, to save him from the gallows, I would crawl on my hands and knees through briers and ignore the bleeding and pain if only I could get to the place where I might offer any testimony, true or false, to save him! This, I submit, is a father's natural attitude, and I do not condemn John Tillman." Whether this assumed course of conduct should be so defended involves profound personal ethics, but I never raised this question with my father.

My father then detailed to the jury the circumstances of the discovery of the body, the terrible evidence of Arthur's guilt. He described the return of the tenant and his wife to their former home, and made much of the fact that the very proof of death—"the corpus delicti"—was identified with the reappearance of Arthur Tillman. With a fine display of his gifts of flowery eloquence, my father said to the jury, "Providence had set the silent sentinels of retribution in the proper place and at the right time to make sure that such a cruel crime would not go unrevealed."

The defendant was convicted but, after a reversal of his conviction by the Supreme Court on technical grounds, a second trial was ordered. He was again convicted and sentenced to death by hanging. The sentence was sustained, and Arthur Tillman was hanged. It was the last legal hanging in Arkansas history, for the legislature soon thereafter adopted the more merciful method of electrocution.

I was saddened by this tragic end of a former schoolmate, but did not begin to formulate my conviction that capital punishment ought to be abolished altogether until I witnessed an electrocution a half dozen years later, an experience I shall describe in a later chapter.

In the early days of my practice I had to struggle to defend my dignity. To everyone I was "Steele Hays' boy," and even the small children around town called me "Brooks." Soon after the new firm opened for business, I was acting as host for a distinguished visitor, Dr. Doak Campbell, later president of Florida State University, and walking down the main street of the town with him I suddenly heard a piercing soprano voice exclaim, "There goes my little lawyer." It was "Aunt JoAnn," a popular and colorful former slave who in her eighties was still vigorous. According to a Russellville legend, she was the author of the expression "Plum Nelly." It was derived from her answer to the question, "Where do you live?" "Plum out of town and nelly to nowhere," she said. I have heard that it was adopted as the name of a home by a member of the famous Mayo family at Rochester, Minnesota, one of whose family married a Russellville young man and who consequently knew Aunt JoAnn.

During one of my political tours as a member of Congress twenty-five years later, an attractive young black lady introduced herself to me in Kansas City, and said, "I am Aunt JoAnn's granddaughter and am a lawyer here in Missouri." It gave me real satisfaction that a home town girl of the other race could rise above her handicaps in this fashion.

My boyhood quadrangle had been bounded by the lines from home to school, to courthouse, to church. After I outgrew activities at the school, I would have had to call it a triangle except for the new civic and economic concerns which I became a part of.

I organized a Lions Club within a few months after the new law firm started, after declining Rotary Club membership on the theory that there was a lot of leadership talent among the younger business and professional men which needed harnessing. The Rotary leaders agreed. Our new little club supplied the town with civic pep pills. We immediately launched a campaign for a public library, the members accepting the drudgery of collecting books, and doing some of the manual labor on a small frame building to house it on the yard of the Presbyterian Church. It was made available by the youthful pastor, William Hodgson, with whom I had been associated in the Rose Hill Mission at the university. The town loved our clownishness. We brought overalls to the noon meeting one week, donned them at the close, and went out with paint buckets to paint the light posts which were becoming very rusty. We helped the county agricultural agent organize calf clubs over the county, and even sponsored a beautification campaign. Petunias bloomed all over the place the year that the Lions called for flower beds to replace the weeds. Finally, as president of the club, I interested the Harmon Foundation of New York City in buying a tract of land within the city to be developed as a playground.

When Marion and I moved to Little Rock in January, 1925, I transferred to the Lion's Club there, soon became district governor for two years, and have continued my interest in the club during these fifty-odd succeeding years. The Lions' best work is in the smaller communities like Russellville, but like other civic luncheon clubs is interested in good causes and has significance in the larger centers too.

Meanwhile, our family life pursued a normal course and I was made very happy one spring day by the news, happily conveyed to me by Marion, that we would become parents. At three o'clock a.m. on October 23, 1923, Marion woke me. "I think it's time to go get Miss Mary," she said. Miss Mary Finley was a practical nurse who had helped bring scores of Russellville babies into the world and was not only experienced and efficient but much beloved. Marion wanted to have the baby at home, so we had made arrangements with Miss Mary months before.

I didn't spend much time on my dressing, just threw on enough to keep me from getting arrested, and dashed downstairs to the car. I don't think that old Ford had ever made such good time as it did that morning! Miss Mary had kept her suitcase packed, so we were back in record time. I phoned the doctor, my uncle, Dr. Fred Hays, and he came before dawn. But the baby didn't get there until noon. I was worn to a frazzle, and could hardly take it in when Uncle Fred said, "Well, Brooks, you've got a fine girl!" Later on, when I invited a little sympathy for the ordeal I had been through, my wife exclaimed, "What do you mean 'ordeal'? You sat there in the bedroom and entertained Miss Mary and Uncle Fred while we all waited!" My defense was that I was so nervous I just couldn't stop talking!

Our baby was tiny, seven pounds, but perfectly formed. We named her Betty Brooks. Within a few weeks we moved into our new home, a small house we had built for four thousand dollars, and Marion exulted, "What else could you provide me with, now that I have a little house, a little car, and a little baby?"

The car was the product of the firm's biggest case, not biggest in terms of work or property involved, but a case in which we represented a wife suing a very wealthy husband for divorce. The judge awarded us a three thousand dollar fee, and my part, six hundred dollars, was enough to buy a car of our own—a Ford coupe—so we didn't have to borrow Dad's five passenger touring car. And when summer came our favorite evening recreation was a drive into the countryside. Once we ran out of gasoline two miles from town, but I knew a man who lived a short distance from the road, and I walked to his front porch and gave the usual "Hello." It was dark, and I wanted him to know it was a friend in trouble. "Hello, Mr. Wells," I called. "I'm out of gas." He came to the front porch. "No gas," he said, "but let's try coal oil. I've heard it works if the engine is hot." He brought me a gallon can filled with coal oil, a potato plugging the spout, and it did work! We drove home on kerosene!

But not all excursions in a Ford had pleasant and easy outcomes. On a business trip (I believe it was in connection with that divorce case) with Marion and the baby, then ten months old, a hundred miles from home, we had four flat tires in a five-mile stretch, and the thermometer was at one hundred degrees. Fixing a tire in those days was a complicated and nerve-wracking chore. Cars did not carry extra wheels, just a patching outfit and a pump, a jack, and big tools for plying the casing off the rim. The process called for placing a rubber patch on the tube and then painfully replacing the tire and pumping air into it. When it was completed, a fellow was near exhaustion. I repeat—four in a five-mile stretch! No one welcomed the spare tire arrangement more than I did.

My "man about town" reputation had an interesting coloration. My friend Owen Cooper, Mississippi businessman, introduced me to an audience forty years later by giving this mythical account: "I stopped in Russellville to get gasoline and asked the operator, 'How is my friend Brooks Hays doing?' I got this reply, 'Doing all right. Works hard to support a wife and baby. He's upstairs there, now, working on a law suit, or maybe he's across the street helping his papa try a case. But come night, he'll be out speaking at a Baptist meeting or a singing convention or a banquet somewhere. You might put it like this: he's a ball of fire by day and a bag of wind by night.' " It would have been more accurate if the gas salesman had added, "If not working on a law suit, at least helping a veteran make out papers for hospitalization, or advising someone on an uncompensated basis about his legal rights."

Every small-town lawyer has a certain amount of "pro bono publico" activity, and if I carried more than my share it was perhaps because of my inordinate sociological interests. I was interested in what was happening at Raspberry, Nogo, Booger Hollow, Lost Corners, Buttermilk Valley, indeed at every village in the area, and the people were aware of my concern. I began to take notice of the economic and social problems of rural Arkansas, an interest that was to flower in my service as assistant attorney general of the state, and in my political activities for sixty years.

Gradual liquidation of the area's social assets was taking place. Soil conservation problems piled up because not enough farmers had learned that water erosion must be restrained by policies affecting a whole watershed, and that cooperation between federal and state agencies would be essential to a solution. Added to this, was the mining of the soil, the region's basic resource. Also the depletion of timber and mineral resources was taking a terrific toll. Experts at the University of Arkansas and elsewhere were beginning to talk about these problems and I was beginning to wonder how I could help do something about them.

The political year 1924 might have offered me an opportunity, had I yielded to a mild impulse, to run for the state legislature. I passed it up. Also as the 1924 political season approached, some of my fellow-townsmen wanted me to run for prosecuting attorney. My refusal might be regarded by some as quixotic but my reasons seemed valid then, and they still do. One of the older lawyers, Bob Ragsdale, who had made an earlier race for the position and had worked toward another campaign for four years, was eager for the place. My happiness did not depend upon it, and apparently his did.

Still there was political recognition for me. Senator Joe T. Robinson was rising rapidly as a national figure in the Democratic party, and when he was scheduled to speak in Russellville I was picked by the political elders to offer a resolution at a luncheon in his honor proposing a "Joe T.

Robinson for President Club." It had an enthusiastic response, and I was mentioned on page one of next morning's *Gazette*, the first time for a "page one" story since my clash with the university authorities five years earlier.

The Baptists took a good deal of my time. I was elected superintendent of the Sunday School and a member of the Board of Deacons. The pastor was a Klansman, and this was displeasing to some of the congregation, particularly to my father and me, but we were doubtless a minority. One Sunday evening Klansmen paraded up the aisle into the pulpit stand, ceremoniously handed the minister an envelope which contained a check for himself, and just as solemnly paraded out. The preacher was ecstatic, his cheeks flushed with enthusiasm and gratitude. It was a profaning of the church, but we non-Klansmen could do nothing about it except to enjoy kidding them the next day, having recognized some of them from their posture and shoes. The reaction set in within two or three years, and the Klan strength vanished as quickly as it grew. It did considerable damage, however, in the estrangement of neighbors and the sowing of seeds of religious and racial distrust and prejudice.

It may be difficult for those who have not lived in small southern communities to appreciate the extent of the influence of the church on the lives of the people. It is the center of social interests and the stimulus for the cultural life of many people, not limited to religious concerns. The democracy of my church and its gospel of love, anchored to the Bible and Baptist tradition, were the magnets that held me. I found much to criticize in the evangelistic methods employed, but on balance found the church's institutional life rooted to the interests of "the common people," hence justifying my enthusiasm. This, in spite of the fact that prejudices were invariably reflected in church policy. Our hope to overcome this is the emerging of a progressive leadership, and a responsiveness by the churches to youth's demands for change. My "liberalism," a mild form, was tolerated at Russellville.

However, there were in time pockets of opposition to me for what was deemed by some who regarded themselves as defenders of the faith as youthful independence and dubious orthodoxy. This dissatisfaction resulted in my being denied an honorary degree by Ouachita Baptist College.

One of the young theologians said to me at an Ecumenical meeting in

1968, "You don't know how it inspires us young radicals to see an old radical around." I was glad for him to point out that the word *radical* is derived from the Greek word for root. So we are dealing with root problems, he said.

The Russellville church had changed a good deal during my seven years of college life. Returning from law school in 1922, I found a new building, with Sunday school rooms and other facilities to replace the one room used for all services. This change also affected other rural churches, and the fact was quaintly put by a Methodist, "We are now wearing shoes, and respectability pinches." Still many of the old values held on.

The conventional revival meetings had a constructive side. It was the community's conscience struggling with the problem of individual commitments to the Christian life, and some of the conversions were genuine, even though, as in one notorious case at Russellville, it had to be done all over again every year. He was one of the town drunks who seemed to enjoy parading his repentance. The pattern was followed in the rural sections of the South and West. Jim Trimble, my colleague in Congress from another Arkansas district, told me of a feud between two farmers growing out of a charge by one that his neighbor had stolen one of his hogs. There was never any satisfactory proof, but the old gentleman stuck to his charge that Ewing Hasper had stolen his hog. At one of the annual revivals, Ewing made a "profession of religion" and joined the church. When it happened, everyone under the big tent looked back to where his detractor was sitting to see how he would take it. Finally the latter walked along the sawdust path, straight to the new convert, held out his hand and said, "I'm glad you've done this, Ewing. You'll make a good Christian, and I wish you well." Then, walking away, he looked back over his shoulder and said, "But, of course, you did steal my hog!"

Church gatherings even reflected something of the political mores. For example, there was the story of the deacon who was very politically minded. Someone asked him, "How was the service yesterday out at Bethel Church?" He got this reply: "Very good." Then he asked, "How was the attendance?"

"Oh, I'd say about a hundred voters . . . er, ah, wurshippers." Some unfriendly souls might have suspected that my own motives through the years were tinged with politics, except for my long history of church activity, and further, that I did not become a candidate for office during the three years' practice at Russellville, and for three more years after moving to Little Rock.

The most satisfying disclaimer of this kind came near the end of my congressional service, nearly thirty years later, when a Little Rock lawyer, who had always been aligned with my opposition, came to my office to say this: "I used to think your religion was a pose, but I was terribly wrong about that. I know now that it wasn't, and because I am not a religious person, and may be near the end of my road, I want your opinion. Do you think God would let me slip in a back door, forgive me for everything, and let me mix with those who have done better by Him in this world than I have? I want your opinion." Before giving him an answer, I said, "Well, no finer statement has been made with reference to my faith than you have expressed." Then I told him, "No, you won't go in the back way. The Lord will roll out a carpet for you down the front steps." And I explained why I thought it would be that way. It was a bit of religious counseling that gave me a lot of pleasure and I believe comfort to him.

In the past we were sometimes sloganized out of an imaginative approach to a faith that should take account of our social sins as well as of individual sinfulness. Today it is different. Students are challenging the old assumptions. For example, they picketed one of our 1969 Baptist conventions with a placard reading, "Christ is the answer, but what are the questions?" In my rural environment, however, I have discovered occasional nuggets of wisdom from such homespun sayings as "The best way to get Christians is to grow 'um." Again, a homespun ungrammatical utterance from a rugged old Baptist, J. B. Gambrell, one of my predecessors as president of the Southern Baptist Convention: "A man don't know nuthin' he didn't learn." But one of the first things a young churchman learns, if he is wise, is that he cannot learn all he needs to know for survival. Some things he must inherit from the race. It must be granted that this acquisition may leave a fuzzy line between faith and knowledge.

It was precisely at this point of dealing with social problems that I became somewhat critical of church policy. It was partly a matter of developing a common vocabulary so that the impingement of Christian ideals on the human environment would be felt. There was a feeble effort in the period I refer to, even in the Baptist community, but it was a northern influence, chiefly Walter Rauschenbusch's, so it was dismissed as modernistic by many Southern Baptists.

And even with my enthusiasm for efforts to define the social expression of the gospel, I conceded the essentiality of its individual expression. The problem originated really from the reluctance of Baptists (and others) to go further. We were oversimplifying the matter. "I believe," says the new convert and the transformation was regarded as ended. The democratic tradition which Baptists appeared to cherish was not as thoroughgoing as I wished. As a general practice the dialogue was not a part of congregational procedures except in the deacon's handling of routine problems and in the fervent arguments in Sunday school class over the meaning of certain scriptures. The approaching social crises of the thirties received little attention either in the sermons or in the Baptist literature which plugged for conservative theological views.

The woman who did my mother's washing sat on the same pew with my parents. "Miss Helen," mother called her, for she had status too. She could not preside over the Women's Missionary Society as Mother did, nor give anything like as much as my father to the church treasury, but in the congregational decisions, Miss Helen's vote had the same weight as theirs. I think of Miss Helen on that pew as a symbol of Baptist equality. However, years later I had a humbling thought about that symbol. If Miss Helen's skin had been black she would not have been there.

We needed at that stage to do something to improve our relationships, white and black, Baptist and non-Baptist. Had we at Russellville and elsewhere in the South made a beginning in the twenties or earlier in promoting racial justice and goodwill, and finding answers to social questions, the ecumenical movement would today be much further along.

It is heartening to find a new consciousness of these problems in the Baptist community, but the progress must be more rapid if we spare ourselves the tension and suffering that come with neglect of them. Much of the ridiculous isolationism which has plagued our young people is passing. Our family smiles now at the statement of the mother of one of my father's friends who, moving from a rural community to Russellville, joined the Presbyterians, a church unknown in her village, "Well, anyway, praise the Lord," his mother exclaimed, "he didn't line up with them sprinkling Methodists."

These lingering signs of a nineteenth-century rivalry bring only chuckles now, but the rivalry was very real until a few years ago. It was illustrated for me by John O. Gross, a prominent Methodist leader who as a young man held a revival in an eastern Kentucky village. It was in

January but in spite of the cold weather the meeting was a success. There were fifteen conversions. In a conference with the stewards at the end of the revival he said, "I'll be back in the spring to baptize them." (In Kentucky, as in many other areas, "baptize" meant immerse in running water, even among the Methodists.) The chairman said, "Spring, nothing! You wait 'til then and the Campbellites will have 'em, ever' one." So Mr. Gross broke a thin layer of ice on a stream and baptized them.

A fine by-product of Baptist informality in church life is enjoyment of humor to brighten daily life. Rarely did a Sunday pass without something happening that could be passed around at the whittler's club on Monday. For example, one of the popular laymen, President J. R. Grant, of the state college at Russellville, was filling the pulpit one Sunday in the pastor's absence and he undertook to tell the familiar story of Sam Jones's comment in a revival meeting. "You women," said the famous evangelist, "are apainting and apowdering your faces like a bunch of Comanche Indians. Is there one among you who didn't do that before you came to church today?" At the rhetorical pause one very homely member of the congregation stood up. Startled out of his gallantry, Sam Jones said, "Well, Sister, I believe a little would help you." When Mr. Grant reached the point in the story at which the question was asked, "is there one among you who didn't apply the paint and powder before church," one very saintly member, not grasping the story, stood up. Whereupon Mr. Grant stuttered interminably before awkardly abandoning his story. "Well, thank you Sister," he said and announced the closing hymn.

Baptists and Catholics stand out as frequent objects of gentle church humor (sometimes not so gentle). The explanation, I believe, is that their constituencies have a wide range of economic, political, and ethnic ties; both are "of the people," they cover the whole spectrum. This Baptist likes it that way.

Danny Thomas, in a dinner meeting in Washington in 1961, implied that other church groups would be glad to have the same prominence. He said, "My pianist complains that I never mention the Lutherans. I just never saw a funny Lutheran." Well, Danny wasn't looking hard. Some good yarns were given me by Lutherans, some being at their expense. For instance, a Catholic priest who enjoyed teasing a nun called her on the phone, disguised his voice, and said, "Sister Margaret, this is Martin Luther." Without a second's delay she said, "Well, Brother Martin, where in hell are you?"

Chester Lauck, who created and portrayed the radio character Lum Edwards in the Lum and Abner team was a friend of mine and a political ally in Arkansas long before he became famous. He and Norris Goff (Abner) were among my leading supporters in my first campaigns. In later years Chester presided at more than one Sigma Chi affair when I was the speaker, and I was always sure he would find a way to exploit my Baptist ties. In our last appearance he suddenly shifted to his Lum Edwards accent and said, "Ole Brooks ast me 'while ago how the new preacher at Pine Ridge wuz adoin'. I could tell him 'cause las' Sunday I went over there and heerd him. I will say this that oncet he mounted the platform, rared back, took a deep breath and cleared his throat, he come forth with the best out-loud talkin' I ever set under. And it wuz such a change, 'cause the feller before him wuz mediander—just mediander. Facts is, when he finally made up his mind to move on he told 'em at church meeting, 'Brethren I have had a clear message from Jesus after talkin' to him about going' on and Jesus tole me it's time I move on to another place.'

"Then," said Lum, "the congregation stood up and broke into the song, 'What a friend we have in Jesus.' "

Also there were smiles when one of our Baptist ladies attended an Episcopal service and said to the rector, "I just love your 'piscopalian lethargy." Pulpit humor is generally welcomed in the rural worship services although one of my friends, C. E. Bryant of the Baptist World Alliance, encountered surprising resistance one Sunday a few years ago in my boyhood church. When making reference to his pleasure in being "in Brooks' home church," he told a couple of my anecdotes, only to be interrupted by a stern old deacon with the admonition to "cut out the levity and start preaching the gospel."

The Russellville beginnings constitute a body of cherished memories, and when the roots were pulled up in January, 1925, for the Little Rock base there was a pang. I resolved, however, that I would never fail to contemplate "the pit from which I was digged and the rock from which I was hewn" (Isaiah 51:1).

Chapter 6 NEW PROSPECTS
1925–1928

But yield who will to their separation,
My object in living is to unite
My avocation and my vocation
As my two eyes make one in sight.
Robert Frost

IN July of 1924 Marion and I put a suitcase and our six-months-old Betty in the Ford and drove to Siloam Springs for a Baptist Youth assembly. It was an inexpensive and, by present day standards, a rather unexciting vacation, but we were with congenial church friends and it was a welcome respite from our routine. One couple whose company we enjoyed was the pastor and his wife, Clyde and Amy Hickerson, who had married the preceding October. I had served as a member of the committee which picked him for our minister, and my hopes were pinned on him to check the rapid turnover in pastors for our church. This he did by declining other calls for eleven years. His friendship and association for the eighteen months we were in his congregation more than counterbalanced the misery we suffered under one of his predecessors, the Klan sponsor.

Our vacation was interrupted by a phone call from Judge Priddy. He told me that the leading candidate for attorney general of the state wanted me to manage his campaign. While it had not been mentioned in the judge's conversation with the candidate, precedents supported the assumption that, if successful, he would make me his assistant. Both the judge and my father wanted me to do it. We drove at once to Russellville for a final huddle and decided I should accept. We made arrangements at once for a six weeks' residence in Little Rock which would take us to the date of the primary, which in 1924 was decisive.

Our candidate, H. W. Applegate of Jonesboro, won, and in November he announced my appointment. This time the *Gazette* carried my picture on the front page, something that signified its importance from a political standpoint. A new chapter in the Hays family story had begun.

Leaving Russellville brought some pangs. It was fun to live near my parents and to be able to see my kinfolks and boyhood friends every day. Also to be so much more a part of community life than I could hope to be for a while in the big city—for we always thought of Little Rock in those terms. But the heritage of my small-town life would always be visible in my activities and my political posture. The rural people were "my people," and I would be seeing political issues largely through their eyes, even though many of them, like myself, had become a part of the big-town complex.

About this time I spent a night with a farm family in the Arkansas valley, the guest of a young farm couple in a small house built of rough timber. It was in the piney woods. During the night I felt the presence of an army of bedbugs. Sleep was impossible. In disgust I got up and walked into the yard. The moon was high, and I could see the outlines of the house and barn and the trees that surrounded them. The Arkansas River only a few hundred yards below me was beautiful in the silver light. I have experienced the stillness of midnight in the woods a few times, but never such stillness as this.

As I stood by the fence in enjoyment of my escape from the misery inside, I thought of the little family's struggle against many handicaps. These very trees, which add so much to the beauty of the landscape and the comfort of the home, are breeding places for loathsome insects. The important fact about the rural people is not that they live in such beauty or that they have such handicaps, but that they are people of character. They will ultimately win out in their struggle. The storms, droughts, and epidemics that bring temporary distress will not down them. They are accustomed to the struggle, and they will keep on. "Life is an offensive against nature's repetitive mechanisms," said A. D. Whitehead. They don't know that Whitehead said it, or might not know what he meant if they were told he said it, but they are proving its truth very well.

On March 25 of our first year in Little Rock (1925) our second baby, a son, was born. We named him Marion Steele for his mother and my father. He is now a judge on the Arkansas Supreme Court. A lady judge on the same court of six members is also named for my wife (Judge

Marion Penix). Having one third of a judicial tribunal named for her is quite a distinction for a person who thinks a subpoena is a new sandwich!

Shortly after we moved to Little Rock, I was drafted as teacher of a young men's Sunday school class of the Second Baptist Church. It met in a tiny building of its own back of the church, and in the twenty years I devoted to this service we outgrew two buildings and reached an enrollment of three hundred and fifty men. It was originally the Baars' Class, named for a revered former teacher, Mrs. F. D. Baars, but shortly after I became teacher the name was changed to the Brooks Hays Class. I was once introduced to the Dallas Rotary Club as "the only man in the United States who was named for a Sunday school class."

The members were careful, with my cooperation, not to involve the class in any of my political campaigns. This made possible a rather bizarre situation in 1930 when I, the teacher, and two of the members were all running for governor of the state! The others were former governor Terral and the state auditor, Carrol Cone.

This was not an ordinary class. It represented a fine cross section of Little Rock life, for many men who belonged to other churches attended regularly, and then went to their own worship services at eleven o'clock. Also there was a wide range of economic and intellectual interests. We had millionnaires and people on welfare, Ph.D.s and some who had never gone to high school. I remember a feeling of chagrin I had, but only for a moment, when a young man whose brother was in the Fort Roots mental hospital said to me, "I hope you don't mind Brother coming every Sunday. This class is the only thing during the week that he seems to understand and enjoy."

On the theological front there was also a considerable range of viewpoints, which often presented a problem for me. When there was more than a trace of liberal thought in a lesson, it was not uncommon to get a vocal (though pleasant) dissent. One conservative brother always sat on the first row, and I felt that this was so he could be conveniently situated to monitor my comments. It was not an easy matter to present an honest interpretation of the Bible without offending those who believed in "verbal infallibility."

One morning toward the end of the lesson I noticed a brother dozing on the front seat, and I instinctively raised my voice and stepped up my delivery. The stratagem was effective. He woke up, and from there on never took his eyes off me. At the conclusion, he rushed up, and grasping my hand, exclaimed excitedly, "Brother Brooks, you know what? This morning you had a visitation of the Holy Ghost! I seen it when it struck you." Snapping his fingers, he added, "juss like that!"

One of our class features was an annual duck dinner. Since Arkansas is a big duck hunting state, it was generally easy for our members to go hunting and bring in plenty for dinner. But one year there was such poor hunting, it began to look as if the dinner would have to be canceled. While we were still uncertain, it was noticed that Brother Drake, one of the most faithful members, had not been coming. Someone checked and reported that Brother Drake had said there was too much talk about the dearth of ducks; he had been afraid the temptation to barbecue him might be too strong!

At the Arkansas Baptist Convention in 1927, I introduced a resolution to provide for a study of the problems of rural churches in our state. The convention approved the resolution and I was named chairman. The report was well received by the convention the following year, but progress in carrying out its recommendations was slow. It did, however, give me the satisfaction of getting the state organization at least to consider a realistic rural program. At a subsequent convention, I introduced a resolution to endorse United States' participation in the World Court, at that time being debated in the United States Senate. This too, was approved. Activity of this kind was new to Baptists, but many applauded the moves, and most were tolerant of me as an activist.

The case receiving the greatest publicity during my two years service as assistant attorney general was the test suit involving the validity of pardons issued by Acting Governor Pete McCall, who decided, in the absence of Governor Terral, to extend clemency to seven inmates of the penitentiary. Governor Terral was irate. Upon his return he asked the attorney general to establish, if possible, the invalidity of these pardons. The attorney general assigned to me the duty of pursuing this in the courts. The supreme court, by a three-to-two vote, held with me on the ground that statutory requirements regarding the manner in which the pardons were granted had not been complied with. The victory helped my prestige, but I derived little satisfaction from that fact. I entertained too much doubt as to the merits of the case. Liberty is such a priceless thing that I questioned the soundness of any rule abrogating it because of irregularities in the papers which certified to its enjoyment.

In the case of one of the prisoners, Arthur Gurley, it was a pyrrhic victory for the state. He quickly went to Texas and resisted the extradition requested by Governor Terral. The attorney general sent me to Austin to present the state's case to Governor Miriam ("Ma") Ferguson, whose husband Jim, having been impeached, successfully promoted his wife's candidacy in the subsequent election. Her husband sat by her during the two-hour arguments presented by the prisoner's lawyer and myself, and I felt sorry for the governor: she looked terribly bored. Not a word was said by her, but Jim had plenty of questions. At the end of the argument, the governor said, "I will give you my decision at three o'clock." At three we returned and there was only Jim to greet us. He said, "The governor asked me to write her opinion, and at her request I did so." He denied the requisition.

When I returned to Little Rock I had to take some good-natured kidding from my associates at the Capitol. A fellow assistant became lyrical, having been inspired by some rhymes in the New York *Times* beginning:

> The Governor of Texas
> A dauntless one are they,
> Tho' frenzied foes assail her
> He never shows dismay

Other ribbing I took was also in verse, composed by John Carter, one of the other assistants. He summed up my experience like this:

> Brooks makes his plea for Gurley
> Directing it at Ma,
> But found when he had finished,
> He should have talked to Pa.

In Dallas in 1926 during a freight rate hearing, Mr. John E. Benton, a Washington attorney, originally from New Hampshire, asked me to arrange for him to attend a Negro church service. He was particularly eager to hear a Negro choir. The doorman at the Baker Hotel directed me to the St. John's Institutional Baptist Church just a few blocks away.

It was an amazing Sunday evening experience. When we reached the church we were told by a friendly usher, who insisted on taking us to a front seat, that the regular minister was away and that we would hear an unplanned and informal program but plenty of singing. And it was magnificent. My yankee friend was not disappointed.

The presiding deacon spotted us, their two white visitors, and announced boldly that we would be heard from. "Our visitors have the privilege of the floor," he declared. Mr. Benton hastily and unequivocally yielded his time to me. I had spoken to Negro audiences in Arkansas and was assured of a friendly reception by the recollection of the audible expressions of approval on those occasions. As I walked to the pulpit I structured my talk: "The Relation of Education and Religion: Booker T. Washington, the Educator, and John Jasper, the preacher." These would be the heroes and the foci of my remarks. I had read books about both.

I devoted more time to John Jasper than to Booker T. Washington. John Jasper was the eloquent uneducated minister of Richmond. I was able to quote his sermon which pictured the glories of heaven and described—in very colorful language—the golden streets; I added that something he said about his own humble origin was very appealing to me since I came from a very humble background. The home where I was born was a three-room rented house with a purple clematis vine at the end of the porch, and I tried to identify myself with those who had known poverty, which would be true in a larger measure with a black congregation than with a white. I quoted John Jasper's words: "After I have seen the streets that are paved with gold and the mansions of unbelievable beauty, I am going to ask the Saviour to turn into a little side street and show me the house where he set my mother up to housekeeping. I will know it by the roses in the yard and the vines on the porch." You can imagine, however, how I felt in Washington months later when Mr. Benton regaled an audience with that story, saying, "Would you believe that Brooks Hays is going to have Heaven segregated?" In 1973 while I was a guest at the Dallas Athletic Club, the head waiter, Mr. Ransom, a member of that church, told me that the older members of the congregation still speak of that evening's events.

Among the important cases which I handled for the state were two that had to do with tax policy. One was the effort to uphold the constitutionality of the severance tax which I strongly favored, and aside from the legal question involved, felt was an essential part of both tax and conservation policies. This tax was, however, invalidated by the United States Supreme Court. The other case was the effort to uphold a very modest income tax, which was invalidated by the state supreme court.

The experience that interested me most was defending, in the federal courts, the constitutionality of a minimum wage law requiring payment of not less than $1.25 a day for women workers. This case I also lost, but I was mentally conditioned for it, as there was a clear precedent for the Court's action in an earlier case arising in Washington, D.C. (*Adkins* vs. *Children's Hospital*). However, I was eager to uphold the statute and hoped that the Supreme Court would overrule the Adkins decision. We had to wait several years for a reversal of that case by the Supreme Court, but there was great rejoicing when it occurred.

My connection with the attorney general's office came to an abrupt end in January of 1927 when I accepted an invitation from a growing young Arkansas insurance company, the Pyramid, to be sales manager. It meant an increase in income and the opportunity to try my wings in the business world. After one year, however, I realized I would be happier in politics, and I secured my release from my good friend, Herbert Thomas, president of the company.

Bolon B. Turner and I then formed a law partnership, Hays and Turner, and we continued the association through the Depression years, interrupted by three difficult political campaigns which by 1934 left us bruised and penniless and ready to seek refuge in salaried positions. Bolon went to Washington as a tax expert and a few months later was appointed by President Roosevelt to the Tax Court, and I became a legal advisor to the National Recovery Administration. I had a dual job: "Legal Adviser to the State Director of the National Emergency Council" and "Labor Compliance Officer for the Arkansas Office of the National Recovery Administration." This appointment was inspired by Secretary of Labor Frances Perkins, who had recommended me for the top position, state director, but Senator Robinson had someone else in mind for that job and his recommendation was accepted.

My relationship with the senator had become strained, and I was probably lucky to have his clearance for the second job. He had been angered when, in the previous year I had run for Congress, challenging the political organization with which he was identified, the circumstances of which I will detail later. Although we were ultimately reconciled, his attitude toward me at that time was consistent with his known tendency to intimidate anyone who opposed his wishes.

One of my humiliations took place early in 1934 when he accompanied the new Speaker of the House, Henry Rainey of Illinois, to Little Rock for a political meeting. Senator Robinson stood beside the Speaker and introduced the guests to him. The Senator gruffly greeted me, but declined to introduce me to Speaker Rainey. I put out my hand, saying, "Mr. Speaker, I am Brooks Hays, and I am Democratic National committeeman from Arkansas. We are happy you were able to visit our state." Mr. Rainey spoke pleasantly and shook my hand. My differences with the senator were ultimately resolved because I was aware of his great public service.

I should explain that I held the office of Democratic national committeeman by reason of a political coup which some of my friends achieved in 1932. That was the year I was circumvented in my hopes of making a third try for the governorship. My former law partner, Judge Priddy, had been importuned to run. Some of the urging came from my political enemies, who knew I would be loyal enough to him to stay out of the race if he ran. He reluctantly entered the race and I cheerfully accepted a place in his campaign organization. Some of my friends, disappointed that I had been thwarted, got my permission to file my name as a candidate for the Democratic National Committee, which at that time was chosen in the primary by popular vote. I made no campaign whatever, as I felt committed to give all my time to Judge Priddy's candidacy, but I carried 73 of our 75 counties, and received the largest popular vote given any of the candidates for any office.

My work for the attorney general had included not only the trial of civil cases for the state but day-to-day counseling for the proliferating agencies. I liked best the contacts with the Department of Education and the office of the supervisor of juvenile courts. The latter was largely a pioneering service, encouraging the counties to strengthen their facilities for dealing with juvenile offenders. One branch of the Education Department also was in the pioneering stage, the library service. At the request of the library director, I drafted a bill to promote a county library service and helped put it through the legislature. It was the first library law for Arkansas.

Some of my cases were very technical. I decided, for example, that an understanding of freight rates, if ever acquired, should qualify me to teach Sanscrit. I argued before the Interstate Commerce Commission an important case for Arkansas shippers, having to do with grape and strawberry shipments to high-consuming territory, but the case and the decision were so complicated I was not sure whether I had won or lost!

The serious character of my duties yielded to an occasional touch of levity. Our office force did not have mid-morning breaks but our noon recesses were relaxed and pleasant, and the resource of Arkansas folklore was fully exploited. In addition, my hobby of cartooning supplied a light touch now and then. The mail one day contained a rather typical letter asking the attorney general to advise the writer as to his legal rights. (This we had to decline to do, since our function was to advise and defend officials only.) It appeared that this troubled citizen was harassed by the practice of his neighbor's bull in disregarding the boundary line between the two farms. The writer told of his fervent efforts to contain the animal, and his detailed description of his fence seemed to fit the traditional requirement that a fence should be "horse high, bull strong, and hog tight." In desperation he appealed to the attorney general with the pathetic query, "What are my rights?" The attorney general handed me the letter with a chuckle and an instruction, "Hand it to Judge Abercrombie when he arrives."

The Judge's delayed arrival gave me time to do some sketching. To add a realistic touch, I drew in a penciled picture of a bull in triumphant posture standing in a gap in the fence, and following the familiar Bull Durham advertisements, showed great smoke exhalations from his nostrils. It was a formidable picture! I placed the letter at the bottom of the judge's stack of letters and awaited the reaction, having let our associates in on my little trick. We did not have to wait long. The Judge emitted a roar and came running to my office. "Look," he exclaimed, "this poor idiot thought I couldn't understand his problem, so he drew a picture for me. Ain't that bull a beaut . . . and look at the snorts on him!" He enjoyed showing it to visitors all day, and I could hardly bear to disillusion him. The expression, "Look at the snorts on him" became one of the office legends, and in due time the judge seemed to enjoy it himself.

In November of 1924, Tom J. Terral had been elected governor for a two-year term. The governor was a big, bumbling, likable person, young and vigorous, with a native flair for politics and extremely ambitious. His education lagged far behind his aspirations, and he came to the governorship poorly equipped to handle its complicated tasks. His basic purposes were good; he had an easy rapport with rural people and a simple faith in democracy as it had been defined to him in his almost primitive early environment, an environment in northern Louisiana which nurtured another politician named Huey P. Long.

One of Tom Terral's first mistakes was to announce that he would pardon no one. He literally spelled it out: not a single pardon would be issued while he was governor. It was shocking and irresponsible and had a good deal to do with the political adversities that denied him a second term.

Another giant error was his adamant refusal to do something about the bonded indebtedness of those counties that had plunged into road building on the thoroughly unsound plan of taxing the lands adjacent to the improved roads. The costs had often been excessive. The highway leaders had been unwilling to wait for legislative help to secure rights-of-way, so the hard-surfaced roads built in this nineteenth-century fashion often followed a serpentine trail. This was only one of many blunders.

The agricultural price and market problems of the 1920s, coupled with the burden of these ruinous acreage assessments for highways, that should have rested upon highway users, not the farmers, were producing disaster. The governor declined to do anything of a substantial nature. His difficulties began to mount, but as one of his opposition said, "He's like a blind mule on a bluff. He doesn't know he is near the brink."

I was eager to see him come forward with a constructive alternative to the plan advanced by the farmers' and bankers' blocs. But the governor was confident that, since more voters were unaffected by the emergency than were suffering from it, he could weather the storm. He failed to take into account the fact that an infuriated minority can put a quiescent majority to flight. And the bonded counties *were* furious.

Little Rock's chancellor, Judge John E. Martineau, one of the candidates defeated by Terral in 1924, announced against the governor and began with an enormous following in spite of the unbroken practice of giving Arkansas governors a second term for the asking. The judge's strength lay largely in the obvious need for the relief of the landowners in the bonded districts. Terral was defeated. He carried fifteen more counties than Martineau, but the judge's big majorities in the distressed areas wiped out this advantage.

The 1927 session of the legislature undertook to correct the injustices by adopting what came to be known as the Martineau Road Law. There were omissions in the measure, however, and I tried vainly to prove it to the voters. The bond brokers and construction men were interested in the juicy new construction projects for the nonbonded counties authorized by the new law which shifted the debts to the road users by gasoline tax and auto license provisions and were having a field day at the people's expense, for the bonded debt was skyrocketing.

The principal architect of the law was a brilliant realtor and investor, Justin Matthews, of Little Rock. He became a member of the State Highway Commission, and the dominant voice in highway affairs, in spite of the fact that the department was headed by an elected official, Dwight Blackwood.

My differences with Mr. Matthews were entirely impersonal but they were substantial. I appreciated his vision and his progressiveness. As a developer of real estate additions to the growing cities of Little Rock and North Little Rock, he rendered a great civic service. But his unconventional fiscal operations were from the public-policy standpoint highly questionable. I shall, in defining the issues in my race against the Mathews candidate in 1928, give some specific illustrations of the highway program presented to the voters.

My objections to the new road program piled up, and further there were things to be done in the school and welfare areas that I wanted to tackle, so I began to think about running for governor myself. I had had enormous publicity during my two years on the attorney general's staff. My acquaintances extended to every part of the state, due to my seven years of intensive civic activity and my university contacts.

Later, in my role as president of the Social Work Conference, I advocated the adoption of a workman's compensation act for the state. Arkansas was one of only two or three states without the benefits of this salutary provision for injured employees and their families. In more than one legislative session I urged its adoption, but we were always blocked by the "personal injury lawyers" who made a specialty of representing the plaintiff in damage suits. And some of the employers also opposed the measure. It was not until the leading industrialists of the state were convinced that the failure to have such benevolent provisions was not only penalizing the employees and their families but also producing very expensive and unjust results for employers, that passage of the workman's compensation bill was assured. It was accomplished in 1938 by use of the Initiative and Referendum provisions of the Constitution. While the business leaders must be given credit for this enactment, I have always derived some satisfaction from my share in the pioneering struggles to achieve this reform.

On March 2, 1928, my family and I were Russellville-bound for a visit with my parents. We rode the bus because part of my meager compensation as the bus company lawyer was free transportation. At Atkins, twenty minutes from our destination, I heard a newsboy peddling the afternoon paper and announcing a headline: THE GOVERNOR WILL AC- CEPT FEDERAL JUDGESHIP. Thus, a new political vista appeared, for this meant a wide-open race in the approaching August primary, and the hopes which I and my family and friends had been entertaining were sud- denly given life. There was real excitement during the remainder of the bus trip and at the supper table, as my father and mother helped evaluate the prospects. I was twenty-nine and a half years old.

I was surprised at my father's enthusiasm. I could explain it only in terms of the favorable publicity I had enjoyed for three years, and further the persistent feeling among friends and well-wishers that I should run at the first opportunity. We had not anticipated that the opening would be in 1928, but thought rather of 1930 or a later date.

By nine o'clock that evening after phone calls to my "cabinet" in Little Rock (which included Bolon Turner, Beloit Taylor, John Wells, and others) the "go" signal was given. I authorized the *Gazette* to an- nounce my candidacy, being the first to make a positive statement of in- tentions. Within a few days, however, the lieutenant governor, Harvey Parnell, who succeeded to the office, was picked by the highway organi- zation as its candidate. Next morning's *Gazette*, in carrying my short announcement, declared that I was "the youngest man in Arkansas history ever to seek the Governorship." (Arkansas' pre–Civil War gov- ernor John Selden Roane was elected at thirty-two.) We did research in preparation for defending a youthful candidacy. We discovered that one governor of Louisiana was only twenty-six, but it did not help much, for he was of the Reconstruction era.

My announcement seemed to galvanize my support. Young people were enthusiastic. Most of the social workers rallied to me. School teach- ers (except for some of the state establishment) were generally in my corner. Organized labor and many small farmers were friendly. Univer- sity friends quickly organized for me. It was a tonic for all of us.

The old guard was caught off guard. But they were not frightened at first. "Nice boy," was the usual comment, "will run fourth" (this was after the list closed with seven including former governor Terral in the race), "may get twenty thousand votes." But a month later my ground- swell support was visible. I was not such a nice boy, after all. I was a "trouble maker," and some even said, after I unfolded the proof of mis- handling of the highway funds, "he's a mudslinger." This was diversionary, of course. It was not mudslinging to discuss public records and public policies. I was not hurt much by that phony charge. The thing that hurt most in the closing days was the undercurrent talk that Tom Terral, by this time feared by thousands as a potential wrecker of the highway program, would win unless people voted for Parnell "to beat Terral." The word they circulated was don't waste a vote on Brooks.

We were also terribly handicapped by lack of money. My father and I put up five thousand dollars, all we could afford, and it was estimated that all expenditures for me by self-constituted committees and friends at the local and state levels did not exceed twenty-five thousand dollars. The Parnell organization spent many times that amount, much of which was supplied by road contractors and bondbrokers.

I made it clear that I subscribed to the principles of the Martineau road law, that is, parity for the nonbonded counties by building their roads at state expense, and good-faith assumption by the state of the local district bonds. At the same time I would replace political factors in locating new highways with sound economic and social factors. Other planks in my platform were: an income tax for schools and eleemosynary purposes, a new hospital for nervous diseases, a runoff primary, and a thorough and independent audit of highway expenditures.

Governor Parnell favored only the hospital proposal, so there was a clear joinder of issues. Former governor Terral talked only about his record and pleaded for a second term. State auditor Carroll Cone capitalized on his reputation as the treasury watch dog.

Of all the campaigns, mine was perhaps the most intense. The usual schedule called for four to eight speeches a day—once I did nine—and totaled three hundred and three for the summer. We ran out of money for daily expenses a time or two. One Monday morning as I was preparing to leave Little Rock headquarters for a week's tour, Bolon Turner, who was our treasurer, said, "Here's a dollar and a quarter. It's all I've got, but the boys (meaning my campaign committee in Conway County) will meet you in Perryville. They promised to pass the hat before leaving Morrilton, and they'll have enough to get you and your driver through the week." They did, but barely!

Campaigning was fun. I felt sorry for those who had to stay at headquarters to wrestle with problems of a state race. My health was excellent. My voice held up in spite of heat and dust and inadequate amplification. One newspaper called me "the Cheerful Crusader." The age factor was both a help and a hindrance. I could understand the objections. I remember telling some Little Rock business men who were friendly to me, but who thought I should delay a race for governor, "All right, if you can induce an older person to run with the point of view I have on these grave matters and with a potential for winning, I'll withdraw tomorrow."

My Grandmother Hays's comment was, "Well, Brooks is not interested in the honor—he just wants to do something for the people." I told her, "You're partly right, Grandmother. I do want very much to help the people, but I can't say I am not interested in the honor. I would like to be called 'Governor.' " I did not regard it as ignoble, and she didn't either.

The problem of my age was accentuated by the fact that I did not look as old as I was. I weighed only 125 pounds, and I could have passed as a youngster just reaching voting age. When I developed a slight ailment, the doctor expressed fear that I had chicken pox, and the campaign committee unanimously agreed that if it proved to be that, they'd withdraw me! "Bad enough to be called the kid candidate, and if he has a child's disease, we've had it," the chairman said. Fortunately it was just a cold.

One thing I did not mind was the reference to me by one opponent as "the Boy Scout candidate." It helped rally the young people. When I was elected to Congress fourteen years later, I said, "Those who were too young to vote for me for governor elected me to Congress."

When I reached Alpena Pass in the Ozarks in time to greet people before the speaking engagement, my local chairman told me that I already had a friend "whooping it up" for me. "Uncle Steve Jones is a red hot Hays man," he said. "Let's go see him."

We found him sitting in the center of a small group, regaling them with my virtues. My companion, laying a hand on my shoulder, said, "Uncle Steve, here's your candidate for governor." Uncle Steve's jaw dropped and his face registered incredulity. "Who?" he exclaimed. "It's Brooks Hays," I gently interjected. His countenance fell in bitter disappointment, as he said, feebly, "Brooks Hays! Shucks!"

While I was enjoying the campaign tours, my unpaid and dedicated workers at headquarters were working on ads, on fresh material for my speeches, and on finding answers to the hundreds of questions that arose each day. One of the hardest workers, John F. Wells, had a tremendous gift for ferreting out relevant facts in the public records, a quality that had made him a star reporter for the *Gazette*. This, coupled with his ability as a writer, also made him an invaluable adjunct to our organization. He gave most of his spare time and all of his vacation to our campaign, primarily because he believed in what I was trying to do. In later years, his political philosophy became ultraconservative, and led him to a rather critical attitude toward me. He disapproved of some of my positions in Congress, notably in the field of race conflicts, but we never lost the feeling of affection for each other that had ripened in the 1928 race. I remain under a heavy debt to him.

My hopes of victory were buoyed by the support I found in localities I had never visited before, and I stopped in many communities between speaking engagements, sometimes for a few fleeting handshakes, to make it possible for friends to say, "Brooks came to see us." If I found enough people around the post office or general store, I would even make a short talk, to give them something to pass on to the uncommitted. It was fun!

One Sunday morning as we were returning early to Little Rock for a rest and an afternoon pep meeting, our car developed motor trouble, and I hitchhiked the rest of the way. I was delighted to learn when picked up that my benefactors were supporters on their way to Little Rock for my rally, Mr. and Mrs. Jones, of El Paso, in White County.

Lots of things happen in a campaign that are unscheduled and unexpected. For example, Marion and the two children, Betty, then four, and Steele, two, along with a big group of Little Rock friends, met me for a Saturday evening outdoor talk at Bauxite, twenty-five miles from home. I was standing in the center of a big circle on the school house lawn giving my exhortations, when Betty suddenly broke loose from her Mother and ran to me. I think the crowd expected something sentimental from her to the father she had not been seeing much of, but what we all heard was, "O, Daddy, I wish you were the hot tamale man!"

One of the most enjoyable experiences of that hectic summer was the homecoming at Russellville, where all political factions had swung into my column. Elaborate plans were made, including a grand entrance for me, perched on top of a special float prepared for the occasion. The driver of this impressive motorized vehicle met me on the edge of town, and I climbed to my pinnacle. We headed for the ball park on the other side of the railroad tracks. Just a few yards before we reached the first of five tracks, I saw a locomotive bearing down on us. I yelled to the driver to stop, but the noise of the train and the motor drowned my voice, and the aperture on the side was too small for perfect vision. In desperation, I reached down and grabbed his hair, giving it a hard jerk, and he slammed on the brakes. In the exuberance of the welcome we received a mile further on, we soon forgot that narrow escape.

Not all of the fun was on the hustings. When I went into Little Rock for the weekends, the staff would always have humorous incidents to report. My favorite was the one involving an old friend, Jim Bland, a north Arkansas political leader. During the final stretch he called Judge Priddy one midnight with a grim story. "Judge," he cried, "somethin's got to be done up here in Lawrence County."

"What's wrong, Jim? I thought we were in good shape up there."

"That's right, we were," Jim said. "Had it by a thousand votes, but we're losin 'em fast, Judge. I'm tellin you, its just awful what's happening."

The Judge was impatient. "Well, quit stammering and stuttering and tell me what it is."

"Well, they've got it out on Brooks that he's an evolutionist."

It was the judge's turn, then, to be agitated. "Oh, that's awful, that's awful! And it's not true, Jim. Deny it, deny it, deny it, Jim!" he shouted.

The answer came quickly. "Deny it? Hell! We're denying it, but to tell you the truth, I believe the little squirt is!"

My earlier-declared opposition to the bill to prohibit any instruction on the Darwinian theory did my candidacy little damage, since it was obscured by other issues. I made no reference to it in my speeches. However, the proposal to ban such teaching was approved by the voters in the general election which followed the primary. It lay unenforced on the statute book for forty years, until the United States Supreme Court wisely proclaimed it to be unconstitutional.

The long campaign finally ended. We had had our moments of great expectations. Indeed, if polls had been available in 1928, I am confident I would have been shown to be ahead two or three weeks before the end. The bandwagon vote was rather sizable. We could "feel" it leaving us in the last few days, and this was to a large degree attributable to the great amount of money that the Parnell forces could release in the final stages. The official score does not reflect the closeness of the race, since Parnell not only had "the bandwagon swell" at the end, but also was the beneficiary of a vicious practice in some counties (after the result is known) of switching enough votes to put the county in the winning column and thus curry favor with the victor. The final tally in round figures looked like this: Parnell – 90,000; Hays – 60,000; Terral – 33,000; total for the three minor candidates – 20,000. Since all of the other candidates were with one possible exception violent opponents of the administration, it was apparent that a runoff would have given me a big advantage. But the results were cheering to my friends, and I was unscarred and unruffled. Someone said to me the following day, as I smilingly received congratulations upon "a great race," that it was believed I was running "for second place." I carried Little Rock by a good vote in spite of the administration's extreme efforts to swing it away from me.

The nomination of Al Smith for president in 1928 presented a problem for me. I had not favored his nomination and I was critical of the method Arkansas used to select its delegates to the Houston Convention. It was done by the small State Central Committee (thirty-five members) with no opportunity for rank-and-file consultation. Though unsuccessful, I had emerged from the primary fight with an impressive following and considerable popularity among the Democrats, and the party machinery was committed to the ticket: Joe T. Robinson was Smith's running mate.

I concluded that I ought not to sit it out, as I would like to have done, thereby sparing myself the disapproval of many Baptists and other church friends. I made a few speeches for the ticket and near the end of the campaign was given a major spot on a key statewide radio program to discuss my reasons for believing that Smith's Catholicism should not be an issue. I could do this sincerely in spite of my feeling that Governor Smith had not exhibited statesmanship nor perceptiveness in apparently dismissing questions as to his religion as "bigoted."

There were understandable and reasonable questions raised by some Protestants, and they should have been answered by Smith himself, just as in 1960 another Catholic, John F. Kennedy, speaking in the same city of Houston, answered them in a brilliant confrontation with Protestant ministers. The situation did, however, give me an opportunity to voice my strong feelings regarding religious tolerance. The governor's race of 1928 had at least provided me with access to the sentiment-forming influences in Arkansas.

Brooks Hays, aged two, with his parents and Aunt Maude, photographed in his father's law office.

1919   Graduation from the University of Arkansas.

The Phi Alpha Delta gathers on the south lawn of the White House for the initiation of President Harding as a member of the law fraternity. In the second row: President Harding, General Pershing, and Chief Justice Taft. In the front row, from the left: Bolon Turner, Brooks Hays and Joe C. Barrett.

Brooks and Marion's first home, Russellville, Arkansas.

Four generations. Ella Dale Hays, her son Steele, her grandson Brooks, and her great grandson Steele II. Taken in 1928.

This is the front porch of a store in eastern Pulaski County, photographed by Ben Shahn in 1935 during a tour of the Arkansas "Resettlement" project. Brooks Hays is in the back, fourth from the right.

President Harry S. Truman signs a bill introduced by Congressman Hays providing land opportunities to war veterans.

Getting directions from two London officers, 1944. Hays's first trip to Europe.

On a congressional committee visit to Berlin, 1951, Hays meets with Mayor Ernest Reuter and Jacob Javits. *Foto-Engels, Bonn*

(1949) *Arkansas Democrat*

Madame Pandit of India signs a wheat agreement authorized by the Humphrey-Hays Amendment. On the back row are Loy Henderson, Brooks Hays, Hubert Humphrey, and Herbert Lehman. *Department of State photo*

President Eisenhower saying good-bye to Governor Faubus and Congressman Hays on September 14, 1957, after meeting in Newport, R.I.

ARKANSAS RESCUE SQUAD

ST.LOUIS POST-DISPATCH
SEPT. 19, 1957

TO THE
HON. BROOKS HAYS.
D.R. Fitzpatrick

(1957) St. Louis *Post-Dispatch*

Receiving honorary citizenship of Nashville, 1958. The Hayses are greeted by Mayor Ben West and James B. Sullivan, with the colonel in charge of Tennessee affairs. *Official photo, City of Nashville*

Hays and his colleagues Dr. Clarence Cranford, president of the American Baptist Convention, and Mrs. Cranford are greeted in Moscow by a reception committee of Russian Baptists. 1958. *Wide World Photos*

Dean Rusk greets Hays as one of the assistant secretaries of state.

Brooks receiving the regalia of his new office—"member of the tribe of Zor Zor."

With Prime Minister Balewa of Nigeria and American Ambassador Joseph Palmer in April, 1963, shortly before the assassination of the prime minister. *Federation of Nigeria*

Chapter 7 WRESTLING WITH THE ESTABLISHMENT 1929–1933

It is a popular saying that "whoever aspires to office is set upon an excellent occupation."
I Timothy 3:1 (Moffatt translation)

NINETEEN hundred and twenty nine was a good year for "Hays and Turner." The campaign of 1928 had made my name well known, and clients came in sufficient numbers to keep us busy. Bolon Turner had to carry more than his share of the work because of the "pro bono publico" work piled on me. And because of my avid interest in things "for the good of the public," it was hard to say no. Before I knew it, I was finance campaign chairman of the Community Fund, president of the Tuberculosis Association, president of the Children's Home and Hospital, and member of the YMCA Board and the Baptist State Executive Committee. I asked the Boy Scout organization to spare me from duties on their area council. On top of this, I let County Judge William Sibeck talk me into being chairman of a special committee to plan a new county home for the indigent. I worked hard at the job, interjecting some modern ideas about care for the sick and aging. Partly as a reward I was appointed referee for the Probate Court, which produced more revenue for the firm. My law partner agreed that "gathering goat feathers" (Ellis Parker Butler's phrase for doing public work without compensation) had some unexpected advantages after all.

The stock market crash hit us during the Community Fund drive. Not having had surplus money to invest in stocks, I did not appreciate its significance. Few others foresaw the extent of the disastrous results of the country's overextension. But within a few months, unemployment was rampant and we were sinking into the Great Depression.

The ominous clouds were over us when 1930 arrived. Our family felt it as all nonsalaried people did. There had been plenty to do, but few paying clients. A classic statement was made by a lawyer in answer to a fellow attorney's query, "Did you have a good week?"

"Oh, a fine one. Had one ten-dollar fee, one five-dollar fee, and two or three little bitty ones."

My father sent me fifteen dollars a week out of his meager income, and it was a great help in keeping food on the table. I supplemented our income by teaching evening public speaking classes.

By February, 1930, there was intense interest in the governor's race, the primary being but six months away. It was evident that the Parnell administration's opposition was centering on me as the one to lead the struggle to oust the highway commission and the governor who kept them in power. There were other issues, but this was the paramount one. The lieutenant governor, Lee Cazort, had broken with Parnell and wanted to run himself, but he was convinced by his own friends that if anyone could defeat the powerful organization, I was the person. He made a gracious public statement, expressing the fervent hope that I would yield to the plea of many people to make another race.

It posed a difficult question for me. I was still in debt, and another race would put me in deeper. It would be tough on my parents and my own family. Many of my friends found themselves under obligation to the incumbent, and consequently would be immobilized or even active on the other side. One of them, former governor Charles H. Brough, one of my close friends, was one of the administration's emissaries to picture an attractive future for me if I would not run. The establishment was forgiving as to my 1928 race and would help me realize my political ambitions in the future. All very ambiguous, but the idea was that I would have a claim on them for the governorship the next time around. Also, others with power to commit the political organization spoke of law business, at least ten thousand dollars a year in tax service. This could be discussed without the taint of bribery because Bolon Turner had drawn the rules and regulations for administering the state's new income tax law. We were, in other words, already getting business from the administration. To run would, of course, cut off this source of income. Moreover, the administration had done some things I approved of, including the income tax law itself which I had advocated in 1928, the building of a new state hospital, and a more generous provision for the schools. The last-named meant loss of some of my support among the teachers.

There were good reasons, therefore, for "playing safe"—leaving the bruising struggle against the State Highway Commission and the governor to someone else, an older person, and someone better able to bear the financial hazards and other hurts. The final and most painful appeal came from my own father. The arguments against running appealed to him, and he sent word that he hoped I would not heed the siren call.

Bolon made the decision a bit easier by saying I should not let the loss of tax business influence me, that I should decide it on the basis of its effect on my own career. He said, "Don't overlook one fact, however: if you decline to run you are out of politics for a long time, maybe forever. You would not have an answer to the charge that you weakened in your opposition to what's going on, and that your 1928 campaign was opportunism. Unfriendly people would put it more bluntly; they would say, 'you sold us down the river.' "

This tended to wipe out whatever lure there was in the picture of a quiet retreat, for politics had become my vocation and I was not ready to give it up. My mother, I knew, would accept my decision cheerfully either way it went, and Marion had the same attitude. She scarcely admitted me to her inmost thoughts, she was so eager for the decision to be mine alone.

But what about Dad? He made it hard for me. He came to Little Rock for a man-to-man talk. He did not accept Bolon's reasoning, which had seemed so logical to me. Dad's attitude became my big problem, for my devotion to him and my desire to spare him every discomfort were stronger than ever. He was emotional. He appealed to me as he had to hundreds of juries, pleading for the decision he earnestly wanted. I stood by the window in the northeast corner of the Rector Building, gazing at the old Gleason Hotel where twenty-eight years earlier he had introduced me (a three-year-old) to this intriguing business of politics, deeply pondering it. I finally broke the news to him.

"Really, Dad," I said, "there's a little more than a career under consideration here. I see this as decisive from another standpoint. Sometimes the right thing to do is the hardest to do. You brought me up to think in those terms and since the decision has to be mine, I cannot do it your way and be true to myself." This grieved him, but I believe that he was proud of me. He later told an audience at Conway just that, and I at last had the satisfaction of knowing he did not think I had let him down.

In March I announced my candidacy. It was obvious that the race would be between Parnell and myself, although the situation was somewhat confused by the announcement, shortly after I entered the race, by a former county judge, John C. Sheffield of Helena, of his intention to run. He purported to be opposing the administration, but a dramatic action by him near the end of the campaign indicated that he was intentionally serving the interests of the administration. More about that episode later. There were two other minor candidates, so for a while it appeared that the absence of a runoff primary might again obstruct the principle of majority rule; but toward the election date the other three dropped so far behind Parnell and myself that the runoff idea lost significance.

The issue was almost altogether the highway situation, not the essentials of the basic law of building roads in the unbonded counties and the paying out of bonds of the special districts which had built their roads before the state assumed responsibility for a system of highways, but rather the administration of the law and my promise of changes in the law to tighten up on expenditures.

My attack was based on the facts that the state was issuing an inordinate number of bonds and stretching our credit to a dangerous degree, and that certain district debts had been assumed that should not have been underwritten by the state, since their roads were not roads at all but parts of speculative real estate additions to the cities, particularly Little Rock. This involved the real estate developments of Justin Mathews, who, as the dominant figure in the Highway Department, was personally profiting by the law.

The Parnell administration was the beneficiary of the idea of bonds for permanent improvements, whether roads or school buildings, and the politicians were reveling in the affluence it temporarily created. Our per capita debt climbed so rapidly that charts showing the debts of the forty-eight states had a single category for Arkansas. No other state approached ours in this index.

I made much of the weakness of the law which permitted the Metropolitan Trust Company of Little Rock, owned by Mr. Mathews, to channel $365,000 of the road funds into its own private coffers. It was accomplished in this fashion: at Mr. Mathew's behest, the legislature had passed a bill authorizing assumption by the state of all outstanding bonds on streets in suburban residential developments. That law also included authorization for the state to buy such bonds before maturity (at discount, of course). Thus, since payment of the district bonds under the law did not depend on whether the roads they were to pay for had actually been built, it was possible to secure payment in advance of maturity. In one instance cash exceeding $300,000 went out of the State Treasury into the treasury of one of Mr. Mathews' investment companies, the Metropolitan Trust Company, although not a foot of pavement had been laid down.

It was an amazing procedure in that neither fraud nor deception was practiced. Actually, the bill was put through without any attempt to conceal facts, but in the usual high-handed, hard-driving fashion followed by the subservient legislature during the days it was on the highway spending binge. The shocking thing about the transaction was in this sloppy handling of vital financing procedures. The fund which wound up in the Metropolitan Trust Company to pay for streets which had not been built was obviously a trust account subject to the trust obligation to build or to return the money. There was no proof that Mr. Mathews was disputing the trusteeship.

There was another issue, a difficult one to define but thousands of thoughtful people responded favorably to my handling of it. It was the erosion of political standards in the handling of a public trust and the corrupting of the sturdy ideals that had generally characterized our state government, antiquated though much of its structure was. Mr. Mathews sincerely believed that the public was served by his progressive ideas as a builder of streets and houses and real estate improvements. And what he did was not disguised. It was not corruption in the criminal sense. What he did not see as one not versed in government and politics, but only in the peripheral matter of a business with a governmental aspect, was that he could not get *his* aid without creating situations in which others could get public money and other forms of political largess which represented *their* private concerns. The total results were disastrous. My slogan was "The public good above private gain," and in the light of revelations regarding diversion of public funds it seemed an appropriate one.

The Parnell campaign was magnificently financed, chiefly by bond brokers and road construction companies with some help from the banking interests of the A. B. Banks Company, which owned a chain of banks and a group of insurance companies. Its condition was shaky during the year 1930, and a few months after the election the structure collapsed.

We knew about this shaky condition, and it was a temptation to say so in the campaign, since Mr. Banks's institutions were being favored with the deposit of state funds; but it would have been unethical to use the issue, since to spread the information we had would have exacerbated the situation by destroying faith in the banks.

The money controlled by my opposition enabled them not only to overwhelm us in radio and newspaper advertising, but to hire hundreds, perhaps thousands, of workers near the finish date. In a period of stark unemployment, this was decisive. Moreover, some of the money went to shockingly illegal uses. For example, a prominent Arkansas attorney told me years later that on election day he was working on a highway crew, and that the foreman gave each of the workers five dollars and gave them time off to vote for the governor. "You voted against me?" I asked him. "No, I took the five dollars and then voted for you," he added. "But not many of them were that unethical." And a friend of Judge Priddy's apologized to him for having carried two thousand dollars to my home county for distribution to key township leaders, including some election officers, the night before the election. One of the Parnell headquarters staff told me months later that they tried hard to keep me from carrying Little Rock again. "We spent twenty thousand dollars there," he said. It was unavailing. I raised my plurality in that county from eight hundred in 1928 to three thousand in 1930. It is easy to see how a huge total expenditure results from the use of money in these proportions. The purchase of individual votes and the unrestrained buying of newspaper space and radio time mounts up.

My pledge to give the state a complete and independent investigation of highway costs and campaign spending bore fruit. The 1931 legislature, unlike the 1929 session, was not under the administration's control, and they not only ordered the audit and investigation, but by formal resolution declared the administration to be "the most corrupt in the state's history since Reconstruction." Later, another resolution softened this language, largely to avoid the implication that the governor had personally profited by the condemned practices. The audit reports were detailed and sweeping in the exposure of corrupt campaign practices, showing an estimated total of $350,000 spent in the governor's behalf in the 1930 race, which in those days was astronomical.

The tie-up of big money and local politics was too much for me.

There were enough men willing to sell their votes, even in ordinary times, to swing a tight election, and in a depression like 1930 it was a tremendous factor. The practice of bloc buying of votes persisted for a decade or more, and still is an obstruction to honest elections in isolated localities. I recall in a later election when I was in a small town on election day, I stopped near the polling place to talk to a friend, and was curious about a crowd of about fifty men sitting in a group a few yards away. I asked about them and got this answer from my friend: "They are waiting for the courthouse crowd to send some more money out here for them. The amount passed out to them earlier in the day was less than they expected for their votes, so they are waiting. The money will probably get here."

I made only 227 speeches in the 1930 race compared with 303 in 1928. Use of radio, coupled with the fact that I was much better known in 1930, lessened the need for public appearances. Campaigning was still fun, but less so than in 1928, for the suffering brought about by the Depression was compounded by a drought and a heat wave. I remember seeing roadside stands operated by desperate people having few farm products to sell, but with pleading expressions directed toward the passersby.

The heat was intense. Thirty-seven years later I was giving a lecture at the University of Colorado summer session when a teacher rose during the question period to say, "Mr. Hays, I heard you speak in Arkadelphia, Arkansas, in 1930 in your race for governor. A young professor introduced you. My question is, 'Do you remember the occasion?'" I convinced him I did. "Yes, the professor was named Matt Ellis, and he later became president of his college and we both stood in a wagon bed a few yards from the Caddo Hotel. I should add that the thermometer had reached 112 degrees earlier in the day." I remember something else that happened. One of my volunteer workers was with me, and he said as we started into the hotel lobby, "Just give me fifty cents and I'll stay around here at the wagon yard. I can do some politicking with the country folks." We conducted that kind of economy campaign.

And now back to the John C. Sheffield episode. About two weeks before the primary, we had indirect word from Judge Sheffield that he was giving some thought to consolidating the anti-Parnell forces, and would be willing to discuss it with someone from "the Hays Headquarters." Without any decision or formal action by our headquarters, and without my knowledge, Lieutenant Governor Cazort and former governor Tom

Terral, who was also supporting me, went to Helena to see Judge Sheffield. The talk produced nothing. The next morning Judge Sheffield issued a statement charging that "the Hays Camp has attempted to bribe me out of the race." The trick had some effect. It was treachery of a shocking kind. Of course there was no basis in fact for his charge. Denials were made by both of these friends but there was no way to determine how much damage was done. I am inclined to think that it changed few votes, but it did slow our campaign down, and had a depressing effect on the morale of our workers.

Finally, the primary rolled around and the tension was relieved. I was mentally conditioned for the second defeat and so were my family, all of them. It left me with a disrupted law practice and six thousand dollars or more in debts. On the plus side was the preservation of my political integrity and perhaps a better image than before the race, for running for governor at thirty in 1928 had given some color to the cry of my opposition that I was "a star gazer and an impractical dreamer." My strength in the voting had climbed from 60,000 in 1928 to 90,000 in 1930. The governor's plurality was 45,000, giving him a total of 135,000, but few people thought that the defeat had taken me off of the lists.

The year 1931 was *not* a good one for Hays and Turner. The tax business was gone, and the bus and truck business which I had pioneered (having drafted the law regulating the new industry adopted by the General Assembly in 1927) was shrinking, largely because, as one of the regulatory commission members said, our clients were "sending the wrong lawyers out to the Capitol to argue their cases." And the fees that were earned were not always collectible; too many people were penniless.

Fortunately, prices were low. We could enjoy a small steak lunch for twenty-five cents, and no restaurant would think of charging more than a nickel for coffee. One of our clients owned a little hole-in-the-wall lunch room, and he informed us that he made a living on his coffee sales. "I break even on food sales," he said, "but make a cent and a half on every cup of coffee, and I sell five hundred cups a day. I can live on that penny and a half if the volume stays up." I bought shirts for one dollar apiece, and ties for fifty cents. Once I found a handsome tie for fifteen cents at a sale. For my wife's present on her birthday, I found a tea table on sale for one dollar and seventy five cents, and grabbed it. But it grieved me to see old friends, once prosperous, slipping around to the welfare office for free commodities. Closing of the banks and the wholesale termination of payrolls accomplished this condition. It reached the nadir in 1931. This is a familiar story, and the experience of the Hayses is typical of millions of situations.

But with a little help from my father, and fees for teaching the public speaking classes to supplement our meager law practice, we managed to survive. We entered 1932 with expectations of some exciting political developments. I have already disclosed the reason for my not making a third attempt for the governorship. An amazing sidelight on the early maneuvering is that Governor Parnell told two friends of mine that he would support me, on the theory that I could defeat the Blackwood highway organization which had turned against him. I make a record of this partly because of the satisfaction I derived from the fact that two vigorous campaigns against him had not embittered him toward me. My speeches and advertisements had been impersonal, and I had stuck to the public records of the men he had entrusted with highway affairs. If this is revealing as to my own philosophy it is certainly revealing of a broad and tolerant attitude on Parnell's part, and on the part of Justin Matthews, with whom I had been less gentle, though I believe always fair. He voted for me when I ran for Congress in 1933. It is easy to let the conflict of rivalries create deep feelings, but, as indicated by these two expressions of friendliness, this need not be the result in every case.

The year 1932 stands out in my memory as the period in which for the first time I achieved some reforms in the party rules, only to have them undone by later organizational action. The two objects of my condemnation had been (1) the refusal of the Democratic State Executive Committee to authorize a procedure for securing a representative delegation to the national conventions, and (2) to call for special primaries to select nominees for unexpired terms of officials resigning or dying during the term for which elected.

In the biennial state convention in 1932, without revealing my strategy in advance, I put the proposals for a democratic procedure up to the Rules Committee, and to my surprise and great satisfaction the members agreed with me and adopted the changes. The convention confirmed this action. My proposal called for special county conventions and a special state convention to name the delegates, with provisions for acquainting the rank and file with the issues and the individual candidacies, a great improvement over hand picking of the national delegates, but it was never tried out, since, at the next convention in 1934, the executive committee talked the convention into reverting to the old method.

The other reform bore fruit in two situations that developed in 1933, but it too went out of the rule book in the 1934 repeal by the state convention. It had to do with the nomination of candidates for the unexpired terms. It also provided for special conventions rather than leaving the executive committee with power to pick the party nominee. In 1932 nominations were tantamount to election, and there was widespread dissatisfaction with the prevailing practice.

The two reform measures that I proposed figured in the story of my struggle for the nomination for a congressional seat in 1933, occasioned by the resignation of our congressman to accept a judgeship. My advocacy of changes in the method of picking nominees was influential in getting later action by the legislature to outlaw committee nominations, and it was augmented by court decisions nullifying such action.

It was in 1932 that tensions began to develop between myself and the old-line professionals. By 1932, they began to tire of my reform efforts. Earlier, some of them called me "the cheerful crusader," but the strain of fighting to hold their advantage put a strain on our friendship and utterly alienated those who were not interested in democratic processes. I had appeared at the state committee's spring meeting in 1932, which was called to select delegates to the national convention, and secured the floor to appeal to them voluntarily to give up this prerogative, and let the people have something to say about the matter. They smilingly declined (almost unanimously), but the smiles had vanished by 1934.

The story of 1933 is a heartbreaker. The agonies of the Depression had spread to most families in Arkansas in one form or another. I was dividing time between the law office, the work of the welfare agencies, and the duties of Democratic national committeeman, the single asset I had retrieved from five years' hard work. My welfare activity had taken on a new dimension. I had been picked in a meeting of concerned citizens of Pulaski County in which Little Rock is located, to serve on the first Public Welfare Commission of five members to do something about the plight of the unemployables. The government was doing little for the welfare cases at that stage. The voluntary agencies' income had shrunk, and they simply could not meet the demands. We tried various ways to dramatize the problem, including an appeal for voluntary welfare tax on each utility bill—ten cents with each payment of an electric, telephone, gas, or water bill, the utilities having agreed to receive the money and transmit to our treasurer. The refusal of many people to share to this small extent was disillusioning, but it was more a reflection of lack of information of the conditions than of indifference, though to be sure there was a bit of that too. This experience convinced me of the impracticality of complete dependency on voluntary giving in meeting the welfare problems. I recall the pain of our commission members and staff as we struggled to meet the needs. (One week we had for each family only one dollar and sixty-five cents for groceries and other requirements.)

On March 4, 1933, I was in Washington to witness the inauguration of Franklin Roosevelt, and to inquire about a job for myself. Having campaigned in Arkansas for the ticket and raised a few thousand dollars for the party, I was known to party leaders. My membership on the national committee at least would open doors, and maybe with some breaks I might get something that would mean a change of fortune for the Hays household. We had hoped Marion could go with me, but there just wasn't money enough. She and the two children went to Russellville to stay with my parents, and since we assumed that I would have to remain at least a few weeks, the children were enrolled in the Russellville schools. We had not expected, though, that my mission would stretch out. April passed, and still no job was offered me. My expenses were kept at a minimum by the kindness of two old Sigma Chi brothers, Dick Doyle, later national head of the fraternity, a New Hampshire Republican, and Dean Davis, a Georgia Democrat. They literally took me into their homes for weeks at a time. And one day Dick steered me into his tailor's shop and instructed the craftsmen to outfit me in their "best double-breasted blue." The best was plenty good enough for this poor jobless Arkansas lawyer who had never owned a tailor-made suit! Dick wanted me to present a good front when talking to potential employers.

Getting the kind of job I had in mind required political contacts, aggressiveness, and a little bit of luck. Weeks later I was still jobless in Washington. So were a lot of other deserving Democrats, and some not so deserving. One teenager had been in our inaugural party, a favorite with his elders, apparently without family moorings since he decided to stay in Washington and get a job. He had achieved fame in Arkansas as a flagpole sitter but had not other claim to distinction, unless a head of beautiful red hair should entitle him to it. I was spokesman for the Arkansas group in trying to dissuade "Red" from remaining among the job seekers. He scoffed at our idea that he return home with the others.

As it turned out, he quickly established himself in the good graces of Vice President Garner, and was the first to land a place on the payroll—a good place, that of special page. I decided he was entitled to comment, "Mr. Hays said I'd be stranded here without any money or any job, but look who's out of work still, and I was on the payroll a week after I got here!"

It developed, however, after I returned to Arkansas, that I had been effective, for Secretary Frances Perkins invited me to become assistant to the secretary of labor, and it was indeed a tempting offer. But at almost the same time Congressman Ragon of our district resigned to accept a judgeship, and this left a wide-open race for the seat. My friends thought I could win it. So I declined the Labor Department position and set my stakes for the congressional office.

The party rules which I had secured the adoption of in 1932 were in effect, so the committee had to assemble a convention or order a primary. The latter course was desirable and would have met with popular favor, but I had little hope that the state committee would do more than assemble a special convention of Democrats from the eight counties in the district. Then suddenly there was another development, a vacancy in the office of chief justice of the Supreme Court. This too called for a special convention, so we prepared to ask the full state convention to order a primary for the congressional seat.

Everything was cut and dried for the judgeship. The Futrell administration's candidate, C. E. Johnson, was already serving on an interim basis through appointment, and was unopposed for the convention nomination. The administration, for reasons of expediency, chose not to take sides in the congressional fight, and to put to the delegates the question, "Shall there be a primary in the congressional race?" It looked like an uphill fight even with that concession, for a majority of district delegates were committed to Sam Rorex, a prominent Parnell lieutenant, and the assumption was that the state convention would merely refer the matter to the district convention.

My father was convinced that it was hopeless and that I would suffer humiliation by asking for a primary. But a caucus of my friends in Little Rock decided otherwise, and I had to go against my father in another major political dilemma.

Floor plans were carefully worked out. We agreed to let the state organization get their nomination out of the way (it would have been fruitless to urge a primary in the judge's race, and, of course, it would have meant defeat on our issue, had we asked for primaries in both races. We accepted the taunt of inconsistency in return for the organization's neutrality in the district fight.)

I spent the preceding evening with my parents at Russellville trying to reconcile my father to our strategy, but he was unyielding and miserable. He and mother did, however, want to attend the convention. During the seventy-five mile motor trip from Russellville to Little Rock, he was silent most of the time. I was going to "embarrass him in a futile gesture that would anger the political leaders in the area." He wanted peace! We entered the convention hall about noon. Everyone thought the proceedings would be over in an hour's time, a nominating speech for Johnson, the nomination to be made unanimous, then a quick motion to authorize the district delegates to act on the other vacancy. What our opposition did not know was that the chairman had agreed to recognize one of my friends to move for a district primary. When that surprise tactic was revealed, the convention was shaken. The Rorex headquarters was full of flowers, and telegrams of congratulations on his nomination were already arriving. The first edition of the afternoon newspaper declared that the district convention was then "in the process of nominating Rorex."

I spoke in favor of the motion for the district primary, and the response was tumultuous. I stole a glance at my father, who had been sitting forlornly on a back seat. He stirred excitedly, glanced around at the delegates, and began to nod appreciatively at the friendly ones. The debate was brief; the roll call began. We were ahead from the start, but the margin narrowed and there was tension. But not for my father! The first outburst had convinced him we had won, and he was ecstatic.

Finally the chairman declared that our motion prevailed and the convention promptly adjourned. I was limp, so much so that when one of Rorex' friends stepped up to me I thought it meant congratulations; but then I heard him say, "Step out here with me and I'll give you the pounding of your life." But a lame man standing by me said, "You lay a finger on Brooks and I'll break this cane over your head." I have loved all cane carriers since that day!

But this was only the first stage. The big battle had been quickly won, but the war was not finished. We girded ourselves for the primary fight.

Rorex and I announced at once. Then a surprise announcement came from D. D. Terry, a respected member of the state house of representatives and son of a former congressman. There were few issues. I promised bold action to deal with the Depression, and stressed economic factors as distinguished from pork-barrel and patronage advantages. Our forces were optimistic throughout. Rorex was a good campaigner and popular with the establishment, but bore the tag of the discredited Parnell administration.

On election night it soon became apparent that I had a plurality but that a runoff would be necessary; but it seemed obvious that it would be between Rorex and myself. Suddenly the returns showed a shift from Rorex to Terry. The story can best be told in the words of a Rorex friend who in later years supported me, and he felt that telling the story to me tended to purge him of a portion of the guilt for what took place.

"At midnight," he said, "the Rorex people decided that Sam could not beat you in a runoff, but we preferred Terry to you, so we decided to shift enough of Sam's votes to Terry to put him in second place. Rorex kicked like a steer, but we went ahead. I was one of those designated to carry the word to county and township key men, and I spent the early morning hours on that mission. I went into the office of one of our men at sunup and gave him the decision. He said, '*What*! I've been up all night stealing 'em from Brooks to give 'em to Sam, have I got to steal 'em the second time?' I told him that that was the message, so he got busy again."

The runoff came only two weeks later. We recognized the disadvantage that the outrageous actions had placed us under. Mr. Terry had not been a party to the fraud; he was merely the beneficiary. What he was about to receive was forged in the fires of bitterness toward me for the independent courses I had pursued.

Came the second primary. The vote was light, for the registration was based upon the one-dollar poll tax payment, and many people, particularly in the rural areas, had felt that they needed to save every dollar, and so did not buy a poll tax in that off-election year.

The ballot had only the one race, so the returns came in quickly; that is, from all except Yell County, Sam Rorex' home until he moved to Little Rock some six years earlier. With reports in from practically every box in the other seven counties, I was 545 votes in the lead. In spite of my familiarity with the unsavory practices in many of the Yell County townships in that period, I felt like relaxing. How could they possibly wipe out my lead when, if everyone in Yell County voted, it would total only 1,662 (less about 300 known Republicans), and it was recognized that I, too, had a strong following in Yell County. But we were in for a shock! The county, holding out its votes with no explanation, finally reported 1,850 votes for Terry and 616 for Hays, a total of 2,466 on a registration of 1,662! That was forty-seven years ago, but today in Arkansas old timers will tell you it was the most fraudulent election in Arkansas history. There was not even the semblance of irregularity in the reporting of votes in the other counties, and the ratio of votes reported to the registration in the other counties ranged from only 60 percent to 80 percent.

One not familiar with election machinery would doubtless wonder how an excess of 800 votes over the registration could be accomplished. Perhaps I can help convey an understanding of how some precincts achieved it. Let us look at little Richland township, for example. It is a sparsely settled area on a mountain top. In 1933 there were fifteen persons eligible to vote. Our survey showed that only nine of them actually voted and that only one of the nine was known to have voted for me. But the reported vote certified by the judges and clerks was 114 for Terry and 1 for Hays. The record of persons voting which must accompany the ballot box to the courthouse at the time of certification had interesting entries. After listing the nine known to have voted (including the officials themselves), the register carried in sequence the names of almost every house-holder in the area, always in this order: Mr. John Jones, Mrs. John Jones, Mr. Brown, Mrs. Brown, Mr. Smith, Mrs. Smith, Mr. Johnson, Mrs. Johnson, etc., 106 names being thus listed. The officials, in order to meet their quota as fixed by the county machine, simply falsified the records. Even if they had had poll tax receipts, it is hardly conceivable that fifty-three couples would have appeared at the polls in such a pattern. All of this would have been revealed if the suit had not been dismissed.

We went to court at once, filing the suit in Little Rock where we knew the Yell County irregularities could be exposed if procedural problems, always an obstruction in election cases, could be solved. The single issue was: who received the larger number of votes, Terry or Hays? And the only way to determine it was to open the ballot boxes (all of which had been impounded), cast out the ones shown to be illegal, and count the remaining ballots.

Here I must decide whether to write for the lawyers who may read my story, or for the general reader who would not be interested in the technical phases of the contest. I shall follow the latter course, though the temptation is great to give the legal aspects of an involved case which contains an abundance of material for the student of election contest law.

The hearings occupied about two months and were the subject of three Arkansas supreme court rulings, all of which were adverse to me and rendered solely because election contest provisions had been too rigidly construed and the court had rationalized their escape from the tough job of deciding between political interests. (Further, there was obvious favoritism by some of the judges.) Election contests procedure is one area in which the old axiom "a remedy for every wrong" seems not to apply, for the boxes were never opened, and my petition for a recount was dismissed. The state supreme court's rulings obstructed us at every stage. The trial judge, looking at the Yell County returns, could tell that fraud showed on its face, and he felt that the ballots should be examined. However, his hands were tied by the technical rulings of the higher court and he followed the only course left to him in dismissing the case.

There is some comfort for all who resent the injustices of election irregularity in the fact that the publicity given Yell County by our case prodded the consciences of the people of the county, and they began to take steps to correct conditions. Further, the poll tax was ultimately abolished, and that helped. Finally, the installation of voting machines makes election thievery very difficult, and Arkansas localities are beginning, under a new law, to use the machines.

The pain of having to bear the injustices of being denied my election credentials was very great, but the greater offense was done to the people. They were denied the right to have the choice of the majority occupy the office, and something precious in democratic life is damaged when this takes place.

I resolved that I would not let the experience hurt me inside, for I knew that if I were not hurt inside I would not be hurt at all. I firmly resolved not to be bitter or cynical, not to lose faith in the people or even in the system which, in this instance, had broken down. Three years after this event I was candidate for a second term as national committeeman, and Yell County gave me a big majority. The tide had been reversed.

Chapter 8 REBOUND FROM ADVERSITY 1934–1942

The World is infinitely cruel;
The World is infinitely kind.
Walter Hines Page

WITH the beginning of 1934, following the failure to get a recount of the ballots in the congressional contest, I was more in need of employment than I had ever been. My debts had climbed to $8,000. The time had come for me to stop crusading and concentrate on making a living.

Federal employment offered the best hope. Emergency agencies were still being staffed. My membership on the Democratic National Committee, a rather prestigious position in Arkansas, was the one thing retrieved from five years of political activity which had produced two defeats for governor and the congressional fiasco. I went to Washington to survey the possibilities, with the favorable results already described, my appointment as chief of the legal and labor compliance responsibilities in the state NRA office. The National Recovery Administration, invalidated by "the sick chicken case," relied largely on voluntary compliance with wage and hours standards as fixed by the codes for the various industries. It was only moderately effective. While other New Deal programs made dramatic impacts upon the stricken economy, the NRA gradually lost standing, and its demise brought little sorrow. At best, it was regarded as an interim measure. Senator Joe Robinson, who became the wheel horse of the New Deal, confided to me that NRA was the only legislative venture of the bold new administration that he regarded as a failure.

The senator was probably surprised at the breathtaking leadership of

115

the new president. As he proceeded to carry the Roosevelt banner on Capitol Hill, I recalled a conversation we had had during the 1932 campaign. In a burst of candor, I had said, "Senator, I haven't yet read any speech of our candidate that reaches the height of great statesmanship." His short reply was, "You won't, either." This was before the Commonwealth Club speech in San Francisco, which I thought was great. My own surprise at Roosevelt's brilliant beginning as president was matched by that of Senator Robinson.

Finally, when my job was secure, I returned to Little Rock and plunged into my new duties. I was happy to have a salary again; $4,500 a year looked mighty good in 1934. My most publicized case involved a ladies' garment factory in Forrest City. The owner had adopted an innovation—employment of colored women operatives on a piece-work basis that produced for the worker from six to ten dollars a week. We determined that under the code, the owner was indebted to various employees in excess of $5,000. A Negro national organization represented by James P. Davis attempted to prove that our figures were too low, so I had to defend our position against attacks by both employer and a friend of the employees, although I think that a big majority of the employees were satisfied with our findings. The articles made in the little plant were house dresses. The low wage enabled the manufacturer to make a profit with a retail price of slightly less than $1.00 for each dress, and as one competitor said, the Forrest City plant was "demoralizing the trade from South Carolina to California." The Appeals Board held with me. My experience proved to my satisfaction that prescribed legal minimum wages are necessary to prevent the operation of sweat shops. Industry self-policing is not sufficient.

I continued my interest in state political affairs, although Governor Futrell and some of his aides regarded me as a pariah. The governor was a strong-willed little person, an able judge, and scrupulously honest. He was extremely frugal. One of his opponents for the governorship declared, "He won't spend money for anything but shotgun shells and Copenhagen snuff. He wouldn't give a dime to see his grandmother a little girl again." And the governor felt the same way about the state's money. He consolidated some offices and abolished others. Except for the federal government's activities to relieve the suffering produced by the Depression, the hardships of many people would have been unbearable, since the governor virtually abdicated his responsibility in the welfare field.

My knowledge of J. M. Futrell went back to 1913 when I was in high school. Joe T. Robinson left the governorship after only a few weeks' tenure to accept the U.S. Senate seat made vacant by the sudden death of Jeff Davis. State Senator Futrell became acting governor by reason of being president pro-tem of the state senate. He could have held on to the high office until the next general election in 1914, almost two years away, but he immediately called a special election to fill the office by popular vote. For that action, he became one of my heroes.

I would gladly have supported him for governor in the 1932 election if my former law partner and 1928 campaign manager, Judge Priddy, had not been pressured into running by certain powerful political figures, some of whom had dubious motives. But Judge Futrell never forgave me. Perhaps some of my criticisms of the conservative posture of his campaign irked him. I was not particularly proud of my speeches; in fact, the maneuvering in that 1932 campaign left me a bit unhappy over the entire situation. I regretted that I never had an opportunity for a heart-to-heart talk with Judge Futrell, to explain the complex circumstances that produced the Priddy candidacy and deprived me of the options to run again or to support him. He had supported me in both races for governor, and had said to some mutual friends that he would stay out of the 1932 race and support me if I became a candidate.

My decision to accede to the plan of friends to place my name on the 1932 ballot for Democratic national committeeman was influenced partly by the feeling that this would allay some of the anger of my partisans over the strategy of one branch of the Parnell group to keep me out of the governor's race by luring Judge Priddy into running.

I talked to Judge Priddy about it before deciding to yield to my friends and run for committeeman, and he said, "Go ahead." Later, he may have had second thoughts. At any rate, the interests behind my opponent for the committee post persisted in efforts to get me out of the race, using the direct appeals to me to "withdraw, so as not to hurt Judge Priddy." It was a tough situation for me. I discovered so much resentment among many of my followers over the strategy used to keep me out of the governor's race that I was convinced that giving up my advantage in the national committeeman's race would hurt Judge Priddy more than it would help his cause. I remember vividly the discomfort I felt when one of the opposition, who was outwardly a Priddy man, but a person incapable of unyielding loyalty, called me into one of the headquarters' private rooms to say, "I have in my pocket twenty-five one hundred dollar bills. They're yours if you promise me now to withdraw. The money is yours personally, or for Priddy's campaign if you want to put all or any part of it into his fund."

The purpose of that last suggestion was obvious. The basis was laid for saying that I was more interested in having an honor for myself than in advancing our candidate's cause in the governor's race. Of course, I promptly told him I could not consider it.

I was an easy winner, carrying 73 of the 75 counties without turning a hand in my own behalf, and giving all of my efforts to Judge Priddy in his hopeless undertaking. He was badly outdistanced by Judge Futrell.

Evidence of Governor Futrell's feeling of antagonism toward me was his reply to the importuning by some of his friends to appoint my father to a judgeship. He refused on the single ground that he was "Brooks Hays's father." He directed his staff at the 1936 National Democratic Convention to see to it that I did not attend caucuses or sit with the delegation. This attitude was out of harmony with his sense of fairness as a judge. When he was elected governor I asked a lawyer from his area about Judge Futrell and got this reply: "At least, he will work hard at the job. When he was elected our chancellor he read Pomeroy's six volumes on equity from cover to cover." I interjected, "Like we Baptists study our Bible?" The lawyer quickly said, "Oh, no! He read it with an open mind." I have not been permitted to forget this one.

As I had predicted in the second governor's race in 1930, the state defaulted on the highway bonds. The 1933 legislature was confronted with the task of producing a brand-new schedule for payment of both classes of bonds, i.e., the old district obligations and the new state bonds. The problem was compounded by the fact that the Halsey-Stuart bond firm which marketed the new state bonds did not give the political history of the bond structure in their literature, and their advertisements did not even refer to the existence of the district bonds, which the state was morally bound to pay. Those purchasers of the state bonds, who had no notice of this condition, had a grievance on this score, since it was obvious only to all who knew the history of the district bonds that the legislature did not propose to pay the prescribed interest on the new state bonds at the cost of defaulting on the older district bonds which had been assumed by the state. A Minnesotan, a total stranger, sitting by me on a Washington streetcar about that time, complained bitterly about Arkansas' mistreatment of the bond purchasers. I told him that my own conscience was clear; that I had begged the people in two governor's races to let me put the brakes on the inordinate highway spending. It hurt Arkansas' reputation in the money market, putting us under a cloud that remained for many years.

The payoff came in the Futrell administration, an ironic fact since he had fought against the folly I have described. In April 1934, I received a telegram that had a profound effect upon my career. It was signed by a person I had never heard of, but I was destined to develop a warm friendship with him, and to find myself under an enormous obligation to him for help in understanding the complicated economic and social problems of the region. His name: Francis Pickens Miller. He was at that time a resident of Fairfax, Virginia, a Rhodes scholar, a distinguished churchman and author, and later an outstanding political leader in his home state of Virginia. He became the courageous leader of the anti-Byrd forces of Virginia. The telegram invited me to a meeting in Atlanta of representative citizens of southern states to organize a movement to alert southern leadership to the grave problems of farm tenancy, low incomes, racial discrimination, disfranchisement due to poll tax laws, discriminatory freight rates, elective irregularities, and other social ills.

I was thrilled to be part of such a movement, and found in the Atlanta meeting a congenial group of college men, newspaper publishers and columnists, and civic leaders, generally of a liberal point of view. We set up a formal organization, the Southern Policy Committee, out of which grew the National Policy Committee. Francis Miller and his gifted wife, Helen Hill Miller (whom he met at Oxford), assumed effective leadership in both groups. We functioned for about ten years and accomplished a good deal for the South. Not least of the achievements was the establishment of friendships and lines of communication between the scattered students of problems of poverty, race relations, and election abuses.

In the year 1934, I got around Arkansas a good deal and took an occasional trip into other southern states, generally on missions for the Southern Policy Committee. I had a surprise invitation to speak at a Chamber of Commerce meeting in Anniston, Alabama, in 1935, and for the first time in my life I felt prepared to discuss southern policy. The speech was well received and was given editorial praise by the Anniston *Star*. The Southern Policy Committee's material was soundly organized and could be adapted to Chamber of Commerce meetings. Businessmen were becoming convinced that low wages and low farm incomes were depressants for the business community.

I spent the night with H. C. Nixon, professor of political science at Tulane University and chairman of the Policy Committee, who was living during the summer in an old resort frame house near Anniston, one of many built around the springs in the South's hill country. At breakfast the next morning, Mrs. Nixon said, "It must have been quite a meeting. My husband kept me awake until way after midnight talking about your shaking those businessmen—it was that exciting to him." Dr. Nixon added, "At least we are getting business and civic leaders to listen."

Our committee also supplied documentation of the freight rate discriminations that had made it difficult for southern producers to reach the high consumption territories of the north and west. This, coupled with our advocacy of the reciprocal trade program to deaden the effect of the tariff upon agricultural areas, gave us some respectability in the business community, although the conservative farm groups looked askance at us, largely because of our emphasis upon the plight of the tenants and sharecroppers.

In 1935 I met Henry Wallace. He and his staff were interested in my ideas on the subjects of political and social reform, and I was invited to his office. I was asked to submit a memorandum on conditions in the cotton areas and to suggest remedies. It was a welcome invitation. I knew that it presented an opportunity to participate in long-range measures to lift the standard of living for a neglected group, the rural poor. Every index showed great disparities between the regions, the per capita income being about half that of the northern states. And within the region the poorest families were in the rural counties and in the black community.

Even as late as 1940, the richest of the eight states in the cotton south (Louisiana with a per capita income of $360) was poorer than the poorest state in the north and northeast (Vermont with $505 per capita income) and, except for South Dakota, tied with $360, and North Dakota with only a slightly lower per capita income of $340 was poorer than any of the states west and northwest of the cotton south. And poverty struck hardest at the largest families. As Congressman Luther Patrick of Alabama said, "The stork and the wolf always did pal around together."

My memorandum for the secretary of agriculture was not a scholarly opus, but it probably gave Mr. Wallace a fairly good picture of the human problems growing out of the unhealthy farm economy. I gave instances of family struggles, supplying, where possible, a view of the humor that characterized the acceptance of hardship. For example, I recalled picking up two Negro farm workers who were en route to the county seat to ask about work and free government commodities.

One of them said, "If I can get a little help till June, I can live then on the fish I catch."

"Do you use a hook and line, or seine for your fish?" I asked.

"No, suh, I hogs my fish."

I had thought I was familiar with all folk ways, but this stumped me, and I asked him to explain.

"That means catchin' 'em with your hands. You find a place where the water's still and where tree roots are next to the bank, if you can, and then reach your hand down there, quiet-like. You try to find a sleepy ole catfish lying up against the bank. You stroke him. He likes that. You get your hand in his mouth, and then it's just you against him, and you can generally conquer him." My report to Secretary Wallace included a few such references to folk ways in the hope that some of the secretary's policy makers would be encouraged to help our impoverished farm people. Twenty-five years later, a professor at the University of the Pacific told me he had found my memorandum in the National Archives, properly classified, and had studied it in preparing a paper on the subject of rural rehabilitation.

My appointment to the Resettlement Administration was not sought by me. I was serving at that time as president of the Arkansas Conference on Social Work, and had gotten acquainted with Harry Hopkins and his assistant, Aubrey Williams, in the course of my two years' service as conference president. In the early spring of 1935 I was in Washington and went into Aubrey Williams' office to invite him to be principal speaker at our annual meeting. He begged off, and I was leaving his office when he said, "Wait, let's see if Rex Tugwell can go." He phoned Rex, and, getting a negative answer, was ready to hang up, when as an after-thought, he said, "Rex, I think you ought to meet this young man—he is not only Social Work Conference president, he is Democratic National Committeeman for Arkansas. Anybody having that combination ought to be on your team." I was in Dr. Tugwell's office in a few minutes for a talk about southern rural problems and possible political and legislative solutions. Within a few days I was offered and accepted a place on his regional staff for the mid-south, which had headquarters in Little Rock. It was located there as a concession to Senator Robinson.

Then later, on a pleasant June day, I was having lunch with Will Alexander, Dr. Tugwell's assistant, and an authority on the south's economic conditions, in the Cosmos Club's open-air garden dining room, when we were joined by Dr. Tugwell. I think Rex sensed that I had been fired up about participating in the bold new programs to deal with rural poverty, for Will said to me that afternoon, "Rex wants you to come up to Washington to help us."

I readily accepted. The offer came partly because of the Democratic National Committee membership, which would help open doors on Capitol Hill, but also because Will Alexander recognized me as a kindred spirit who would be congenial with the group of young crusaders gathering in Washington to help fashion economic, social, and political reforms. I reveled in the new assignment. While officially "Special Assistant to the Administrator" (Dr. Tugwell), I was in reality an understudy for Dr. Alexander, and I worked closely with him as a congressional liaison officer. Our chief legislative interest in the early days of Resettlement was passage of the Bankhead-Jones bill to provide liberal terms for loans to purchase family-sized farms for qualified families having the demonstrated capacity to operate farms as owners. The ratio of tenant-operated farms had climbed to more than two-thirds, and tenancy had become a symbol of rural farm distress. At the same time, it was recognized that those renters and sharecroppers without the qualifications for ownership should not be left out of the wise and benevolent new relief measures. Therefore, several types of family aid were being devised. A land purchase program was instituted, and thousands of acres of good farm land were purchased by the government from mortgagees who had had to foreclose on properties, subject to debts that the mortgagors were unable to pay. The sympathies of many urban dwellers had been won, and there was a surge of favorable sentiment for the land purchase program.

I was busy on the Hill explaining our program to senators and House members, concentrating on agricultural committees and southerners.

Now and then I did encounter some resistance. I recall, for example, dropping in at the office of Senator Ellison D. Smith, (known as "Cotton Ed"), an acid-tongued senior conservative senator from South Carolina. The card handed him by the secretary: "Brooks Hays, Democratic National Committeeman," was an eye-catcher for members of Congress, but at times it was deceptive. The venerable senator was certainly deceived. "Well, sit down here, and let's talk about agriculture," he said. "I'm glad to have somebody with practical political sense to talk to. You know, Rex Tugwell sent one of his damn fools out here a few days ago to talk about some wild ideas of that downtown crowd . . ." I tried to disguise my story of tenant needs quickly and discreetly, and left hurriedly, hoping he didn't sense the fact that a second "damn fool" had been to see him.

For several months in 1935 I luxuriated in the work of helping Will Alexander and Dr. Tugwell perfect the Rural Resettlement organization. I was the liaison with Senator Joe T. Robinson, who had already demonstrated his enormous gifts of leadership on Capitol Hill. His anger at me for refusing to yield to his wishes for Sam Rorex to fill the vacancy in the congressional office in 1933 had subsided, and by carefully conveying his desires to the Tugwell staff, I had managed to be useful to him, as well as to the administration. He seemed to sense that, while I had been "off the reservation" in Arkansas politics, I wanted to help advance the Roosevelt program and was eager to maintain a peaceful relationship with his office. I was a good message bearer. I also had the advantage of membership on the Democratic National Committee, the place won in the 1932 primary with a landslide that greatly impressed him. I also had a working and friendly relationship with the "old heads" on the committee, including Chairman Jim Farley, and with the other members of the Arkansas congressional delegation. The senator trusted me. I was not as obsequious as he liked those with political aspirations of their own to be, but I think he respected me, and he wanted to get along with my friends. He had probably been surprised to find me somewhat independent of the Little Rock big wheels to whom he looked for political advice. He told me so one day.

He gruffly said, "Brooks, the boys tell me you're not working with them, or with me."

"Now, Senator," I replied rather firmly, "let me be very frank. I *am* working with you. I am your friend, and I want them and everybody else to be your friends. The difference between us is that they don't want you and me to be friends. I do want them as your friends, even though they will never be friendly to me. You need them and you also need those of us who play by a different game plan. They will continue to try to poison you against me, and all I can say is that you can count on me, and I hope you will trust me to work with you regardless of what my opposition in Arkansas tell you about me." I assume he was convinced because, a few weeks later, he said, "I have told them" (and I think "them" meant a small group led by Homer Adkins, the Internal Revenue collector for Arkansas), "I don't want to hear any more carping about Brooks—not another word. I told them flatly that you and I understand each other."

He made only one patronage demand of me that I remember. He called me into his office one morning to say, "Brooks, when I ran for Congress in 1902, I had one good friend in Pine Bluff, Meyer Solmson. He worked hard and got results, and asked nothing in return. He later went to New York and got a newspaper job, but lately has had hard luck. He needs a job desperately. I want a job for him, and I want it right away." I promised him I would do my best. I went straight to Dr. Tugwell. I was surprised to meet resistance.

"Now, Brooks, we can't give everybody a job just to please a Senator. Let's take our time on this." I had to plead with Rex for that job. I pointed out that the senator's man had had considerable experience in newspaper work, and that in an organization as large as ours there would be something for him where he could render a service. Rex finally yielded, but not until I reminded him of the tremendous obligation we owed Joe Robinson. "And he continues to fight for us," I said. "Tomorrow, our appropriation bill with eighty million dollars for rural rehabilitation will come up for action in the Senate, and you ought to authorize me right now to tell him to have his friend down here before sundown to fill out the papers!" That did it, and my conscience was clear. Joe Robinson had discharged, with my help, a thirty-three-year-old obligation. This could be cited as an argument for civil service coverage, but it is also a case study in practical politics where a department is serving, as we were, a great humanitarian cause.

Joe Robinson needed the spurt that the New Deal gave him to win a special place in the political annals. His talents were geared to producing legislative results, but that required a party majority; consequently his role as minority leader of the Senate during the twenties was undistinguished. His pinnacle was reached in the Roosevelt era. He was not an innovator, but the legislative proposals generated by the Roosevelt brain trust, once placed in Joe Robinson's hands, were destined to return to the president's desk with both Senate and House approval, ready for the FDR signature. Only once was he unable to deliver the votes, and that was not his fault; the so-called "Supreme Court packing" measure was doomed from the outset. The senator did his best in spite of his discomfort over the furious opposition of some of his favorite colleagues, and perhaps the reservations of his own mind, over the wisdom of the idea.

John E. Miller, Robinson's successor in the Senate, then a House member, told me that he was in the senator's office shortly after the senator had returned from the White House after conferring with the president on the subject of a strategic retreat on the Court bill. He told John that the president accepted the senator's report to the effect that he simply did not have the votes and could not muster them to put the bill through. It was agreed that a compromise along lines recommended by Robinson would be sought. The happy senator came back ecstatic over the results, but an hour later the president changed the signals, and Joe Robinson found himself again embarrassed by having to preside over a dwindling Democratic force. John Miller related this to me with a gesture, imitating the senator's throwing his great arms around his own chest in frustration, agonizing over the collapse of the senator's plan to save the president from a humiliating defeat.

On the whole, Senator Robinson's performance as Democratic leader of the Senate from the beginning of the Roosevelt administration, March 4, 1933, until his sudden death on July 14, 1937, was brilliant. He earned the reward that would certainly have been his, appointment to the first Supreme Court vacancy of the Roosevelt era. My certainty that, had he lived, he would have had this reward he worked so hard for, is based on what Jim Farley said to me on the funeral train, "Brooks, the president told me to tell the senator he would be appointed, and I did it. He had that assurance before he died." Later, Jim gave me some of the details. The president, for understandable reasons, had committed him to secrecy. Joe asked only that he be permitted to tell Mrs. Robinson and Pat Harrison, the Mississippi senator and Joe's closest Senate friend.

Joe Robinson had, in addition to the intellectual and temperamental equipment for legislative success, a marvelous physical presence. A large frame and a voice like a bull horn helped him to put to effective use the fruits of hard work and singleness of purpose. In spite of his inability to control his temper always, he managed to get along fairly well with people. The irritations that he showed with me were never long lived, and he probably had a sort of paternal feeling toward me (he and my father were the same age and were old friends). He could not fail to notice that I was at his beck and call every minute of the 1936 Democratic Convention in Philadelphia which he served as permanent chairman, and he may have had something to do with my having the privilege of leading the parade in his honor around the convention hall when he was named the chairman.

The last evening I spent in the company of this remarkable man was at the University Club in Washington a few days before his passing. The new governor of Arkansas was Carl E. Bailey, a strong-willed leader himself. The two had not gotten along very well. However, the senator had said to me soon after Carl's inauguration earlier in that year (1937), "Your friend Carl and I have had a talk, and we understand each other. I know you'll be glad that we are going to work together."

A few days before the senator's death my former law partner, Bolon Turner, a Tax Court judge (appointed by Roosevelt at Joe Robinson's urging), together with Senator Robinson's assistant Fred McClerkin, and I were hosts at a dinner for the senator and the governor with a half dozen other choice friends. Both of the honorees were in good spirits and kept up a lively conversation, seldom having to yield to the hosts or other guests. The senator in particular was in a mellow mood. He recalled his clash with the Ku Klux Klan in the heyday of its power, and mentioned his exchange with Senator Tom Heflin in a Senate debate on that issue. He added, "In spite of the strong feelings I had on that matter, I never entirely lost my feeling of affection for old Tom. His intolerance in that campaign of '28 seemed out of character."

That fall, a few weeks after the senator's death, by chance I rode on the same train with Senator Heflin from Montgomery to Auburn, and when he mentioned his admiration for Joe Robinson, I was glad to be able to tell him of the senator's warm reference to him in my last conversation with him. The mellowness of these comments by Senator Robinson at the dinner and by Senator Heflin on the train were in sharp contrast with the mood reflected by their exchange on the Senate floor in the spring of 1928. Senator Robinson had said some biting things about the Klan when Heflin interrupted to say, "The senator won't go to Arkansas and say that this fall," to which Senator Robinson replied, "I will not only say it in Arkansas, I will go to Alabama and say it!"

At this point, Senator Heflin lost his poise, and slipped badly. His voice raised, he said, "And they'll tar and feather him if he does!" Senator Robinson's gift of eloquence surfaced spontaneously. "Mr. President," he said, "the utterance to which we have just listened only demonstrates the spirit of proscription which resides in the breast of the senator from Alabama." He proceeded with fresh vigor to attack the Klan, and the Senate listened.

Another incident related to me by Senator Robinson in that long dinner discussion was his visit in the White House with President Harding. The two had been Senate colleagues for six years and were on good terms. Senator Robinson went to the White House to discuss a legislative matter shortly after Mr. Harding took office. He opened the conversation with a pleasant inquiry, "And how do you like your new job, Mr. President?" Harding looked tired, and his voice reflected it. "Well, Joe, I would like it just fine, except for the pressures of every imaginable kind. Everybody wants something, and some are unreasonable." The senator then said something on the spur of the moment, a wholly unplanned reply: "Then, Mr. President, why don't you pay the woman off and get rid of her?" The president's countenance all of a sudden changed, and it registered a quizzical expression as if he were asking, "Do you know about her?" The senator promptly shifted to another subject, but when Nan Britton's authenticated story, *The President's Daughter*, appeared after the president's death, Senator Robinson knew why the president stared at him so pathetically that day.

I became a sort of stand-in for both Dr. Tugwell and Dr. Alexander for meetings sponsored by organizations interested in solving the severe problems of rural poverty. Among my more important appearances were (1) the meeting of the National Christian Rural Fellowship in Nashville, at which I spoke on "The Christian's Relation to the Land." I emphasized the need for owners, tenants, and consumers of farm products to hold to certain principles, among them that "all occupants should love the land, and only those who love it should live upon it." I believed that land speculation is a social evil and I advocated the adoption of standards in this field. I did not treat the tenant's obligations lightly. He must be required to conserve the soil and protect the owner's investments, and rights of tenure should be established for the tenant's protection. I quoted the tenant who said, "Every politician ought to be a tenant for a while. About the third time the dust of an Alabama road settled on his household stuff being moved to a new location, he'd decide something oughta be done."

I prepared an article for the Emory University *Journal of Public Law* on planning good tenant-owner relations. I tried in this article to stress the fact that much of the out-migration loss of population to the South could be prevented by sound planning for better farm practices and improved owner-tenant relations. I spoke to the New Orleans Association of Commerce in 1938 on "Problems of the South's Low Income Farmer," and received a sympathetic hearing in my plea for an acknowledgment by the city leaders of the agricultural basis for economic progress in the South. In that talk I drew upon an observation of Walter Lowdermilk, an authority on the Middle East, who described the tragedy awaiting any civilization that neglects its land problems. Dr. Lowdermilk dramatized the experience of Antioch, the great port city of Asia Minor, which had at the time of St. Paul's visits one-third of a million people; but today, largely because the urban interests neglected the tableland and farm problems, there are only a few hundred fisher families residing there.

One of the lasting friendships growing out of my Department of Agriculture service during the thirties was with a parish Catholic priest in Granger, Iowa, Luigi Ligutti, who later acquired international recognition by his work in rural programs. He became the Pope's representative for the Farm and Agriculture Organization, which maintains headquarters in Rome. Now a monsignor, he continues to work for land reform and the improvement of living standards in Latin America, Africa, and Asia. He once promoted a continental conference of Catholic bishops and other churchmen at Bogotá, Colombia, with the prophetic slogan, "There will be land reform with us, without us, or against us," thus signifying the hopes that many churchmen entertain to give moral guidance to the revolutionary trends in land policy.

There was nothing revolutionary in the kind of social programs inspired by the Farm Security Administration (Resettlement's successor), but men like Father Ligutti and myself were certainly targets of the anti-Roosevelt group and were regarded as radicals. Still, the critical conditions of southern rural life forced the conservative South to view with some tolerance the plans of New Dealers to provide sound social and economic changes. There were some political risks, but I cheerfully accepted them: indeed, as one of the links of the Farm Security idealists to the political hierarchy, I was enthusiastic over my assignments.

The staid old minions of the sprawling Agriculture Department were probably skeptical of "the young upstarts—the unprofessional newcomers," but an atmosphere of hospitality to new ideas which we created gradually developed. In some cases such dedicated leaders of the establishment as M. L. Wilson, director of the Agricultural Extension Service, welcomed the inspiriting of the career people who had tended to succumb to routine activity with a consequent loss of imagination and excitement.

With so much land in the hands of banks and mortgage companies it was actually easier to procure farms for the competent renters than to deal effectively with the human problems growing out of faulty landlord-tenant relations. We were accused of trying to make owners out of all landless farmers, a claim that was completely groundless. Our record of selecting only qualified tenants for the family farm purchase program was proof of our essential conservatism. We were not blind to the fact that many renters and croppers did not have the ability to operate as owners. Our hopes for them centered around a program of prescribing duties and rights on both sides, thus enabling each to establish legal pressures for good performance by the other.

I was terribly disappointed, however, in the lack of willingness by some landlords to cooperate in this kind of effort to improve the lot of tenant families. It had a political buttress in much of the cotton plantation country. Officeholders in many instances depended upon the landlords, their suppliers, and related interests for perpetuation in office. Thus we were forced to rely largely upon the graciousness and progressive spirit of a landed gentry, who in their individual relations tried to be just and fair but were nevertheless so steeped in the old patterns and so unmoved by its injustices that this phase of our activity was not impressive.

An illustration of how unreasonable and adamant resistance of the Arkansas establishment was is indicated in the frustration we experienced in a mild proposal to set up an arbitration procedure to settle tenant claims against landlords. Simple justice would support this idea, since, without it, tenants would have to file lawsuits even for small claims. Delays and court costs made this alternative generally intolerable. But the moment we began work on the project some of the big plantation owners and their lawyers pulled wires in Washington and I was instructed to drop it. "The heat is too much for us," our superiors declared. It was one of my first disappointments as a fledgling ombudsman.

In the early days of my work with Resettlement, I shared an office just a few yards from Secretary Wallace and Dr. Tugwell (with a brain-truster having the intriguing name of Morecai Ezekiel); but on my second tour in Washington, after passage of the Bankhead-Jones Act in June, 1937, I had a tiny basement office in the Agriculture South Building. But obscurity and drab daily toil could not stifle our sense of urgency and excitement as we entered the labyrinthine structure each morning to work on loan programs for small farmers and home programs for their families. It was a great period for American agriculture, in spite of the fact that some of the most significant phases of the program were later canceled by the counter political influences of the conservative "big men" in agriculture and politics. Some undramatic, but reliable, studies of the significant Farm Security projects of that period have been made by scholars like the late James G. Maddox and John A. Baker (both natives of Arkansas), and in spite of setbacks, there are permanent results of our "grand scheme" to be cherished. One of our most valuable supporters was Jim Patton of Colorado, a dedicated farm leader—later, national president of the Farmers' Union.

Will Alexander was picked by President Roosevelt, who as a part-time resident of Georgia knew something of Will's monumental work in the struggle for the rights of southern blacks, and in promoting economic opportunities for the poor of both races. He brought an understanding of the southern scene which Rex Tugwell needed, since Dr. Tugwell had grown up as a favored upstate New Yorker. They made a fine team. Rex was breathtakingly bold in blueprinting ideas for change in farm practices, and Will knew how to apply the brakes when needed. Moreover, Will always sought the counsel of those of us who had lived close to village and farm life and could take account of political factors. Rex tended to be very impatient with these "realities."

Will Alexander began adult life as a Methodist minister and was a popular young pastor in Nashville when he came to the decision that he wanted to come to grips with poverty and race problems. He was a logical choice for the directorship of the Rosenwald-financed Commission on Inter-Racial Cooperation. He was responsible for my election to that commission in the early days of my Resettlement service, an activity that supplied an outlet for my concern for black people of the region.

It was enriching in providing new friendships among the black leaders, outside of Arkansas. I had come in contact with some great individual black leaders at the local level in my social work in Arkansas, and was haunted at times by the tragedy of finding unutilized moral and intellectual resources in the professional life of the circumscribed black community of Little Rock. I remember how surprised I was, for example, to find one of the librarians of Little Rock's Negro high school to be a very articulate and highly educated black woman seventy-five years of age whose inspiring life of usefulness to black youth had spanned sixty years as teacher and leader. At fifteen, Charlotte Stephens had been picked to teach the first graders in the neglected Negro schools of Little Rock, and when I met her she was in technical retirement but continuing to work in the high school library. The beneficiary of scholarships, she had graduated at Oberlin College and chose to return to her native city to work among her own people. I came to know brilliant professional black men, doctors, lawyers, and educators, but the white community generally moved along in its traditional ways, not knowing of the loss it suffered in not fully utilizing the black leadership.

The meetings of the Commission on Inter-Racial Cooperation were usually held in Atlanta, on the campus of Atlanta University, a school for blacks, since state laws and city ordinances prohibited unsegregated meetings. During the thirties, the police were under pressure to enforce in rigid fashion all of the laws designed to prevent any intermingling. I recall going into an interracial conference in the city of Birmingham in the late thirties in the company of Dr. Charles Johnson, black president of Fisk University, and Mark Ethridge, white editor of the Louisville Courier-Journal. The police at the door stopped us. "You two fellows," he said, pointing to Mark and me, "sit over there," and, gesturing to our black friend, "you sit over on this side." We were furious. Mark remonstrated. "But you are violating my rights; we want to sit with our friend, and you are doing a reprehensible thing in the name of the law in not letting us three friends sit where we want to sit." The expression on the officer's countenance changed to a sour and menacing look, and seeing there was no point in protesting, we moved on to the designated places. The human dignity of two members of the majority race had been affronted as arrogantly as that of the minority member. This was an almost daily experience for black persons, but members of the white race have to endure it less frequently.

The climax of our efforts to secure permanent legislation in behalf of farm tenants, laborers, and low-income owners was the passage in July, 1937, of the Bankhead-Jones Act. The legislation was finally adopted by both houses and was signed into law by an enthusiastic Franklin Roosevelt. Prior to this, the operations under Resettlement had been under executive order. The passage of the Bankhead-Jones Act, with only twenty-nine House members opposing, assured the agency of a permanent status and gave the Congress a better scrutiny of day-to-day operations.

Nineteen hundred thirty-six was Arkansas's centennial year, and one day in early June, Rex Tugwell brought word back from the White House that I would be invited to ride on the president's train to Little Rock for the ceremonies. Senators Robinson and Caraway were included, but none of the House members. I was a bit embarrassed about the seven representatives not being included, since they had cooperated with me in legislative and other matters, and I feared that they might suspect that my standing with the administration was such that I could have arranged for their being included if I had so desired. One of the congressmen actually did ask me to see if I couldn't get him a place on that train. The president's popularity was so high that he believed it would help him in his district. I tried, but was told that the list could not be enlarged.

The route was over the Southern Railway's line via Knoxville, Chattanooga, and Memphis. It required about thirty hours. During the second afternoon Marvin McIntyre, President Roosevelt's top aide, said to me, "The boss wants you to eat with him and a few other guests in his private car. He will look for you at six." The other guests were Senator Robinson, Jesse Jones of the Reconstruction Finance Corporation, Karl Crowley, candidate for the Texas governorship (the president's schedule included Texas, since it was their centennial too), and Marshall Diggs, a Washington attorney.

I walked back through the pullman cars to the president's car with Senator Robinson. An attendant met us at the entrance and said, "The president hasn't come in yet," whereupon the senator said, "Well, he said to be here at six, and it's six o'clock now," and with that he barged past the poor waiter into the dining section. I meekly followed. The others, including the president, soon came. I had been with him on several occasions, including a small stag dinner at the White House, but never under such intimate and favorable circumstances. I was surprised to find myself seated on his left. Senator Robinson, not surprisingly, was on his right.

The great man was in a jovial and talkative mood. He and the senator did most of the conversing, although it was obvious that the others were completely at ease and expected to participate in the talk. I did share in it.

Everyone but the president was served large thick steaks. He asked for scrambled eggs. One of his trademarks was a long cigarette holder, and it was in use a good part of the time. I noticed that the butts filled up his ashtray before the party ended. It did not end until late—nearly ten o'clock; there was nowhere to go, and being an election year, there was plenty to talk about.

The president talked freely of his Groton and Harvard days, and of some of his interesting contacts with other chiefs of state. Before we got around to the upcoming campaign, he mentioned our new interest in the Orient. I do not recall that he had any fixed theories or determinations about Japan, but rather an attitude of curiosity regarding the new power, military and industrial, and new purposes, in the emerging nation. He told us with some enjoyment of his interest which went back to college days. He recalled, for example, that one of his friends at Groton or Harvard was of the nobility of Japan, an attractive young prince. (I am not sure of the rank.) The president regaled us with a story of his using some choice wine his mother had sent him "to get that young prince in a talkative mood."

"I kept pouring Mother's wine down him, hoping to get some insights from a loose tongue, but when the bottle was emptied by the end of the evening, I had no new information."

But he told us a stranger story involving Japan, relating an incident in which Mussolini figured. It occurred after Mr. Roosevelt became president. A close friend of his was to see Mussolini in Rome, and according to the president's account he said to his friend, "Tell Il Duce that the president of the United States is puzzled about Italy's arming to the teeth. Why those military preparations? What nations are threatening Italy?" The answer that his friend brought back was a confusing one. "Tell President Roosevelt," the dictator said, "that Theodore Roosevelt was not mistaken about the yellow peril; he was just twenty-five years ahead of time." Not even FDR on that June evening in 1936 could throw much light on that, but when his famous speech a few years later characterized Mussolini's attack on France as "a stab in the back," and when in 1942 Italy aligned herself on Japan's side, I wondered if the irony of those actions occurred to FDR, and how much of the strange conversation he could recall.

We turned from international affairs to politics. The president mentioned the difficulties connected with our tax reform programs. The subject is too technical and complicated to make it much of a magnet for support. Mr. Roosevelt turned to me.

"You have run for governor. Didn't you find it so?" he asked.

"Mr. President, I have a perfect example," I said. "I was the first candidate ever to advocate an income tax in Arkansas, and I had rough going trying to sell it to the voters in 1928. You will recall the Scopes trial was held in Tennessee in 1925. Well, I was doing my best to make my income tax program sound simple and sensible. One day I was speaking in a small community forty miles from a railroad called Big Flat. I was standing under a large tree in front of a blacksmith shop, surrounded by a small crowd, and pouring out my heart on taxation, when a big brawny fellow, leaning against the door of the shop said, 'Hold on a minute. Can I ask you a question?'

" 'Certainly,' I said, mopping my forehead."

" 'Well, that talk about taxes is all right, I reckon, but what we folks here at Big Flat want to know is—How do you stand on evolution?' "

Everybody about the table joined in the president's laughter, as he threw back his head in his familiar gesture. A few minutes later he came back to the story. "What did you tell that fellow?" Not wanting to bore him with any part of my old speech, I said, "Well, Mr. President, after I had gone, one of my listeners is reported to have said, 'If Brooks is as good a two-stepper as he is a side-stepper, I'll bet he's popular at them Little Rock dances.' "

Before we dropped the campaign, the president mentioned his admiration for Governor Alfred M. Landon of Kansas, his Republican opponent. "We Democrats will have to guard against overconfidence this time, things have gone along so well," he said. "The Republicans have got a good candidate. He's got a good record and a folksy way about him that appeals to people." My memory of his comments is a little vague after these forty years, but I believe the president made the point that the tendency to dismiss "the candidate from a small prairie state," as one prominent Democrat had referred to him, could backfire. Later I was glad to have confirmation of my impressions of Mr. Roosevelt's appraisal of Landon in one of Arthur M. Schlesinger, Jr.'s, books. When I was in Governor Landon's home city of Topeka some thirty years later, I was invited to have breakfast with him and Mrs. Landon, and I derived considerable pleasure from relating President Roosevelt's comments to him.

After passage of the farm tenant measure in July, 1937, there was no occasion for my remaining in Washington, so I asked the Legal division to transfer me back to Little Rock as regional attorney for Arkansas, Louisiana, and Mississippi. It meant a fading of the glamour of the New Deal circle, but an Arkansas base was more logical, and my superiors in the Resettlement branch of the service were sympathetic with my wishes.

Dr. Will Alexander, who had succeeded Dr. Tugwell, was ambitious for me and he was constantly looking for openings in the public service that might mean a more prestigious assignment. He had become familiar, of course, with my political handicaps, particularly the difficulties growing out of the mistake of my friend Governor Carl Bailey in trying in the easy way to get the Senate seat made vacant by Senator Joe Robinson's sudden death. Upon Senator Robinson's passing, Mrs. Caraway became the senior senator. Sometime during this period—I cannot pinpoint the date because I did not learn of developments until later—Dr. Alexander and other friends suggested to President Roosevelt that he appoint me to a judgeship. The idea appealed to him, so, according to Dr. Alexander, the president asked Senator Caraway to agree to Senate confirmation. All of us were amazed when she refused, and some of my friends speculated that my close friendship with Carl Bailey was a factor, since she and the governor were not congenial. But friendship with Governor Bailey did not hurt me with FDR, for the governor and his friends were philosophically closer to the Roosevelt program than those in Senator Robinson's political circle proved to be after the senator's death in July, 1937.

One of the strange contradictions of this period was the willingness of the junior senator, John E. Miller, to support my appointment to a judgeship, since I had supported his opponent, Governor Bailey, in the special election of 1937 when Mr. Miller was chosen to succeed Senator Robinson. He submitted a list of six names, mine being one, of Arkansas attorneys he would support as joint sponsor for the vacancy. Mrs. Caraway would not accept any of the six, and induced the administration to accept her candidate, Harry J. Lemley.

There were other evidences of the president's desire to advance me. His appreciation of my long-time support was obvious. In 1939 he learned of my sponsorship that year of a constitutional amendment to repeal the Arkansas poll tax requirement for voting, and wrote me a strong personal letter endorsing it. It began "Dear Brooks," and while ordinarily that would not get notice, it came soon after he wrote the famous "Dear Alben" letter to Senator Barkley, and his message got special attention in Arkansas.

In October of 1938 I received an invitation from Barry Bingham of Louisville, whose father, Robert W. Bingham, had served as ambassador to Great Britain, and whose family published the *Courier-Journal*, to spend a weekend at his home with a half dozen other friends. The purpose was to talk about the Democratic party's future, particularly to counsel together as to a nominee in 1940. I gladly accepted and found congenial friends for the two days in Barry's home. The group included among others my old friend Francis P. Miller and four noted journalists, Bill Waymack of Des Moines, Tarleton Collier of Atlanta, and Barry's *Courier-Journal* associates Mark Ethridge and Herbert Agar.

All were supporters of New Deal measures who had demonstrated in our Southern and National Policy Committee sessions a concern for progressive economic and social policies. There was already talk of a third term for Mr. Roosevelt. It developed early in our conversations that we were unanimous in opposition to a third term on principle, and not because we were unhappy with FDR. All were admirers of the president. We did not reach unanimity, however, in the choice of a successor. We liked Cordell Hull and Henry Wallace (this was before he came under the sway of the "dissidents"), and there were several luminaries whose potential candidacies were appealing, but our chief interest was in getting the third-term idea out of the picture as early as possible.

The consensus was that Barry, being closest to the president, should confer with him and let him know how we as his friends felt about the third term. Barry quickly arranged the private conference with him in the White House, and later gave us in succinct terms the result of their meeting. Like so many engagements with the great man, the dialogue was missing. The president did practically all of the talking. When Barry introduced the subject, Mr. Roosevelt took over. It was apparent, Barry later informed us, that the president had already determined his 1940 course. The rationale was briefly laid out for Barry's benefit. He did not have an open mind, and Barry soon recognized that the president had little interest in what we, his warm friends, thought about his yielding the helm. In short, his decision was based upon the clear assumption that if he should declare he would not run again there would be a severe fragmentation of the party, and that those who opposed his reforms would regain power. We had no further meetings and felt helpless in the rigidifying situation. I do not believe any of us had much heart for his re-election in 1940, though we were all fully committed to him.

In June, 1941, I was transferred back to Washington from the regional attorney's office in Little Rock to the staff of James G. Maddox, a brilliant economist in the Department of Agriculture in Washington. Early in 1942 I learned that Congressman D. D. Terry, who had been the beneficiary of the fraudulent 1933 election, had decided to run for the Senate, Senator John E. Miller, who succeeded Senator Joe Robinson, having announced that he would accept a judgeship. That meant a wide-open race for Terry's seat. I saw an opportunity to win it. I was determined to have one more test of my political strength, and to realize something on the investment of years in political contests, which had produced some tragedies for myself and my family. While I was considering the matter, I received a telephone call from one of the state's leading political figures who was generally on the other side from me. He said, "Brooks, I think you ought to run for Congress. Some of us have been talking about it down here, and we believe you are the logical man to defeat Bob Bailey." (Lieutenant Governor Bailey had announced as a candidate, and hoped to have the nomination without opposition, which, of course, meant election, since at that time the Republicans were not seriously challenging any Democrat for a congressional seat.)

The call excited me because I knew that with this kind of support I would have one source of help that I had never had before. It was this political leader who later in 1942 gave my wife and me some of the details of the fraudulent election in 1933, outlined in a previous chapter. We were eager, of course, to let him feel that he had been forgiven. It would have disturbed me a bit if the newcomers had wanted to oversee my campaign but I knew that we could conduct a campaign free from irregularities. Furthermore this would be a general primary with many offices being contested, making irregularities less likely than in 1933. There would be many other candidacies, all the way from United States senator to township officers being voted on, whereas the corruption in that 1933 special election was for the one office, the congressman, and there was no monitoring by candidates for other offices.

That was the background in which I decided to run for Congress in 1942. I went back to Arkansas at once and was convinced by conversations with many of my old friends that I should run. My father at that time was seventy years old. His health was not good; he spent a good deal of time sitting on his east porch in Russellville, our old home where I had taken my bride in 1922, and where we had lived for about six months before our little home down the street was built. I was by myself on this mission. I was glad Marion was not along, because Dad was in a very resistant mood. He was sure I should not run for Congress. It was a replay of the preliminaries to my second race for governor in 1930, and he alluded to that. He said, "Son, I'm an old man. My health isn't good." He removed his dentures and looked pitiful—he took off his glasses, held his hand to his forehead, and bowed his head. He was doing the dramatics, just as in the court cases when he was famous as one of the best trial lawyers in Arkansas, saying, "Son, I'm afraid you'll put me in my grave. It will be the final blow. You lost the two governor's races; they robbed you of the congressional office, and here we are with a very insecure financial situation. You're not going to do this to me, are you, in my old age?" "Well," I finally said, "No!" Now, this was not on the east porch, because it was in late winter. We sat in his bedroom, Mother having to listen to it, and acting as a mediator.

Finally, I said, "Dad, I want you to be satisfied about it. Of course I'm not going to go against you." Then I made my pitch as eloquently as I could, saying that I had waited nine years to win vindication and to get something out of the efforts we had put in during the past years. I had found that the lieutenant governor was not as strong as some thought, even though the governor, Homer Adkins, would be for him. But there was an informal understanding with my friends who were Adkins men, but not Bailey men, that Adkins would not be active in my race. I presented these pointers to Dad.

About midnight I went upstairs to bed. There were just the three of us in the house. Mother came up after I'd gone to bed. She put her head in the door and said, "Son, you and your Daddy just must get together.

Can I assure him now that you really are not going to insist on running if he isn't satisfied?" I said, "Yes, Mom, you can make that promise." It pleased her immensely. This is the human side of politics, of course, the agony of families often experienced where there are conflicting forces. She told me the next morning that it had made it possible for Dad to sleep. We had a happy breakfast. I had made an agonizing concession, but I was hoping against hope that Dad would see the light.

He came home at noon. I had not left the house. He walked into the front room, and I saw that he had a companion with him. It was a friend with the awesome name of James Harrison Alexander Baker, but we always called him "the Colonel." Dad said, "Son, Colonel's here with me. Colonel says you can win the race." I said, "What do *you* say, Dad?" He answered, "I'm ready to go. Colonel says we can form an organization and go to town."

The news brought joy, because had I not run I would probably have gone to my grave thinking that I had kept out of a race I could have won only to spare my father the misery of another race. I had gone against his wishes in 1930 and again in 1933, and I felt that I should not persist in going against my father's wishes in these matters. Incidentally, Dad was known as a very dominant person, a man of strong will, strong desires, but I doubt, even if I had not been able to convince him, on that first visit to Russellville, that he would have held out. I think that in time he would have seen that it would be unfair to keep me out of the Congress race. Later, somebody said, "How do you think the Congress race is going?" and my hard-boiled tough political-minded Dad said, "Well, Brooks'll win it." And he added, "I'll tell you why I think he will: it's like a dog chasing a rabbit. With the dog, it's just another race; with the rabbit it's life or death." So that was the background for my race in 1942.

I quickly threw an organization together; I had the remnants of the organizations of my previous campaigns, but largely a personal following of young men who believed in me and who were not a part of the political establishment. Among them was Raymond Lindsey, an insurance man, later the international president of Gideons, who said that it was my quiet work in the Sunday school class that convinced him that he ought to have a change in his own outlook on life and become an active churchman. He agreed to be treasurer. (It was not much of a treasury at that time.) Lindsey and John F. Wells, who had been city editor of the *Arkansas Gazette* when I ran for governor, worked well together. Harold Sadler, my cousin, who perhaps was better fixed financially than any of us, became active. He was in the automobile business. Another stalwart was T. Shad Medlin, a young businessman. Jack Stewart, who became the campaign manager, had worked at one time for the state government and was an exception to what I said about having no one from the bureaucracy. He organized the headquarters with volunteer help. We spent in the whole campaign of 1942 only $4,900. I put up about $700 of it in addition to what I spent in travel. We were able to show in our carefully audited report an expenditure of $4,900, $4,200 of which was put up by friends, mostly in five, ten, and twenty-five dollar amounts. I believe that the largest campaign contribution we had was $100. There were a few $100 contributions, not many, perhaps half a dozen, and my long-time friend Dave Grundfest may have put in $300. We had a surplus and instead of holding it for future campaigns, we returned it to the donors. We sent 15 percent of all contributions back to the givers. One of my friends said after he had been away during the campaign, having left $100 and getting a $15 check back, "My goodness, if I had known it was going to pay that big a dividend, I would have put in more."

I went out on the hustings, and I loved it. Our son, Steele, who was at that time seventeen years old, did the driving. We had a simple little battery loudspeaker system. Sometimes there were only a dozen listeners in a village, and I talked to them quietly about what I hoped to do. There were a few big rallies at the end of the campaign. I had some friends who attached themselves to me on a personal basis who had known me in Lions Club work, or in other civic associations. I pondered this question: How much should a civic membership restrict the members in political activity? It could be said, of course, that the mere fact that the friendships grew out of a civic club association does not mean that they ought to restrain themselves. In Clarksville, Johnson County, the one county outside his home county that my opponent carried, four young men took charge of my campaign there against what they called "the machine." I called them "the four horsemen of the Apocalypse." One was a druggist, two were doctors, and the other was a dentist. This provided a weight on the medical side, and they got out and "rode the range" every day for me in the last part of the campaign, coming up with a big vote in a county that had been represented by my opponent in the state senate before he became lieutenant governor.

My opponent spent a lot of time in a hotel room in Little Rock, using the phone constantly. He did not spend much time seeing the people. I left the work of my headquarters to my friends there, and got into every part of the district. Some friends thought that I had developed considerable platform ability. Whatever I had did not come naturally. My first efforts in high school were not impressive, but I was so determined to go into politics that I kept working at it at the university and in law school. I think that by my first race for governor in 1928 I had developed some skill in speaking. Armed with a strong devotion to certain causes, I became rather effective partly because people were warming to those causes. When we had a rally, the people responded, and it was contagious.

Near the end Bailey was told by his closest friends that his race was lost. Then he became desperate. On Saturday before the primary election on Tuesday, everywhere in the district his leaders got great bundles of circulars, page-sized, inflaming feelings on the race issue. It was an attack upon me as "a dangerous radical." Race feelings were intense. The party rules did not permit the blacks to vote, but one of them came to me before the election and said, "Mr. Hays, we cannot vote for you." He was an able black lawyer with the beautiful name of Scipio Africanus Jones. He added, "We can't vote for you, but there are a lot of prayers being offered by Negroes today for your success."

Of course I cherished that, because I had been interested in the black people, in their conditions of poverty, unemployment, and discriminations, from the day I landed in Little Rock in 1925, and even before. I had helped organize the Urban League and was the president of the Tuberculosis Association. I often went to meetings in the black community, and had on occasions done what politicians were not supposed to do, namely, eaten with black friends. That was not a common occurrence, because there was still some sensitivity on the part of our black friends who would, I am sure, have invited me to many more of their affairs except for their consideration of its political effect. Nevertheless, the fact that I was a friend of the black people, and interested in them for no political purpose, was exploited in the 1942 race by my opponent.

He knew of one event in my history: I had attended the 1938 well-publicized Southern Conference on Human Welfare in Birmingham. At that meeting, I had served as chairman of the rules committee, and had received publicity on that point. That publicity was revived as part of the scurrilous attack on me. This eleventh-hour effort to save Bailey's political scalp was frustrated in one county in a strange way. When I went into the office of a lawyer friend, he pointed to a stack of circulars, and said, "There they are, thousands of Bailey's circulars which I am supposed to distribute in this county." I said, "Why did he send them to you? You're my friend." He said, "Yes, but he doesn't know it. And your opponent mistreated me one time. He doesn't know that I learned of it. I had resolved to get even, and my way of doing it was to let him think that I am supporting him. He is counting on my getting these circulars distributed. I will simply let those circulars stay here until after the election, and then they'll be burned. The people will vote, unblinded by this material."

This was not the only county in which my opponent had broken reeds to lean on. In another county one political leader whose heavy obligations to the governor and lieutenant governor prevented his supporting me, something he really wanted to do, told me after the election that the Bailey committee had sent him a big check to be spent in that county. He turned it over to someone who, while a Bailey supporter, was what he called "inept." He said, "I put it where it would do the least good."

When it was obvious that I had won, some of Mr. Bailey's leaders in Johnson County, which gave him a fifty-vote lead, went to my friends, the Four Horsemen, on the next morning to suggest that both sides agree to manipulate the returns to show a majority for me in that county. They said, "Let's switch enough votes over to Brooks to put the county in his column, so he'll feel kindly toward us." My friends said, "Not on your life! You were against Brooks. We're not going to let you deceive him. This county stays in Bailey's column." And I was proud of them for it. I regret to add that in certain counties in certain periods that practice was tolerated.

I won the election with a majority of 3,500 votes. The final results showed that I received 16,000 votes; my opponent received 12,500 (both figures rounded out), which to me is a graphic illustration of how much disfranchisement there was at that time. Just think of it—going to Congress to represent 325,000 people, having received only 16,000 votes. The total vote was 28,588. This is a sad commentary on conditions in Arkansas in the period, and it was typical of the South. It was partly due to the poll tax system, and partly due to the suppression of aspirations of the black community. I should make one other reference to the character of the campaign in the last few hours. It was related by my parents' cook, a part-time employee. She stood on the edge of the crowd in a final rally in Bailey's home town and listened to my opponent say, "Well, we don't want any nigger votes, do we?" and some shouted "No!" It is hard to imagine that kind of utterance in a political meeting, yet that was in 1942, less than forty years ago.

We had quickly planned a strategy of defense against the desperation drive to stir racial feeling. John Wells with his keen journalistic talents produced a page advertisement answering my opponent's circular. My scrapbook contains clippings to prove the groundless character of Bailey's charges, but no effort was made to negate my concern for the welfare of the black people. These clippings showed that I had left the 1939 Birmingham conference before an active minority, some of whom had been influenced by Communist propaganda, put through all kinds of extreme and unrealistic resolutions that were later repudiated by those who had called the conference. Newspaper accounts showed that I was speaking in New Orleans on the day that these resolutions were passed. I would have preferred to reply on another basis, namely, that I sympathized with the purposes of the conference, but found myself in opposition to some extreme measures advocated by the group, rather than to rely upon the fact that I was not present at a particular session. That would have been quixotic, however, since the explanation that "Mr. Hays was in New Orleans, not in Birmingham" was a completely honest reply.

But the crowning part of that advertisement was a resolution by the Women's Society of the Methodist Church, South. It had been adopted before unification. This resolution strongly condemned the use of race as an issue in political campaigns, and was set out prominently in our reply to the Bailey advertisement. Another part of the language showed consideration for me. In a little box in the center of the page was this comment: "When Brooks Hays reads this advertisement, it will be the first time that he sees it. He has not assisted in the preparation of this statement, because he is so charitable by nature that he would doubtless have refused to let us deal so drastically and factually with his irresponsible opponent."

That's the story. As a little footnote, I might say that some few months after my election, when John Wells was paying me a visit in Washington and was sitting in my office, a wonderful lady, Mrs. M. E. Tilley of Atlanta, came in. She was a friend of the blacks, and of the South's poor people. She said, "Mr. Hays, you know we certainly circularized the women in your district, and we believe it was pretty effective.

We used a little statement that I want you to see," and she added, "A lot of women read this statement of the Women's Missionary Society of the Methodist Church." You can imagine how I enjoyed saying, "Mrs. Tilley, I want to introduce you to the man who reproduced the statement you are showing me in an advertisement that helped win the election for me." It was a real thrill for all three of us.

A lot of things grew out of the 1942 campaign that give me satisfaction. My father was ecstatic when my opponent conceded the election. He had seen me go down to defeat so often, and, of course, deprived of the 1933 election by the corruption in Yell County. In the 1942 primary I carried Yell County (the one that changed enough votes to move Terry into second place, and later into first place in the second primary in 1933). One would often hear people speak with great indignation of what had been done in 1933, and because of that reaction I did not have to campaign very much in that county. Bob Bailey had tried to pressure me not to run, but he had robbed himself of whatever claim he had on me by reason of earlier support in the governor's races, since he had abandoned me and my principles in the 1933 crucial election. Some of the township leaders and many of the rank and file in Yell County told me that they had been against me in that earlier campaign, but were determined to avenge it. I remember one man saying to me, as if he were telling me something that I did not know, "Brooks, you know what? They stole you out in our township." Of course I knew they had done that, not only in his township, but in about fifteen other townships. In the joy of the 1942 victory the frustrations and injustices of 1933 were forgotten.

Chapter 9 STAR GAZING AND DOLLAR WATCHING 1943–1951

To count the cost is, in all things temporal, the only wise course, but there comes a time in the life of every man and every nation when eternal principles enter the calculation, and . . . these lie outside the domain of statistics.
Basil Gildersleve

THE period between the July 28, 1942, Democratic primary (the equivalent of election in those days) and the convening of the 78th Congress on January 3, 1943, was exciting. I was free from any responsibilities and could spend considerable time preparing for my new job. I picked for my executive assistant a young Little Rock lawyer, Paul Barnard, with whom I had worked in church and party organizations.

I decided it would be best for Marion to wait until I had made living arrangements before going to Washington, so Paul and I went ahead by train, reached there about breakfast time three days before Congress convened. We went at once to my assigned room in the Old House Office Building (now the Cannon Building), which was at that early hour quite empty. It was a strange sensation—seeing my name on the door in block letters, BROOKS HAYS, and underneath, the single word, ARKANSAS, clearly remembered now thirty-six years later because it was the culmination of long and bruising battles. I think Paul knew that my emotions were stirred by the experience. We were silent as I looked at the nameplate and contemplated its significance—just twenty years after my father's defeat for this same office, twelve years after my second defeat for the governorship, and nine years after the bitter experience of the 1933 special election in which I was deprived, by the outrageous action of one county's election officials, of my certificate to this Fifth Congressional seat.

A new congressman has a lot to do—housekeeping duties, committee assignments, and just getting acquainted. My seven years on the Democratic National Committee and my service in the Department of Agriculture had given me some advantage in acquaintanceships, and I was determined to know at least by sight every one of the 435 members.

Two doors from my office was the one occupied by Howard W. Smith of Virginia, an able conservative and a highly competent big wheel in the Byrd organization. We quickly became good friends in spite of our ideological differences. "The Judge" learned pretty soon of my liberal tendencies and of my personal friendship with Francis Pickens Miller, a mortal enemy of the Byrd machine, but it did not affect our friendship. It would surprise many people, I am sure, to know that the proximity of offices and the close committee associations often produce friendships that are unaffected by strong legislative and philosophical conflicts. The Republican watchdog, Robert Rich of Pennsylvania (of "Where you gonna get the money" fame), and I were warm friends though we seldom voted together.

Next door was another conservative, Cliff Clevenger of Ohio, a plainspoken Republican. I soon had an illustration of his ability to throw barbs without creating tension. We were walking through the House tunnel to the Capitol one morning, not knowing that one of our colleagues was close behind us. Cliff had occasion to mention him, "biggest demagogue in Congress," he said. Just then the named colleague overtook us. Unperturbed, Cliff said, "Well, here he is now. Hello, —————, meet a new member from Arkansas. I was just telling him that you're the biggest demagogue in the House."

"Well," the good-natured one replied as he shook my hand, "Thank you, Cliff, that's quite a compliment."

Later observing this man's performance, I concluded that it was not demagoguery, but a loquaciousness that he could not restrain. He wanted to speak on every contested bill, even when the opposition was minimal. For example, I recall his saying during the debate on amendments to a farm bill, "I shall vote for this farm relief bill even if it means my defeat." For a representative from a rural district, that didn't require much courage. In that same term (1942–1944) a calculation was made by a member that 90 percent of the House *Congressional Record* was devoted to the words of twenty men—less than 5 percent of the total. I believe that this would hardly hold true today, since there have been concessions to junior members' desire to share more fully in the speech making.

There were extracurricular activities that helped provide contacts for me. One, the Hall's Restaurant Thursday Dinner group, with off-the-record discussions was familiar to me because, as an Agriculture Department official, I had helped set it up seven years earlier. One of its unique features was that departmental officers were welcome, and met with legislators on an informal and uninhibited basis, an arrangement that proved very helpful to both sides. I regret that the group finally disbanded. It began with a southern liberal slant, but gradually lost much of this character. Often, men high in the executive branch came: Henry Wallace, Rex Tugwell, M. L. Wilson, Ben Cohen, Will Alexander, and others showed up. Hugh Bennett, the pioneer in soil conservation, was a regular attendee. We owed a special debt to him because of his ability to picture conditions in a way that could carry over into congressional and home district speeches. On his authority I was able to say in conservation speeches, "At one time a person could stand on the bank of the lower Mississippi River and see in its murky waters a forty-acre farm floating down to the sea every hour of the day and night." And another line with a punch was, "And it takes Mother Nature five hundred years to deposit one inch of the precious topsoil that is being rapidly lost." Soil and water conservation had been a passionate interest of mine for many years—so much so that I could understand why one Arkansas voter became confused. When asked, "What branch of the government is Brooks in?" he said, "I think he's in Soil Conversation."

I have never forgotten one of Hugh Bennett's comments at a Hall's Restaurant meeting. "You congressmen know that your part in great undertakings is only the initial one. Important though the act is, really all you do is to lay the dollar down where the action people can reach it. Somebody must pick up your dollar and put it to work to give your legislative action any effect." There were times, listening to ill-tempered attacks on Executive Department officials, when I wished the critic might sense the import of Hugh Bennett's comment in our scheme of things. But Mr. Bennett was only one of several saints of that period in the conservation field. I recently recalled the contribution of Walter Lowdermilk, for example, during a visit to Chester, in England. Chester's harbor, upon which the city's commercial importance depended, was affected by the silt which had moved in great volume down the River Dee to destroy port facilities.

I have dwelt upon this physical aspect of the New Deal activity in which I had such an avid interest, partly because it was so much easier to propagandize, and at times much more pleasant, than the controversial measures having to do with human resources. There was resistance to proposals dealing with the latter from some segments of "the establishment," but seldom resistance to the physical proposals from any source. It has been this way, I suppose, since the Christian era began, for, apparently, Jesus was frustrated in his plea for sympathy for the Amhaaretz, "the people of the land."

My efforts in the Roosevelt-inspired program of relating the rural poor more viably, and thus more equitably, to the land sometimes brought recriminations and violent personal attacks upon me. I was once denounced by a representative in the Arkansas legislature as "a Communist." And even in the more acceptable conservation measures, I found that being persona non grata to some members of the Arkansas political establishment I was blocked in carrying forward comprehensive relief measures. To illustrate: in 1941, the United States Department of Agriculture asked me to bring to the attention of Arkansas' Governor Homer Adkins the need of amendments to the model soil conservation law which his predecessor, Governor Carl Bailey, had put through after I had, on behalf of the Roosevelt administration, requested him to do so (the first such law in the nation). Governor Adkins had defeated Bailey in 1940. When I asked my assistant, a member of the department's regional legal staff and a political friend of the governor, to inquire of him as to its acceptance, he called by phone to ask the governor himself. The assistant sent word to me to listen on an extension line. He failed, however, to advise Governor Adkins that I was listening, and my assistant's face was red for days when the governor's voice came booming through, "No indeed, no objection to the amendments, but if we put them through, Brooks Hays would get the credit, and I'm not about to let that happen!"

In the early period of my sixteen happy years in the Congress I suffered to a slight extent from the fact that among some of my colleagues I had the reputation of being "a star-gazer and visionary." It was largely attributable to my seven years with the Department of Agriculture's program for low-income farmers. That image might have been different if these colleagues had known of my adversities which had given me an appreciation of the value of a dollar. Still, I presume it was inevitable that one who had given so much energy to problems of disadvantaged rural people would be regarded as a dreamer. I was sensitive about it as a young congressman, but in later years had a certain pride in cultivating "hopes and dreams" for an improved life for those below the poverty line.

During my first year in Congress the New York newspaper *PM* ran a story about me under the caption, "A Bureaucrat in Congress." It did not help me with colleagues, since at that time bureaucrats were in disfavor, but it was part of a modest build-up for my rather unique background— Democratic national committeeman, civil servant, Sunday school teacher, and states' rights liberal, as some observers called me. The publicity just alluded to was not sufficient to rank me with that most glamorous of the 1943 freshmen, Congressman J. William Fulbright, but it was sufficient to keep alive the hope of recognition which every politician possesses, else he would not be in politics. So the first of "the happy years" was gratifying.

My anxiety regarding the scarcity of good farmland for returning veterans was accentuated by the policy of the new director for the Farm Security Administration, former congressman Frank Hancock of North Carolina. He seemed determined to get rid of all of the remaining acreage of the government as quickly as possible for as high a price as possible and in large tracts, thus feeding the evils of land inflation and farm tenancy. This, in spite of the fact that these lands had been procured in the first place for the purpose of dealing with these and related evils.

My bill to give veterans with farm background a priority in the purchase of such land in family-sized tracts was intended to promote ownership. Over 600,000 veterans had expressed a desire to return to farming. While hundreds of farms were eventually made available to these young farmers, much of the government's valuable land holdings went into the maw of overcapitalization, farm tenancy, and land speculation. The federal revenue factor was thus pulled out of its proper place in a great social movement, and the revenue from government land sales provided no comfort for returning veterans who wanted to engage in farming.

Among the radio programs I was invited to participate in were two "Town-Meeting of the Air" programs and "Breakfast with Congress," the latter broadcast from the members' own breakfast tables with wives participating. About that time a young local radio master of ceremonies with a small audience in the Washington area named Walter Cronkite invited me to sit in his little studio in the Harrington Hotel to chat about legislative problems.

The congressional salary was low at that time ($10,000), and the allowances for telephone and other services were nil. The travel allowance was designed to provide about enough for one round trip for the member and family from his district to Washington. Congress did a good thing later in liberalizing these allowances, though I think that there should be careful scrutiny of any future proposals to expand them. Belt-tightening may be "around the corner" and the best examples in government economy should come from the Congress itself.

It was my practice to keep my constituents informed on legislative problems, making full use of the media, sending a weekly letter to the paper, and a tape recording of comments and views for the radio stations' use every Sunday. I embraced Walter Judd's axiom, "a representative should be a window as well as a mirror." I also wrote special messages periodically to my leadership group. A sample of these reports follows. It was dated May 16, 1945, soon after Mr. Truman's assumption of the presidency, and early in my second term.

> Dear "Managers":
> . . . I have never been able to express in adequate terms how I feel about all of you. This job which you made it possible for me to have still has tremendous attractions for me, and at this time especially it can be called an adventure. I want to share it with you. You are entitled to an accounting as often as I can send one.
> When I refer to the job with a possessory air I don't mean to be mentally unprepared to lose it if political trends should be against us, and that could happen, but the fine thing about the time spent here is that an investment is being built up that will be useful in some capacity for years to come, even if a defeat creeps in.
> I got up early this morning—to do something else—but decided to try to set down a few ideas that have been taking form in my mind. (This is written with a pencil at 7:00 A.M.—have just put the coffee pot on the stove.)
> *President Truman is still going strong. In some respects the outlook is better than under Roosevelt. It reminds me of the honeymoon*

of 1933, and no matter how violent the later differences may be, it is good to have harmony now.

. . . It was mighty fine to feel that I had FDR's friendship, but the new President and I will get along all right. You would probably be surprised at the infrequency of my need for White House assistance, anyway. The prospect of success in major undertakings like Bretton Woods is greatly improved. The prospects of a Democratic victory in '48 are not good, but why worry about that—the crucial decisions as to the Peace will have been made by that time.

More and more I am finding my place in the legislative set-up. My personal associations in the House could not be more pleasant. It took time to shed the impression that "a professor from down-town has crashed in on us." Now I'm almost "one of the boys"—a member of the lodge—and difference of views on particular bills does not affect these friendships.

There is a certain amount of floor activity that has to be done, but I am far from loquacious.

For a while the civil rights issue looked like a re-run of the pre–Civil War wrangling and is still intense. Some of us have got to steer a middle of the road course or we will square off in warring camps—not of the usual kind between two political parties or factions wanting the jobs, but between zealots wanting their own way about everything including the extermination of the other side!

Let me illustrate. When Mark Sullivan first mentioned my FEPC debate with Charles LaFollette in his column and complimented us both for arranging it, I had letters and long-distance phone calls from extremists wanting to help me "knock these radicals out," meaning the FEPC proponents.

People like us must stick up for the moral side. I would like to say this without appearing to preach. It's hard to say without being trite, but we literally must insist on the *right* thing being done. Moral insight —a sense of justice—fairness even at expense to one's group, if necessary—these are indispensable needs. Those who veer to the left need this counseling just as those on the other side do.

You know how I feel about the fallacy of labels. I have no desire to establish a reputation as a liberal or anything else, only to strengthen the hope that we will pull through with a minimum strain on national unity but it will take sober counsel and perhaps courage at times.

This is all there is time for now. I will elaborate when I see you.

There should be a pleasant banter between congressmen and constituents. Fortunately, many of my Arkansas constituents seemed to enjoy teasing me, and I believe their practice to be fairly typical. I enjoyed the handshaking excursions and was glad to be the target of gentle kidding.

In Yell County during a summer recess, I approached a small group, picking out an acquaintance to greet first, "Good morning, Mr. Ferguson. I'm glad to see you."

"Glad to see you, Brooks. Just yesterday, my wife hollered at me out in the yard. 'Come inside, Jim, Brooks is on the air.' 'Nope,' I said, 'I heard him last Sunday.'" The small crowd laughed and I managed a smile myself.

To a Pulaski County audience, a friendly chairman said, "Had a letter recently from my son, stationed at Quantico, Virginia. He wrote, 'Dear Dad, I went up to Washington for the weekend. Had a good time. Saw Lincoln's Memorial, Lindbergh's airplane, the dinosaur bones, and Congressman Hays."

But sometimes a response is warmly favorable. I accosted a lonely man in overalls one day in a rural community, waiting for a bus. "I'd like to meet you, sir," I said. "I'm Brooks Hays."

"Air you Brooks?" he asked. "Well, I'm sure glad to see you. Never laid eyes on you before, but I listen to you ever' Sunday. It's like this. You come on the Conway radio station about one o'clock on Sunday. I got just time after church to eat a bite, and then, since I ain't got a radio, I walk down the road a ways, 'bout a hundred yards, I reckon to Bud Porter's to listen to you." I thanked him, and as I left I said, "Give Bud my regards."

"Oh, I will, he'll be so glad I seen you."

Another constituent further down the road on that same day asked, "How's the crippled blackbird a doin' that you mentioned on the radio— the one that your Dad takes special care of in his backyard?" The radio and my weekly letter, which always carried a "chuckle of the week," were my best means of communicating with the home folks.

The radio programs were financed largely by individual House members, with a slight subsidy by the House. This was justified, considering the fact that it acquainted constituents with current legislative problems. There has been some abuse of the franking privilege. I remember, for example, a long distance call to my office from a midwestern city in 1948 that went like this: Operator: "Is this Mr. Hays?" Then the person calling identified himself and immediately said, "What do you think about having 40,000 copies of Tom Dewey's last night's speech put in the *Congressional Record* and sending 'em out under the senator's frank?" I said,

"You're talking to a Democratic congressman named Brooks Hays."

"Oh, my goodness. Thought I had one of the assistants to my senator." I refrained from approving the practice, but sportsmanship forced me to add, "Both sides do it."

While such political documents carry the line "Not printed at government expense," the frank puts the cost of distribution on the government, and there is even an element of subsidy in the printing. Still, until an improved way is found to finance campaigns, the practice within reasonable bounds can be defended. This is on the assumption that both political parties will have equal treatment, a situation that does not apply to congressional races if an incumbent is a candidate.

A committee assignment for the new member is a matter of vast importance and often of considerable maneuvering. Agriculture was my first choice, but a long-time friend, Congressman E. C. ("Took") Gathings of the east Arkansas cotton area, was already on that committee, and the House tradition was against having two members from the same state. Older members might have argued in my behalf that the farming patterns of the east and west parts of our state were so different that an exception might have been made for me, as it was later when Mr. Pat Jennings of the Blue Ridge section of Virginia was put on the Agriculture Committee, which already had a senior "southside" Virginia member, Mr. Wat Abbitt. But I probably would not have had a great deal of influence in behalf of the small farm owners, tenants, and farm workers, since the committee was more interested in the commercial type farm operations. I learned this later in more than one confrontation between the two—we were in a dreary period for the little farmer and the farm worker, and still are, though progress has been made in this area.

My next choice was the Committee on Foreign Affairs, since I had strong feelings about the evils of the war system, and hoped to contribute something to the world's escape from its incalculable cost in lives and money. But Mr. Fulbright wanted the single vacancy on that committee, and I yielded to him as an Oxford-trained student of international affairs.

About the only important committee left was Banking and Currency, and I was placed on that prosaic panel. It was one of the best things that ever happened to me. My academic preparation in economics was confined to a semester's course in my freshman year at the University of Arkansas in 1915, a course taught by Dr. E. G. Nourse, who became President Truman's chairman of economic advisers—the first to serve on that Executive Department agency established under a law I helped pass. Dr. Nourse may not have remembered the back-bench freshman who listened to his lectures thirty years earlier, but he seemed to take pride in my recollections of and admiration for him. He sought my advice on some of his agency's policy questions.

The Second World War had two and a half tough years yet to go, and the economic problems related to inflation came before our committee. I had to bend over the papers and testimony in prolonged study in order to vote intelligently upon the issues. It was excellent training. Mike Monroney of Oklahoma was one of the senior members, and he and I became close friends. I developed great admiration for him. In one dramatic struggle we were singled out in the House debate as "betrayers" of the cotton and textile industries—all because we were determined not to permit a ruinous rise in the cost of living. Our position was politically risky, of course, for both Oklahoma and Arkansas are cotton states, but we trusted our people at home to give us credit for acting in their long-run interest and in the nation's interest.

A bitter fight had developed when the textile lobby, which was unhappy with a price ceiling decision of the Office of Price Administration (though they were not being damaged any more than many other major segments of the economy), sought an increase based upon a formula built around "the average" for certain prescribed industries. It sounded reasonable. There was added, as a lure for cotton farmers, a modest provision for an increase in raw cotton. Mike and I recognized its danger and fought furiously in committee and on the floor against this move. We based our opposition primarily upon the fact that it should remain an administrative, not a legislative, question for determination by professional economists with due regard for the overall effect of changes in the price scales. We urged the House not to permit a breach in the wall through which other commodities could quickly move. (One of the points in my speech was that if textiles were favored with a price boost of the kind proposed, then immediately a new average was established.)

As to the carrot for the cotton farmer, we argued that eventual increases for his cotton would be minuscule. I used the illustration of an iron weight with a rubber handle. Since so many middle processors and handlers are involved in the movement of a pound of cotton from the field to the retail counter, we would find the suggested relief for the farmer similar to lifting the weight with a rubber belt—stretching out to unrealistic lengths, and imposing new burdens upon the consumer class —of which the farmers are significant members.

It was in this debate that John Rankin shouted, "Mike Monroney and Brooks Hays are the worst enemies of the South ever sent to Congress." For a new member this was exceedingly painful. I smarted under his and other less abusive personal attacks. Two members made a life-long friend of me by coming over to my seat to put ointment on my wound, Jerry Voorhis of California and Clinton Anderson of New Mexico. And finally, the wounds were healed by the House itself, which defeated this effort to gain an advantage by improper procedures.

Ironically, our problem of holding the price line was made more difficult by the ending of hostilities. The basic cause of the inflation of that period, the imbalance between production and money volume, continued, but with the coming of peace the demand for ending controls mounted. I recall the day in 1946 when the bill authorizing extension of controls came before the House. Seven amendments were adopted—all of them substantially limiting the agency's power to carry out the mandate to preserve the buying power of the dollar, all by roll call after we, the defenders, demanded record votes, leaving the legislation a shambles. The nation consequently coasted rather crazily to a no-control era. We have not yet recovered fully from the effects of that "Black Friday."

Rent control for those cities having a scarcity of dwelling units also presented grave problems for our committee. This was a grievous one for me, because, while I recognized the advantages of having defense installations in my home city of Little Rock, I was aware of the hardships placed upon owners of rental property. I sympathized with them as I did with all of my constituents with fixed incomes. Few of them really understood the basis of my position, and it pained me to have to take abuse from the very people that antiinflation legislation was designed to help the most.

One group of irate rental property owners came to my office in Little Rock to protest, and their anger and frustrations led to abuse being heaped upon me even by some long-time friends. Finally, an elderly gentleman among them who was convinced of my sincerity banged on the floor with his cane and shouted, "Stop. Stop this now, and let Mr. Hays tell us his side!" They did, and I did, and they went away feeling better.

In my speeches in the home district during this period, I emphasized the evils of inflation, and on the basis of one comment, I concluded that people listened. In a civic club talk in Little Rock, I spoke of the monumental war expenditures and made this bizarre comparison, "It costs our government more than $10,000 to kill an enemy, while Julius Caesar, whose marching men required thirty days to move across his mighty empire, needed only seventy-five cents to accomplish the death of an enemy." A member of the club said to me when the meeting ended, "I heard you a month ago in Fort Smith and you used that illustration, but then you said Caesar needed only fifty cents. Is this inflation retroactive?"

Another important, though uninteresting, assignment for our committee had to do with supervising the corporations such as Commodity Credit, which provided the mechanisms for supporting farm prices, and the Reconstruction Finance Corporation to help keep firm foundations under the corporate structure of the country. Some other Depression corporations, such as the Home Owners Loan Corporation, were preparing to wind up their operations. Home Owners did close out as directed by Congress after presenting an impressive record of service for millions of families. It is a unique record. The corporation not only saved a vast multitude of homes for the owners that otherwise would have been lost by foreclosure, but after paying all operating costs turned earnings of $30 million into the federal treasury.

The Commodity Credit Corporation also performed well in emergency, and even in normal situations. For a few years Congress, having followed sound economic policy in authorizing government purchase of basic commodities—cotton, wheat, certain grains, etc.—seemed to drift purposelessly until wise provisions for getting rid of government-held stocks were adopted. I remember that at one time the Commodity Corporation was paying for storage space for the surpluses at the rate of $350,000 a day. The story of food relief for the developing nations by our government is a splendid one, and a credit to the generosity of the American people.

The Agriculture Committee produced Public Law 481 under which millions of dollars worth of food went to hungry families in other continents, and the Foreign Affairs Committee matched the food bill with some other aids that resulted in moving surpluses, sometimes on the basis of grants, sometimes with payments in the currency of recipient nations.

The late Senator Hubert Humphrey and I were joint authors of legislation for the original wheat shipments to India for famine and regular relief there.

But the foreign aid procedures have not always moved efficiently to accomplish our purpose. Much remains to be done in this field. Sometimes even an affluent nation tires of the onerous tasks of feeding less fortunate people. The rare betrayals by officials of our own or other countries retard the implementation of the noble directives of our aid program. And we also find ourselves experiencing irritations over the disproportionate share of the world's total needs carried by us. I am eager to see the United Nations agencies gather greater support in the relief processes that will make our United States activities more palatable to taxpayers.

Henry Steagall of Alabama, gracious but unspectacular chairman of the Committee on Banking, died in 1943, soon after the 78th Congress convened, and Brent Spence succeeded him. He continued in that position for almost twenty years until he retired and was succeeded by the sincere "man of the people" Wright Patman of Texas, who had come to the Congress in 1928. Mr. Spence was a much loved Kentuckian, son of a Confederate Army officer, and a consistent though not narrowly partisan Democrat. His speeches were poorly delivered, but when read in the *Record* next day they were in choicest English and revealed his scholarly mind and knowledge of the subject. I saw him lose his temper only once. The Republican opposition was pursuing a course which he regarded as indefensible, and he turned to me at the committee table during debate and whispered, "I'd rather be a Mohammedan than a Republican!" Having given vent to his irritation, he began laughing at himself for losing his calmness, and in a moment was conferring amiably with Jesse Wolcott of Michigan, ranking Republican on the committee. Actually displays of extreme partisanship in the House were not as common as is ordinarily believed. In the 1970s, however, it should be noted that some committees may have been overstaffed, and results seemed to confirm the idea that the Congress should utilize the departmental expertise as much as possible.

Both legislative and executive departments share in credit for novel devices to meet emergencies. The "dollar pass-through" was an example. This proved to be a workable way to help the producer during the war without feeding inflation. The "pass-through" meant that an additional price as an incentive for the producer would be authorized, the added dollar to be paid by the consumer to pass through the wholesaler and other handlers in the distributive system without percentage markups by them, ordinarily applied.

I was unopposed in 1944 for a second term, but was not so fortunate in 1946. Two veterans of the Second World War announced for the seat, Lieutenant-Colonel Parker Parker and Major Homer Berry. Colonel Parker tried to capitalize on his overseas service, while Major Berry, who had gained prominence before the war as "a rainmaker," had a single issue: "Mr. Hays has not taken seriously the menace of the anopheles mosquito." Congress was in session and I chose to remain in Washington. I received a clear majority over the two candidates. Congressman Patman could not resist announcing in the cloakroom, "Brooks has defeated Parker Parker and Berry Berry."

Many years after the events being recorded in this chapter, I was introduced to speak one evening by a chairman who demonstrated a close knowledge of my activities. He said, "Mr. Hays is identified with two important pieces of legislation, one passed before his election to Congress and one after his retirement from Congress. I know of no one else who has ever had legislative monuments erected both before and after his service." He was referring to the Bankhead-Jones Farm Tenant Act and the rural phases of the area redevelopment legislation of which Senator Paul Douglas was author. The comment added to my pride in measures to improve the status of disadvantaged farm people. It was this concern that induced President Roosevelt to take an interest in me before I came to Congress.

My fear that Mr. Roosevelt would not live out the fourth term was shared, I presume, by many who witnessed his fourth inauguration on the south portico of the White House, January 20, 1945. There were ominous signs of his declining health in his countenance and manner, and I left the White House discouraged and depressed. Our daughter Betty stood with me through the service, and she too sensed the somber mood of the crowd. Marion was not with us, having given her ticket to Betty, but she was at the Sulgrave Club the day of the president's death on April 12, less than three months later, when Mrs. Roosevelt was called to the phone. She returned to ask the guests to excuse her, saying that she had been called to the White House, and expressed her regret that she had to leave. Marion believed that she had not been given the reason for the call. On that day a great era ended, but the Roosevelt legend will continue until the end of time.

Chapter 10 SWORDS AND PLOWSHARES 1951–1958

The common sense of most shall hold
a fretful realm in awe,
And the gentle earth shall slumber
lapped in universal law
Tennyson

IN the fall of 1950 it appeared that there would be several vacancies on the Foreign Affairs Committee and I decided to transfer. Chester Holifield of California, who had another committee membership but of equal rank in the House with me, deferred to me by waiving the right to toss a coin for the top place among the new members. His graciousness in yielding was typical of him. My good friend J. P. (Dick) Richards of South Carolina succeeded to the chairmanship of the committee soon after I became a member, and we worked together in almost unbroken harmony. He found that the State Department also wished to utilize my avid interest in foreign policy. When Secretary Dulles asked that I be named a delegate to the United Nations in 1955, Chairman Richards acquiesced although it involved jumping over some senior members, and it is very unusual to give such assignments to junior committee members.

I felt no diminution of party loyalty in the Foreign Affairs Committee's concern over our bipartisan policy. Walter Judd, Minnesota Republican, and I had formed a warm friendship early in our congressional service. We entered the House on the same day and had had a mutual interest in church life, Walter having served as a medical missionary for ten years in China. Walter had won a committee spot ahead of me, but before either of us became committee members we proposed that the postwar foreign policy be undertaken on a bipartisan basis. This idea was

160

inspired by the fact that world conditions had thrust new responsibilities upon the United States and the idea that we should avoid some of the errors which followed the First World War. Our capsule argument followed the advice of Winston Churchill: "If the present takes up a quarrel with the past we may lose the future." The resolution was never adopted but it provided a good focus for discussion of the great new problems that made narrow partisanship unappealing and even damaging to our foreign policy.

Walter and I devoted a good deal of our energies to these two areas, church and foreign policy. Walter reflected a conservative point of view on the domestic scene and I was nearer the center, a liberal, in fact, by southern standards. The friendship persisted throughout our House service and culminated in our organizing the former members of Congress in 1970.

Our most publicized joint effort was House Concurrent Resolution 64 introduced on June 7, 1949. The text follows: "Resolved by the House of Representatives (the Senate concurring), That it is the sense of the Congress that it should be a fundamental objective of the foreign policy of the United States to support and strengthen the United Nations, and to seek its development into a world federation open to all nations with defined and limited powers adequate to preserve peace and prevent aggression through the enactment, interpretation, and enforcement of world law."

We invited several other members to join us in the sponsorship of this proposal, and I recall that Mr. Richards and a senior Republican, Mr. John Vorys of Ohio, both highly respected, associated themselves with the movement. Again, we failed to win acceptance of the idea by the Congress but it was a significant action, because of its seminal character in the evolving peace program.

Granville Clark, an early pioneer in the studies for a new approach to the problem of outlawing war, thought well of our resolution and referred approvingly to it in his treatise on this theme. He concluded his testimony to the committee on October 17, 1949, with this appeal: "I believe that this resolution is the most important of all the measures before the Congress. I urge its prompt adoption. By so doing I believe that the Congress would lift up the hearts of the world."

HR 64 drew fire from some of the Veterans of Foreign Wars posts, also from a few of the American Legion leaders, and this tended to make it an ideological struggle with the political advantage on the side of our opposition. I remember how unhappy Mike Monroney of Oklahoma was (he had pledged his support for our resolution) in his first race for the Senate in 1952 to find that the resolution was regarded by some as "unpatriotic." This was the mood of the period immediately following World War II.

But we stood our ground, and surprisingly, took little punishment at home. There was some slight heckling, but I think people gave us credit for trying to accomplish something. I probably suffered very little politically from this resolution. Eventually I believe something like the system for world law which Dr. Judd and I advocated, "a strengthened United Nations with authority to promulgate, interpret, and enforce world law for the prevention of aggression and the maintenance of world peace" will be a reality.

The committee's hearings on the resolution were comprehensive. At first the resolution might have appeared to be a platitudinous statement of principles but eventually the implications were recognized. Dr. Judd and I certainly did not want it viewed as a bland assertion and were glad for its purpose to be explained and understood. When it did appear that the resolution represented a solemn commitment to the rule of law with new powers, carefully defined and limited, for the United Nations, then the extreme isolationists condemned the proposed action. One member called it "treasonable" on the theory that the United States would alienate a part of its sovereignty—its options, in other words, would be reduced in some future international controversy. The absurdity of this extreme view should be seen when we consider the innumerable treaties that have given up some of our freedom of action. Senator Robert Taft, who would have been among the last to view lightly any sacrifice of true sovereignty, said (in another context) that the time will come when the United States will have to recognize that some decisions affecting the world's peace and American interests must be made by tribunals not constructed strictly according to our wishes and control.

While the resolution is no longer an issue in congressional debates, the quiet but substantial movement to mobilize sentiment in support of the broad principle that the United Nations should be able to "promulgate, interpret, and enforce world law to preserve the peace" continues. We are moving undramatically through a period in which world opinion is coming to bear upon the conflicts that provoke hostilities.

The struggle in previous centuries to win acceptance for freedom of the seas and many other principles governing the conduct of world commerce and international affairs had some of the same difficulties to surmount. The Dutch statesman Hugo Grotius devoted a lifetime to winning acceptance of those simple principles and is rightly credited with erecting some great landmarks in human progress. My admiration for him is so strong that on one of my trips to Europe I made a pilgrimage to his home town of Delft in Holland to see the place where he lived and died.

My service at the United Nations in 1955, its tenth anniversary, provided valuable experience. I was assigned to the Economic Committee, which gave me a good forum. There was worldwide interest that year in the proposal to establish a Special United Nations Fund for Economic Development known by the intriguing acronym SUNFED. My first impression was that someone had come up with a novel idea for harnessing solar power.

Able staff experts, particularly Nat King, Bill Stiberve, and Dorothy Crook, convinced me that the idea was too grandiose, and while having the noble purpose of helping the developing new nations of Africa and Asia, had not gone through the maturing processes of discussion so necessary for launching sound international programs. The United States would have been the chief contributor, and understandably our attitude was sympathetic but noncommital. However, it had great momentum among most of the other nations, with even the Soviets praising the plan, and I suspect enjoying our discomfort while they played their role.

I sensed the need of our country not to temporize while hopes were building up among the Asians and Africans, but it was very difficult to convince those in Washington who were responsible for a final decision that a mere "No" would be highly damaging to American prestige. We had to have a viable alternative. The staff and I came up with one. It was sent to the Department of State with our urging for a speedy response. But since fiscal policy was involved, it had to have Treasury Department clearance, and Treasury officials simply had not been exposed to the dynamics of international politics, and they were taking too much time to pass on our alternative proposal.

Urgent calls to Francis Wilcox, assistant secretary of state for international affairs, always induced action—he would again pressure Treasury, explaining that the debate was being concluded with no contribution of opinion from us and not even a signal to evidence sympathy for the SUNFED goals. Still, when the time came for a statement of our position, we had no word from Washington. We managed to get a vote postponement, and as memory serves me now, more than one. It was obvious that we were dragging our feet. When at last the moment of truth was approaching, and on the very day we had to say something or suffer a severe diplomatic loss, I told Henry Cabot Lodge just before leaving our embassy offices on Park Avenue for the crucial Economic Committee session that I was desperate. It hit him at an inconvenient time, for he was having some tough problems himself in the Political Committee. He said, "Ride with me to the UN Building and let's talk about it on the way." I gave him the simple facts. We could not buy the SUNFED plan but we could ill afford to offer nothing in its place. We had to submit an alternative, and I then assured him that we had a good alternative—one that was modest, realizable, and with experimental phases that gave us a chance to correct any built-in weaknesses. Mr. Lodge liked the idea.

"What do you think we should do?" he asked.

"Just authorize me to submit it with our country's okay," I told him. He quickly said, "Do it!" And I did, knowing that Cabot would back me up if Washington should explode.

The American plan was well received that morning, and we won breathing time. But when I called Wilcox, he exclaimed, "Great guns (or its equivalent)! You didn't?"

"Yes I did," I said. "And you should feel all right about it." I think I reminded him that in battle a field general who has no orders from the commanding general has to act on his own when emergencies occur. In the final analysis my argument against SUNFED as originally conceived was accepted.

Our suggested first steps in the development of a long-range program for United Nations-sponsored aid of various kinds for the emerging nations of Africa and Asia were favorably received, but progress has been slow and the multilateral help lags. This is unfortunate for two reasons. (1) The obligation rests upon *all* favored nations and (2) there is waste in the overlapping and competitive unilateral programs.

I was impressed while at the UN with the quietly effective work of Mr. David Owens' Specialized Technical Assistance agency, a related international organization. He described the measures taken to short-circuit cumbersome aid procedures and to maximize special services by the favored countries. A good illustration was the help given the island of Santa Lucia in the Caribbean area by engineers and other technicians of Iceland's government in making use of thermal waters from the hot springs of the little island. Iceland's experience with similar phenomena was thus made available to a less fortunate but aspiring people.

Service at the UN in 1955 differed considerably from the hectic life of today's representatives. As I have indicated, there was controversy, but it was not of the traumatic character of current sessions. There were only sixty member nations, less than half the number now enrolled.

There is some disenchantment with the UN, not only in our country but in many other areas as well, but there are many things to cheer us. This agency for peace has lasted much longer than the League of Nations and has charter powers which, though far from adequate, occasionally prove effective in dealing with incipient wars. In 1955 the delegates discussed three proposed charter changes: (1) means of preventing use of the veto by the great powers to obstruct genuine correctives in international tensions, (2) modification of the "one country, one vote" rule so as to reflect world sentiment in assembly decisions more accurately, and finally, (3) viable plans for a permanent policing force to prevent localized ruptures from spreading. These problems remain largely unresolved.

In the delegates' lounge I found that the cheerful banter which I had always believed in as a tension softener could be indulged, though not with the same abandon which we enjoyed in the congressional Democratic and Republican cloakrooms. In my service in the assembly I developed a half dozen friendships with representatives from other countries. When I met the Afghanistan delegate, for example, I said, "You will be glad to know, sir, that your country has good standing in my home state, Arkansas. Last year in ridiculing my interest in foreign affairs, my opponent said, 'Mr. Hays' heart bleeds for Afghanistan.' The vote given me in that election proved that the people believe that an interest in your country does not disqualify one for membership in the Congress. A graduate of the University of Texas, he was among those who appreciated my effort to invoke wholesome humor on occasion.

My best effort had to do with the 1955 Soviet proposal to admit Outer Mongolia to the United Nations. In one of the lounge conversations I came up with a compromise. "Let's take Outer Mongolia in," I said, "and to cancel out her vote take in Texas, on the theory that Texas is just as autonomous and independent as Outer Mongolia, and generally will be as loyal to our foreign policy as Outer Mongolia to Soviet policy, but we will then change the name of Texas to Outer Arkansas." I had just made a forty-minute UN speech on economic policy, but the mention given it in the Arkansas media, compared with the notice my Outer Arkansas plan received, was like the space given a Slippery Rock College football game against that given a Razorback victory over the University of Texas! I could have been elected for life if an election could have been held next day. The explanation is that Texans and Arkansans have enjoyed a long and friendly feud. One chairman had used this as the basis for a line in introducing me to a Texas audience: "Mr. Hays is the only Phi Beta Kappa ever to receive his key barefooted." Considering these friendly taunts, the reception given my Outer Arkansas quip, even in Texas, was a sweet experience.

My experience at the United Nations accentuated my interest in the problems of the developing countries. I was happy to find that the great powers and others were finding that President Truman's "Point Four" program can, if sustained and free from red tape, bring vast benefits to the disadvantaged. Keeping such aid from becoming a pawn in partisan struggles was one of the factors that Dr. Judd and I had in mind in presenting our resolution pertaining to bipartisan policy. Progress has been made. During President Eisenhower's reading of his first inaugural address, Senator Monroney, sitting by me, said, "Sounds like Point Four will become Point Six," and we agreed that the digital designation was not important. The loyal opposition should not carp about language. The first name generally sticks. The Republicans might prefer "Good Friend" to "Good Neighbor" for Latin Americans, but the older phrase persists, and, anyway, it is the essence of policy, not its name, that matters.

All through my congressional service I supported the aid programs with enthusiasm, including the Marshall Plan, which cost seventeen billion dollars. It was one of the wisest of postwar policies, for it set the wheels turning again to revive a stagnated economy in Western Europe. There are often double motivations in programs of this kind, and it is quite consistent with altruistic claims that our long-term economic interests are also served. However, I fear that we congressmen made too much of the national interest claims and not enough of the humanitarian purposes underlying many of our programs.

My neglect to stress this aspect of the Marshall Plan and other programs received an unconscious rebuke from a blind friend of mine in Adona, in Perry County, Arkansas, in 1947. I had stopped at his village on my regular "post office tour" in late summer and in the midst of the handshaking that goes with such a tour I heard a question in a raised voice from across the road, "Is it Brooks?" When the blind constituent, an elderly man, was told that it was, he said, "Then lead me over there, please, I want to ask him something." He began like this. "Now Brooks, I been hearing about your going over there to Europe and other places, and about the president asking us all to pitch in and help hungry people get on their feet again. What I want to know is—do those other folks have less to eat than we do? Are conditions as bad as the president claims?" Having been in Western Germany, Holland, Belgium, France, and England earlier in that year (1947), I knew from a firsthand view of conditions how severe they were, and I told him so. He ended the little talk with a penetrating comment, "Then I'll go along. My wife and I don't have a lot—in fact, when we have our dinner we push back what's left and eat leftovers for supper, but I don't want any country or anybody not to have enough to eat, and we'll go along with the president to help other people because *it's our Christian duty.*"

The Christian duty part struck me because I had been reluctant to speak of what we owe others. I believe this is a mistake that is often made by representatives in the government. We are inclined to rest policy exclusively upon our narrow national interests. My speeches during the rest of the summer included a reference to a blind man's feeling of compassion for foreigners.

In April, 1963, during my White House service, Marion and I were viewing some of the Baptist installations (schools and hospitals) in Nigeria. Near Ibadan, north of Lagos, I met with some American Point Four workers. One of them, Lester Ariail, introduced himself and said, "I am here in Nigeria because of something you said in Wake Forest, North Carolina, a year ago about Point Four. You described it as the governmental equivalent of foreign missions. I had not fully decided to be a foreign missionary, but felt an urge to help the people of Africa, and I concluded from what you said that I could contribute to a vital program while making up my mind." He assured me that he was pleased with his decision. Almost everywhere we found traces of this kind of idealism among American technicians, teachers, health workers, and others.

On my first trip to Mexico, I met a teacher, Thelma McCamie, in a girls' school in a rural village. It was a church-sponsored school. At a Methodist Church meeting in Arkansas some months later, I mentioned the school and the young lady, knowing only that she was an Arkansas girl. A pleased Methodist in the audience said to me at the end of the meeting, "Thank you for mentioning my daughter." There are thousands of these dedicated young men and women in Latin America and elsewhere, using their talents in both public and private agencies to make happier the lives of disadvantaged peoples. One I recall—Virginia Smith, a missionary to Costa Rica who had come in to the capital, San José, to get Christmas candy and toys for the children in remote mountain areas. Our son-in-law, William Bell, a sanitary engineer who was in water resources work in Costa Rica, invited me to join Virginia's church group in preparing the packages for distribution. I inquired of Virginia, "Where is your mission field?"

"In San Carlos," she said. I registered ignorance of San Carlos but asked if it were near Villa Quesada. "Well, a bit north of it," she said. "The bus stops there and I ride horseback on into the mountains a few miles, and when the road ends I walk four miles the rest of the way to my little mission."

Every encouragement should be given both church and government officials to achieve better coordination of their programs. One need is greater flexibility in the missions program. Some of our Baptist missionaries in Nigeria complained that a traditional objection by homeland Baptists to the mixing of church and state programs (missions and Point Four) was hampering their work, although the Nigerian Baptists were eager to work with government officials, unhindered by doctrinaire positions.

Nigeria might well become a proving ground for effective work by aid officials and the professional missionaries from American churches who have buried themselves in service to the back-country people who wish to enjoy the fruits of full independence and greater progress.

Another incident involving a Baptist medical missionary was an outgrowth of my 1958 defeat for a ninth term in Congress. I received a letter from a Dr. Joanna Maiden, writing from Nigeria. She had read of my activity in the Little Rock school crisis and of my views as president of the Baptist Convention regarding equality for black people. Without quite saying that she was glad I had been defeated, she said that it was a help to her as church worker and physician to be able to say that "the president of the Baptist organization which supplies the funds for our work in Nigeria was concerned enough for the rights of the minority race to risk his seat in Congress." Naturally, I derived some inner satisfactions from her letter. I mentioned the correspondence in church talks and once in Elizabethton, Tennessee, again one of my listeners said after the service, "The medical missionary you mentioned is my daughter."

My activities in support of a strengthened foreign affairs committee did not divert me from the concern for an improved status for the South's low-income farmers, black and white, owners and renters. Also the migrant workers. All were within the orbit of my legislative concern. They were then (as now to a slightly less degree) the forgotten people in our economy.

As a step toward a centralized approach to the problem, I proposed that three departments of government, Agriculture, Labor, and HEW, be given responsibility for assisting the migrant workers. I proposed a legislative mandate for these departments to set up a program, defining the functions of various agencies, and then to provide some directives leading to substantial help for this neglected group. I was unsuccessful. It seemed impossible to interest the powerful economic groups in the plight of these disadvantaged workers. There is activity among the church people, but it generally takes the turn of emergency aid, or child care, the palliatives that mean taking care of the families when there is unemployment, looking after some of the immediate needs, such as housing, but there has not yet been a substantial program by the federal government on their behalf.

Another thing that I attempted during the first Eisenhower administration I hoped might have good results. Theodore Roosevelt had in 1906 appointed a commission to study rural life, and it was a landmark study, "The Country Life Commission." In 1956 I introduced a bill for a similar study on the fiftieth anniversary of that 1906 experience. Some of the Republican congressmen warmed to it. Congressman Albert Quie of Minnesota, elected governor of his state in 1978, asked my consent to introduce a similar bill and it became known as the Hays-Quie bill. There were hearings on it, but we were unable to get it out of committee, primarily because the secretary of agriculture, Ezra Taft Benson, was not favorable. Here is unfinished business for the friends of rural America. Studies to update the Theodore Roosevelt report and dramatize the continuing plight of the rural poor should be authorized.

In the 1942 campaign my most emphatic commitment had to do with the development of the Arkansas River, not so much with navigation, because in 1942 we were thinking more in terms of agricultural life, and not much with hydroelectric power and recreation, but with the idea of saving the best land we had in the hill country counties. The Arkansas forms a narrow valley, and it was very important, from the standpoint of productiveness, that the bottomland be protected against the recurring floods; so I had a good deal to say about flood control and I said little about multiple purposes, because it was recognized that Arkansas would not have, as Tennessee and Alabama had, a valley authority. Senator Robinson had opposed an Arkansas valley authority, although Franklin Roosevelt was prepared to advocate the same kind of total valley development, with a federally directed and controlled plan for the entire Arkansas Valley that had been developed earlier in the seven states of the Tennessee Valley. I knew that it was a forlorn hope, although I would have been happy to sponsor it.

It appeared that nothing could be done in the way of a substantial attack on the river problem until World War II ended. That occurred almost three years later, and then came the Korean War. Although we had had in the budget and by appropriation of Congress some funds for the Arkansas, a presidential impoundment followed, which was understandable, since President Truman, acting within his authority under Korean War powers, wanted to hold down nonmilitary expenditures. This was accepted rather gracefully by the people of my district, although it put the burden on me of explaining why we could not proceed quickly to give the river the attention that it deserved. Even after the Korean War was concluded it was necessary to make vigorous fights on the floor of the House to get any river items at all, particularly for the Dardanelle Dam, about eighty miles west of Little Rock, which became the symbol for the river development.

For a number of years we tried in the House to break down Chairman Cannon's adamant position that only Budget Bureau requests would be included in Appropriation bills, but the "economy bloc" was powerful in the House, and the money bills always went with little or no change from Budget Bureau figures to the Senate for action there. Politically, this was painful, because the Senate, with more flexible procedures, found it possible to get credit for items that showed up in the final appropriation measures, the House Members getting little credit for action. It was noticeable that Senators Kerr and McClellan, who were always alert to river needs, had nothing like the obstacles to fight that we had in the House. We were generally successful, however. Once the conference committees brought back items for the river development, favorable House action followed, and it is something to give the entire country great satisfaction that we now have a virtually completed, all-purpose Arkansas River development with several hydroelectric dams, a number of navigation dams, and recreational projects, all of which constitute a well-controlled river. From the mouth of the Arkansas to the Oklahoma-Kansas line we now have a burgeoning commerce that is bringing a great increase in prosperity to the valley. However, I do not feel that the results of river development have yet reached the villages and the agricultural population generally with a comprehensive restructuring of economic life.

What has happened is certainly in the interest of most of the people, but there are still islands of poverty in the area that should have both federal and state assistance. The river program had priority but I also had what I would call backup plans, such as the rural industries bill, to secure, in the absence of a comprehensive river program, an alternative, the program that Senator Flanders of Vermont and I were pressing during the last few years of our service in the Congress. This bill would have provided a loan program for cooperatives and small industries to establish facilities for the processing of agricultural and timber products through small plants that would mean employment, full-time or seasonal, for a large number of people in the small communities of the hinterland.

This was designed to add stability to the economy by creating part-time employment for those classified as marginal farmers. I do not like the word *marginal*, but this was the theory on which we advanced our rural industries bill. The final legislation, known as the "area redevelopment program" for the stranded population of the troubled industrial areas was largely due to the imagination and fine leadership of Paul Douglas, senator from Illinois. Senator Douglas told the Senate that the agricultural features of his bill followed the patterns of my bill. (That was after Senator Flanders had left the Senate.) Senator Douglas gave me credit for contributing something to the significant legislation extending government aid to private industry to meet unemployment and underemployment problems.

I would like at this point to insert an observation, that while I have mentioned Senator Kerr and Senator McClellan, others pressed for action just as vigorously. I refer to Congressmen Norrell, Mills, Trimble, Gathings, Harris, Cravens, and Tackett, who carried their share of the load, also Congressman Edmondson of Oklahoma, who was picked by us to make the key speech in the House at the time we overrode Chairman Cannon of the Appropriations Committee in breaking the rigid rule against amending appropriation bills by including unbudgeted items. It was a happy day for us rebels, for we felt that Chairman Cannon had been unduly restrictive in his rigid policy of opposing any change in Bureau of the Budget requests. Ed Edmondson made a stirring speech. Trimble and I followed him with a plea for the Dardanelle Dam, and on that day we broke the resistance of those who would oppose all items not requested by the Budget Bureau. This pointed up the need for an improved Congressional Budget Control procedure.

Ironically, during all of this I received criticism from a few members of the strong lobbying group at home, some of whom did not appreciate our difficulties. And as always, any representative faces criticism from those who expect immediate results. These critics are often indifferent to the reasons for delay or failure. Two militant members of the Arkansas Development Association were critical of me and other members because of postponement of appropriations. I remember a phone call from one who was caustic. He said, "If you don't get this appropriation in the House, we're going to send somebody up there who can."

"Wait a minute," I said. "Come over that again," and it was repeated. I said, "Now, let me say that I am not interested in this program because of a fear that if I don't give it my best I will be deprived of my seat in Congress. You are not going to intimidate me or affect me, nor will you inspire more activity on my part. Just remember that you'll get the same vigorous service out of me whatever the prospects for my reelection." Occasionally "the hired hand" is entitled to speak firmly in his own defense.

There are a number of people in the private sector who deserve credit for mobilizing sentiment while we in the Congress were trying to utilize that sentiment for legislative results. As long as Arkansas was alone in the fight it was difficult to make progress. I remember that Mike Monroney, then a representative from Oklahoma City, whose commercial interests seemed to clash with those of Tulsa, which was on the Arkansas River, opposed us at first. He was very unhappy about having to be on the other side, since we were warm friends. I felt sure then that eventually Oklahomans would recognize the wisdom of river development. When they finally did we began to make more rapid progress.

No treatment of economic programs would be complete without a reference to the "Hays-Fulbright Act" (as it is known at the Department of Agriculture), which required that government-owned farmland should be sold on liberal terms to veterans with a farm background. I sponsored this bill and got Senator Fulbright's help to secure Senate approval. It was approved by President Truman and resulted in several hundred veterans' procuring farms on favorable terms.

My membership on the Foreign Affairs Committee necessitated some travel to other countries. For example, in 1951 I went with a subcommittee on the House Foreign Affairs Committee to make a study of occupation policies in Germany. My friend Clem Zablocki of Wisconsin was chairman of the committee. Other members were Edna Kelly of New York, Senator Jacob Javits, then a House member, also from New York, and Chester Merrow of New Hampshire. When we were received by Chancellor Adenauer and were seated in his office, Mr. Zablocki said, "Mr. Chancellor, I shall ask Mr. Hays of Arkansas, our senior member, to open the discussion." (He had reference to age, not service). I had had no advance notice that the chairman intended to do this but on impulse I looked up at "Der Alte," a stern old statesman, revered by his people. I said, "Mr. Chancellor, perhaps there is some logic in our chairman's request, for I am the only one of this committee who comes from a state that was once occupied by an invading army."

The chancellor looked a bit quizzical at this point, but I quickly added, "I know, Mr. Chancellor, that an occupation army is never popular, but if you fear that your people can never come to love us, please look at this scene." Then I made a sweeping movement of my hand around the circle. "I love these yankees. The people of Arkansas and other southern states have come to appreciate and love the yankees. I trust that in a much briefer period the great German people will come to love us and will not fear us."

In my White House office, years later, when I was serving as special assistant to President Kennedy, a German newspaperman, Mr. Peter Pechel, came to see me. I began to relate this incident. He stopped me immediately. He said, "Mr. Hays, I know about that. You see Chancellor Adenauer himself told me about it, and added, 'The Arkansas congressman relaxed us all.' "

Finally, I must include in this inventory of legislative actions a reference to the prayer room. My recollection of its early history is clear. Coming out of a meeting in which Billy Graham had spoken, Mike Monroney said, "Brooks, why don't you throw in a resolution tomorrow to establish a place of prayer in the Capitol?" It originated with Mike. He is an Episcopalian, with strong religious interests.

He did not seek Senate action immediately, but waited for the House to act. At first there was little interest in it. Neither of us sought publicity. I hoped for a ferment of opinion, and there was one. However, Mr. Rayburn approached me one day with this appeal, "Brooks, please don't push for it." I agreed not to. I respected his feelings, but was hopeful that he would, in time, be convinced of its desirability.

Justice Brandeis warned against the careless use of "conjure words." A word may conjure favor or disfavor, and, of course, "prayer" conjures favor. But I knew when I found Mr. Rayburn somewhat opposed to it that I should not press for immediate passage. So we put it on the shelf for a while. Senator Guy Gillette of Iowa raised a question: "The Bible says that one should go into his closet to pray, he should not pray in public." That was easily answered. I replied, "Senator, that is exactly what we propose. The prayer room will be a closet, a place of retreat. No one will see you pray there, and members will not sound the trumpet, or at least they shouldn't."

Our arguments rested on the simple idea that just as the Congress provides a restaurant for nourishment of the body, it should provide a place for those so minded to seek nourishment for the soul. The results have vindicated us. One member said to me while I was still in Congress, "Brooks, I have just spent thirty minutes in the meditation room, and what it did for me to restore my spirit is worth all that it cost."

Early in 1953 in the first session of the 83rd Congress, almost three years after its introduction, the Republicans acted on my resolution. I did not want it to have either a Democratic or a Republic label. It is to the credit of Speaker Joe Martin that he felt the same way. After the resolution was approved, he said, "Brooks, you're going to be chairman of the Prayer Room Committee. I'm going to put Katharine St. George and Karl LeCompte on it with you. It will be an unofficial committee, and you three will be expected to carry out the purposes of the resolution." So I happened to be the only Democrat chairman of a committee in a Republican House. It belonged to the House for "housekeeping" purposes, since it was on our side of the Capitol, but, of course, the room itself was for the use of both Senate and House members. Both Senate and House votes on the resolution were unanimous.

It is not generally known that the designated room was at one time the congressional bar where some Senators and Representatives went for a libation. That use went out even before prohibition, and was never revived.

I believe that the fears of some that the prayer room would be exploited have been dissipated. One member of Congress did propose to have a picture of himself taken standing before the altar but we prohibited that kind of action. Public sentiment supported us in discouraging such a practice.

The physical attractiveness of the room met the expectations of the sponsors, thanks primarily to the special interest of the Capitol architect, J. George Stewart. The House and Senate chaplains, Bernard Braskamp and Frederick Brown Harris, made sure that the facilities were consistent with our Judeo-Christian traditions. In this, they had the counsel of Father Edward J. Herrmann of the Archdiocese of Washington and Rabbi Norman Gerstenfeld of the Washington Hebrew Congregation.

My action was quite consistent with my devotion to the doctrine of separation of church and state. This distinctive doctrine has to do with structure, and was likened by Jefferson to an "impregnable" wall. But to be impregnable it need not be impenetrable. The doctrine anticipates communication between religion and politics. Commerce between leaders in the religious community and political leaders must be maintained. According to this doctrine, ecclesiastical power must not dominate political authorities, and at the same time the politician must never give orders to the churchman. Separation of power is in the interest of religion. For example, Cardinal Koenig of Vienna said, "Surely Catholics around the world can see that in countries that have separation of church and state it is easier to maintain moral power and spiritual strength than in nations where there is reliance upon a political prop."

Members of Congress are inspired by two pressures to pray, one being personal difficulty, and secondly one's concern for his nation and his world. I remember having had a strange and baffling problem in

1953—an illness that defied diagnosis—and it affected my morale. I became somewhat depressed at times and utilized the prayer room on several occasions, meditating on the resources that were available to me as a harassed individual. It had nothing to do with politics. The prayer room is therefore valuable as a symbol of our moral foundations, but more importantly as a practical facility for individual use. Whether there was wisdom in the establishment of the prayer and meditation room will depend on whether over the years its use is free from pretentious pietism and whether the symbolism of our pluralistic character as a people of faith is preserved.

One of my most interesting assignments was in my last term in the Congress, working with a younger member, Frank Coffin of Maine, to develop plans for improved Canadian–United States relations. Our trips to Canada in 1957 and 1958 to confer with parliamentary leaders, including Prime Minister Diefenbaker and the opposition spokesmen, produced enlightenment as to the sources of tension. We learned, for example, that Canadians were not happy over the extensive holdings of Americans in Canadian industries. Our report submitted in May, 1958, dealt with this and other sources of discontent. We recommended that Congress pursue conversations with members of the Canadian Parliament by establishing informal joint committees of the respective legislative bodies.

Our report stressed the need for a continuing dialogue. Paralleling our action was a report to the Senate of findings by a committee chaired by Senator George Aiken of Vermont. Coordination of American action with the Canadian procedures was achieved without violence to our constitutional concept of executive powers.

Frank Coffin was not with me when I invited Mr. Diefenbaker, also a Baptist, to address our Southern Baptist Convention, of which I was serving as president in that period. "I'll try to do it," he said. "Let me call you at eleven in the morning to give you a definite answer." I told him I would be meeting in Toronto with the board of the Canadian Chamber of Commerce. Accordingly, I said to the receptionist before the board convened, "When Mr. Diefenbaker calls, just slip in with a note, and I will come out of the meeting."

But she didn't do it that way. Just at eleven she opened the door and in a loud clear voice that reminded me of Fishbait Miller announcing the president, said, "The Prime Minister wishes to speak to Mr. Hays."

Silence fell over the room. While the silence prevailed I paused at the door and said, "I told her to do it like that." What they did not know was that it had to do with a Baptist meeting, not profound matters of state. However, the prime minister's interest in our efforts to develop stronger bonds of friendship was evidence of progress toward final solutions.

Our report (commonly known as the "Hays-Coffin" Report) was widely publicized in Canada because of its sympathetic analysis of our northern neighbor's complaints. It pointed out that American investments in oil, mining, and manufacturing represented 49 percent of the total, with Canadians having only 43 percent (Britain controlled practically all of the remaining 7 percent).

In 1981 an imbalance remains a problem, and accounts for the occasional public protests by Canadian officials, but Congress is generally credited with wanting to find viable answers. The Canadian ambassador, Mr. Peter Towe, has expressed appreciation of our continuing concern. This concern is based upon the fact that seventeen years after we completed the study, United States capital invested in Canada adds up to $25 billion of the total foreign investment of $30 billion. This is startling to the Canadians when they observe that all foreign capital investments in the United States are a bit less than our investment in Canadian industries.

The time spent on this report was a diversion from my exertions to surmount segregationists' opposition to a ninth term, but had virtually no relationship to my defeat—though I did tell Frank Coffin that I felt, when the phrase "Hays-Coffin" got into the news, that it had an ominous ring, particularly when friends of my opponent read it "Hays's coffin"—the same opponent who said, "Mr. Hays' heart bleeds for Afghanistan." Frank much preferred the play on his name that I quipped when he finished a lucid presentation to the House on the subject. I said to the House, following his speech, "I have been to a wake," explaining that the dictionary defines a wake as "sitting silently and reverently in front of a coffin." My defense of this dubious effort to induce a smile is that the subject matter was rather dull, and I hoped to bring just a faint touch of lightness to a complex but important foreign policy problem.

The little elves who guard the chest of my legislative memories keep telling me to dig into the obscure material lying on the bottom. I will spare the reader, except for a brief reference to some measures that had limited public interest. My friend Felix de Weldon, the famous sculptor, enlisted my help in securing legislative authority for the erection of the Iwo Jima statue which now rises magnificently on the west side of the Potomac. I introduced the bill providing for dedication of the land and authorizing the construction of that impressive monument. In 1950 Brigadier General James Devereux, who had a distinguished career in the Marine Corps, climaxed by heroism on Wake Island, became a member of Congress from Maryland, and we acted jointly in pushing the legislation through the Congress.

Mr. de Weldon had made his first models of the Iwo Jima Memorial while serving at the Patuxent naval base, and a monument there today commemorates his work. A facsimile of the page of the *Congressional Record* which carried my speech on the subject is set in bronze on one side of the stone. The purpose of this unique Patuxent memorial was to preserve a record of Mr. de Weldon's work at Patuxent and to honor the Marines for their heroism in the Iwo Jima battle, a few of the details being described in my address to the House.

One bill that I introduced at the request of a New York friend, W. H. Baldwin, president of the Urban League, provided for changing the name of Bedloe's Island to Liberty Island, having made sure the representative in whose district the island is located did not object. Since the Statue of Liberty is the only distinguishing feature of the tiny island, there seemed to be logic in the change. It passed the House, and the Senate concurred. The president signed the bill, and today it is officially Liberty Island.

Chapter 11 WEARING A WOUND STRIPE 1959

'Tis not always ours to command success; we can do more, Sempronius, we can deserve it.
Addison

I N the preface to my book *A Southern Moderate Speaks*, I said, "This is the story exactly as written before the eight-day write-in campaign that cost me my seat in Congress in November, 1958. The significant events connected with that campaign, in which my opponent had the support of Governor Faubus, belong to another narrative." The "story" has reference to the Little Rock desegregation crisis, including my part in the Newport Conference between President Eisenhower and Governor Faubus on September 13, 1957. This chapter is the additional narrative.

My allusions to the civil rights struggles of the forties and fifties have been sketchy primarily because the earlier book, published in 1959, describes in some detail my involvement in the Newport meeting and in efforts to avoid the confrontation on September 23 when the president sent federal troops to Little Rock to ensure the peaceful admission of the black pupils as ordered by the courts.

I hope that this book will be regarded as an appropriate response to Dr. Arthur Schlesinger's friendly invitation to say more about my political philosophy. It is contained in his review for the New York *Times* (June 23, 1968) of my book *Hotbed of Tranquility*. He asserted that that book "does not relieve Brooks Hays of the obligation to write his serious memoirs—a book which could tell us a great deal about the Old South and the New, and about the dilemma of a moral man in democratic poli-

179

tics." I am indebted to this warmhearted friend and White House neighbor for this prod.

From 1945 through 1958, my last year in the Congress, I was constantly involved in efforts to make headway in meeting at every level of government the aspirations of our black minority for complete equality. I introduced a number of bills to achieve this, some of which were designed to induce my southern colleagues to share in the enactments that were essential to progress in this vital area. There were four general categories of my activity in the struggle, as follows:

(1) Abolishment of segregation in all forms of interstate travel—air, rail, and bus. I contended that Congress should not wait for the courts to outlaw segregation, that making it unlawful for the carriers to impose segregation in interstate travel, which Congress had the unquestioned power to do, would shortly cause a collapse of the intrastate segregation system over which congressional authority was dubious.

(2) Repeal by congressional amendment of the poll tax requirement for voting which was clearly the only valid way to accomplish it. Ultimately this was the agreed-upon procedure.

(3) Adoption of an effective antilynching bill with special pressure applied to the states to assume primary responsibility for prosecution, but authorizing prosecution by federal authorities where the prescribed standards were not met and prosecutions begun by the states.

(4) A federal fair-employment-practices statute with an emphasis in the early stages on educational and counseling procedures that would make it easier for southern employers to cooperate with federal officials to eliminate discriminatory policies.

Obviously there were some political risks for me in these endeavors but I weathered every storm until the 1958 election. On October 27, 1958, I spoke to the representatives of the plumbing supply industry in their national convention in the Roosevelt Hotel in New Orleans. As I finished the speech I was told that I was being paged. It was a long distance call from my Little Rock office assistant and close friend Dick Emerson. It was bad news. Dick was shaken by the confirmation he had had of the rumor that the Faubus administration was launching a write-in campaign against me. They had picked Dale Alford, a Little Rock eye doctor, and were going all out to deprive me of the seat in Congress, which everyone thought until that moment was made secure by my nomination in the July primary and the failure of the Republicans to nominate a candidate against me.

Dick's information was based upon a phone conversation with Marlin Hawkins, sheriff of Conway County. Governor Faubus had driven to Morrilton to the sheriff's home on the previous evening, reaching there about 10:00 P.M., and for two hours had pressured Marlin to join in the vendetta against me. This, Marlin vigorously declined to do. About midnight, the governor left to return to Little Rock. Only his police guard and driver had accompanied him. We later learned that the master strategist was not the governor, but one of his aides, Claude Carpenter, who was immediately granted a leave of absence by the governor to manage Alford's campaign. There was considerable irony in the fact that Carpenter was serving as the official director of the Democratic fund-raising campaign while engaging in the eleventh-hour attack upon one of that party's nominees! Furthermore Alford had voted in the Democratic primary, the same primary in which Governor Faubus and Carpenter had pledged to support all of the nominees.

The Conway County sheriff told me later of the arguments he advanced in support of his position of loyalty to the party and to me, and he did not mince words in branding Carpenter's actions as dishonorable. If dissatisfied with me, they could at least have had an independent candidate formally file for a printed ballot position, instead of staging a sneak attack at the last minute.

At that time Dick had not learned of the dishonest plan for the illegal use of printed stickers to be passed out at the polls (and in some Pulaski County precincts by the judges and clerks of the election where the Faubus organization was in control of the election machinery). The stickers bore the printed name of Alford and a printed X following his name. This was prior to the use of voting machines. The state law provided for "a write in" but not for the use of stickers in cases where a printed name, as in my case, appeared on the ballot. The whole scheme, Hawkins rightly argued with the governor, was scandalous.

The final phase of the midnight conversation between the governor and the sheriff came to light later. This is a good place to relate it, though I had absolutely no knowledge of it until after the November election. Marlin told me afterwards of the following significant exchange with the governor. The sheriff walked in the darkness with the governor to his waiting car. He made a final plea to the governor to call the whole thing off. The governor succumbed, "Yes, you're right, I'll tell the boys in the morning not to do it." I presume that the reason Marlin did not include this bit of information in his talk with Dick Emerson is that he was waiting to see if indeed "the dogs were being called off." He could hardly have served our cause by saying at the conclusion of his cry of alarm, "but don't worry, the governor will cancel it out."

Long after the election Marlin told me of this curious aspect of the unhappy episode and he pieced various known bits of knowledge together to form the conclusion that the governor had passed "the point of no return," that he had lost control of his game plan. Claude Carpenter confirmed this in a talk with Marlin after Alford became congressman. Marlin's question was, "Did the governor countermand the directions—did he change signals?" and Claude said, "Yes, he did, but it was too late— we knew that all we had to do was to go ahead with our plans, that nothing the governor could, or at least would, do could disrupt our campaign." All of the available evidence supports the assumption that, whatever second thoughts the governor had, he continued to cooperate with Claude Carpenter and Dale Alford and conformed to their arrangements for an all-out drive for the segregationist candidate. The presence in every county of the district of leading figures of the Faubus organization in the final hours of the campaign negates any claim that the governor was not responsible for the outcome.

I relate this, not to help the Faubus image, but to give all of the story as it has come to me. Image building is secondary. My personal view is that the governor is not helped by the fact of his change of inner feelings expressed in his farewell to Marlin that night. If his political conscience had really been stirred, he could have publicly renounced the Carpenter-Alford plans. His course in the write-in, stick-in campaign is, sadly, of a piece with his weak posture in most matters involving political strategy. I record this judgment with sadness, for I have always, in reflecting even upon injustices at his hands, a feeling of wistfulness rather than anger toward him. At the beginning of his career, many of us thought of him as a wise and good man as well as a clever politician, but his weakness became more prominent and more tragic as the Little Rock story unfolded.

Now back to the call from my Little Rock office with Dick's summons to get home to be with our scattered troops for the crucial encounter. From New Orleans I could not go straight to Little Rock. On the following day I was due in Nashville, Tennessee, for what had been designated by the mayor and Southern Baptist officials as "Brooks Hays's Day." Nashville is the headquarters of our executive committee and of our Baptist publishing house. So I went on to Nashville, where I was met at the airport by representatives of officialdom. There were the usual things that go with a publicity gambit—appropriate certificates signed by my friends, Governor Buford Ellington, County Judge Beverley Briley, and Mayor Ben West, keys to the city, and a police escort to the hotel. The sponsor of this pleasant ceremony was the Broadman Press, publishers of my first book, *This World—A Christian's Workshop*, which was located in Nashville. It would have pleased my mother, who had attended the University of Nashville in the nineties. That teacher training college became the George Peabody College, and I have been one of its trustees since 1938.

By the time I reached Nashville the wire services were carrying word of Alford's plans to announce. So I was asked by newsmen about my own plans. I had to compose a quick response, the substance of which was that I would hurry on home after meeting Nashville engagements to fight hard to hold my congressional seat. It was a difficult situation. The development revealed that the political winds were not favorable (due almost wholly to the integration hysteria) and I recognized that a resource—my personal acceptation by the people of Arkansas—which had, in calmer times, seemed impregnable, was now greatly impaired.

When I reached Little Rock my fears were confirmed. My friends, though not disconsolate, were obviously worried. We were disorganized and baffled, not only by the sudden thrust of the administration forces, but by the absence of any blueprints for action, or criteria for determining our strategy. I was pretty miserable.

I would not understand the indifference of my opposition to the unwritten code of simple political ethics. In July I had handily won the Democratic nomination over a strong segregationist, Amis Guthridge, who had made my civil rights position an issue. Actually, I received 12,000 more votes in the July primary than Alford received in November, and the total number of votes cast in July was 71,000 compared with the November election total of 61,000. Alford's alleged majority was about 1,200. These figures tend to prove that the earlier vote was a more accurate indication of sentiment than the general election, which seldom reflected the interest induced by the vigorous Democratic contests.

There was, however, one development between July and November that worked against me, and that was an inflamed feeling against the federal government, resulting from the decision of the Supreme Court on September 12 ordering the Little Rock School Board without further delay to proceed with desegregation. The justices had been called into a special session by Chief Justice Warren, interrupting their vacations, to pass upon the legal problems generated by Little Rock's resistance to the admission of black high school pupils.

The publicity given that bit of drama was highly damaging to me, for on that very day I was guest of the National Baptist Convention (predominantly black) at their annual meeting in Chicago, giving one of the principal addresses. Almost simultaneously with the Court's unanimous ruling I was pictured in the newspapers and television programs on the platform of the Negro convention, thus allowing the racists to capitalize on my longtime concern for minority aspirations. The provocative caption on thousands of anonymous circulars dropped from airplanes just one day before the election, another violation of Arkansas election laws, was, "We know you, Brooks."

My opponent had a good television style and conducted an impressive campaign, hammering away constantly on the segregation issue. This was enhanced by his praise of Governor Faubus, whose fanatical segregationist following had produced unprecedented political strength. A sentence in Alford's speech suffices as an example: "Not one time have we heard Congressman Hays say a single word in praise of our great and wonderful governor."

Alford and Carpenter fully exploited the near fanatical feeling for this "defender of the southern way of life," as they described Orval Faubus. The candidate added, "I am an Arkansas Democrat; Mr. Hays is a national Democrat. I am a Faubus Democrat; Mr. Hays is a Paul Butler Democrat." (Mr. Butler was chairman of the Democratic National Committee.) They continually played upon the theme that their congressman was "selling Arkansas out."

They also found ways to capitalize on the feelings of alienated groups, such as some of the postal workers who felt I should have signed the discharge petition for their increase in pay. I had taken the position that the Post Office Committee should be given time to produce a satisfactory pay raise plan. But the postal workers were pretty upset about their lag in pay increases. I could understand that, but I had resisted the pressures because of my convictions on sound legislative procedures. I refused to sign their discharge petition to bring the bill to an immediate House vote without committee action.

Then there was some opposition among the veterans. I had voted to uphold President Truman's veto of a bill that raised inordinately the payments for non-service-connected disabilities for the veterans. I never had opposed any increase in allowances for service-connected disability, but this was for non-service-connected claims, and it would have reached ultimately $400 million a year. Mr. Truman vetoed it on what I thought were sound and equitable grounds, and I supported his veto. Then too, my opposition to abolishment of local rent controls, described in Chapter Nine had cost me some support. All of these things augmented the support of the bitter segregationists.

So, considering the advantages held by Dr. Alford, perhaps I did fairly well to come within 1,200 votes of winning, out of 61,000 votes cast. It is estimated by some of my friends who made a study of the election practices and returns that at least 3,000 of the Alford votes were illegal. I would argue that all of the ballots with the stickers were illegal, which would add an unascertainable number to the above figure, since there is no provision in law for a sticker. But even if the sticker ballots for Alford were regarded as legal, there is a strong probability that I received a legal majority. We have no way of knowing exactly, since the House Committee did not take testimony on the irregularities, as they had promised to do in the initial hearing in Washington.

I spent election night with my eighty-six-year-old ailing father at Russellville, listening to the returns, and, except for a brief time as the results outside Little Rock gave me an advantage, I had scant hope of coming out ahead. Our son Steele was with us. Marion was in Washington. We called Marion at midnight to prepare her for the bad news that she would be reading in the Washington *Post* next morning. It was not difficult to cheer her up; she had traversed valleys of defeat before. Steele took over the conversation to respond to her comment that she was reconciled but had wanted me to leave Congress at a peak moment and not in defeat. "No, Mother," Steele said, "This is the finest way for him to go, and when the clouds clear, I think you will see why." She did.

All of my staff except Dick Emerson and Kitty Johnson had also remained in Washington—there had been no time to transfer our base of operations to the district. If there was heaviness of heart, and there was a degree of it, of course, it was more for them and for our daughter Betty and her family in Cincinnati, who had to watch the scene from a great distance with a feeling of helplessness. I could count on Marion's gameness pulling her through. Steele and I drove back to Little Rock early the next morning.

Telegrams of sympathy and indignation poured into the Little Rock office. My decision not to file a contest was rather quickly reached, though of course I owed it to my campaign committee and other supporters to seek their counsel. There was scarcely a dissent. My decision was influenced, perhaps unconsciously, by the agonies associated with the 1933 experience, partly by the futility of contests generally, and perhaps most of all by the feeling of exhaustion in trying to represent a divided community.

Near noon we were able to assemble a faithful dozen close friends and workers in the office of Raymond Lindsey, one of my most active supporters, and there we shared an emotional experience. We were just beginning to talk about what kind of public statement I should make when Marlin Hawkins joined us. I am afraid my lips quivered visibly when I tried to thank him for standing with me against "the establishment." He had defied his old political allies to live by his code of ethics, and it had produced a breach between him and his friend Orval Faubus, who had permitted the discarding of that code. While the breach was later healed to some extent, the relation between the Conway County Courthouse and the Faubus office was never quite the same again.

Sheriff Hawkins is an amazing rural leader. (He has since retired from politics.) His grip on the political structure of his county was based on his continual enjoyment of doing favors for individual voters from the Morrilton county seat, a town of about seven thousand, to the remotest wooded area thirty-five miles away. I have never discovered him doing anything in violation of what we would regard as the basic requirements of political honor. True, he is tough on occasion and also a partisan, but what he believes serves the people's interests is always a first consideration with him. Those who belong to his school of politics have quoted him as saying in appeals for support for me, "Mr. Brooks will work with us, but he won't do just anything we ask of him—if we're entitled to it, we'll get it." And I can't remember his asking anything of a dubious moral character of me. He was one of the very few who called me "Mr. Brooks," and this practice went back to the days when he was a neophyte and I was even then a veteran. There have been times when I wished he would be more congenial with the "reform" group, but the reformers at least knew where he stood and that he would not be engaged in shoddy practices. Finally, I wish all sheriffs were as humane and compassionate toward the jail inmates as Marlin Hawkins.

In accordance with his practice of "good sportsmanship" and with the thought of "another day" and "peace in the ranks," Marlin advanced the idea of my going at once to the Alford headquarters and congratulating the doctor. Dick Emerson doubtless spoke the sentiment of the rest of us when he rose from his chair, his voice trembling with indignation, and said, "He ain't a gonna do it." Sensing the mood of our feelings, Marlin quickly capitulated.

I did, however, call Alford headquarters. I got this answer: "Congressman Alford's office"—I had to swallow to keep from acknowledging that in a sarcastic vein. When I identified myself as Brooks Hays, not as "Congressman Hays," Dr. Alford came to the phone. "Yes, Mr. Hays," he said. He had never called me that before. I wanted to say "Dale, when you were fitting these glasses I am wearing, you always called me 'Brooks'; why the formality?" But I only said, as calmly as possible, "Dale, I called to say that I am conceding the election." He thanked me stiffly and the conversation ended.

This gesture was the expected courtesy and I did not mind doing it. But our circle of devoted friends wanted to talk about the city's malaise that had produced a sudden change of fortune. No one in the group, I feel sure, was anticipating the widespread national revulsion of feeling that followed the election, giving the extremists their brief day of glory. Rather, we sought in our quiet retreat a recovery from despondency, and a renewal of hope for our city's recovery.

As we were getting ready to go, Clyde E. Lowry, who had gone through every campaign with me as a personal champion, said, "Now wait—I think it would be good to ask Raymond to offer a prayer for Brooks, for all of us, and for Little Rock." I believe that every man there felt that it was altogether proper. I have identified Raymond, but I should add that he was at that time president of Gideons' International and had often publicly credited me, as his Sunday school teacher, with helping him change from a conventional churchman into a Christian activist. Clyde chose the right man to offer this prayer for a distraught closely knit group.

I have never heard a prayer like it. It was offered not in the attitude of defeatism, or as a supplication for their defeated member. Rather the anguish of men who loved their community surfaced in an appeal for "healing of our sick and divided city." With the "Amen," I saw some of them hiding their tears. And Steele, in a successful effort to keep the emotional tide from engulfing us, pulled out an extra handkerchief and tendered it to Dick Emerson whose copious tears gave way to gentle laughter.

Other councils of political warfare had been held in this same room of Raymond's casualty insurance office. It was there a few days before that one of my trusted advisers hammered on the table as he emphasized the point that the city was worked up over the threatened change in its "way of life"—the pattern of racial segregation. "Brooks," he urged, "you have never once said that you are a segregationist. The people are waiting to hear you say at least that much on the subject. It will take it to save the situation." My response was "I can't say that for the simple reason that I am *not* a segregationist." His pressure continued until Steele said, "Please don't make Dad unhappy about this. He isn't going to do it." This was convincing.

I was unaware of how widespread the interest in my defeat was until the national news media representatives besieged me before sundown. I had little to add to my decision not to institute contest proceedings in the House. My decision did not deter my long-time friend John F. Wells, publisher of a weekly newspaper and in his later years a critic of some of my political views. His many admirable fights against election frauds made him impregnable to any criticism that he was inspired by pique or personal animosities. He instituted a strong movement to prevent the seating of Alford, making it clear that he acted strictly as a private citizen interested only in purging the returns of obvious frauds. For a while it appeared that he might succeed. Certainly everyone who knew John knew of his independence, and that he was motivated by conviction and not friendship. His efforts in the Alford case were responsible for his receiving the Elijah Parish Lovejoy Award for "courage in journalism," given by Southern Illinois University and the International Conference of Weekly Newspaper Editors in 1959.

Notice of John Wells's protest was taken by the House Special Elections Committee chaired by Congressman Cliff Davis of Tennessee, and I was asked to appear before the committee of five members to comment upon the petition. My testimony was more in the nature of a statement of my reasons for not contesting, but it confirmed, out of general knowledge of the Alford strategy, what Mr. Wells was alleging.

It became clear to the committee that an inquiry should be conducted, even though the complaint was from a citizen voter, and not the opposition candidate. I presume that a majority of the committee members recognized the dubious character of the use of stickers with the X printed in a box opposite Alford's *printed* name, an obvious violation of the Arkansas law. (The "sticker case" cited by Carpenter and other Alford supporters, 186 Arkansas Reports page 413, decided October 13, 1932, was not in point, since that decision was rendered prior to the use of the X mark requirement and, moreover, was based upon measures to fill a sudden vacancy occurring just before the election, and necessitating the use of ballots with no name at all printed on them.)

The committee unanimously voted to recommend that an investigation of all phases of the election be conducted by the House, but a minority (Cliff Davis of Tennessee and Robert Jones of Alabama) dissented from the recommendation that Alford not be seated pending the results of the inquiry. The three other committee members were Thomas P. ("Tip") O'Neill of Massachusetts, the present speaker of the house, Kenneth Keating of New York, later senator from his state and ambassador to India, and William Dennison of Ohio, the last two being Republicans.

The committee's recommendation created quite a stir. Many southern members were unhappy that what appeared at first to be a clear-cut political victory for the segregationists was not the genuine article. To hold their advantage they had to firm up the old, though often tenuous, coalition with the Republicans. Also, some went so far as to resort to a form of "political blackmail," serving notice on the House leadership that if Alford were denied a seat they would find a basis for challenging the credentials of Adam Clayton Powell, thus embarrassing many northern members. It was a tough spot for Majority Leader John McCormack, who felt the urge to fight openly against the kind of racism that produced the Alford candidacy.

Apparently, there were a number of closed-door consultations, and it was finally resolved in Mr. McCormack's office by a gentlemen's agreement that the standing House Administration Committee would be instructed to inquire into the matter and that, pending a report, Alford would be seated, but without prejudice to later action on his credentials.

Mr. McCormack had to abandon his inclination to participate in the attack on the methods used against me.

Mr. Rayburn was publicly silent throughout, though anyone familiar with his style would have to conclude that, though he doubtless disapproved of Faubus' exploiting race feelings, he fell in line with the southern strategy of 1958.

John Dingell of Michigan, who was not a party to any agreement, was determined to claim his right to object to Alford's receiving the oath on the opening day of the session. Consequently, he addressed the Speaker with his privileged request, and Alford had to wait until the following day to take his oath of office. In the meantime, the parliamentary technicalities were put in order, and the agreed-upon first step of administering the oath to Dr. Alford was taken. But not without a loud protest from Tip O'Neill of Massachusetts, the present Speaker, who vainly sought the floor to oppose the seating.

Then the House Administration Committee began its "investigation." It turned out to be a pathetic "bill of health" for the November election. The committee ignored its commitment to take oral testimony based upon affidavits which had been submitted in the Washington hearing, notably the sworn statement of Mrs. Marie Hildreth of North Little Rock, an election official, that in her precinct the Alford stickers were passed out with the ballots by one of the other officials.

Further, the committee did not even pretend to establish the legality of the use of stickers, or take notice of the distribution on the day before the election of the scurrilous and unsigned circulars carrying the picture of me with my black friend, the Reverend Joseph Jackson, president of the National Baptist Convention, implying that we were engaged in a plot. Proof of the authorship could probably have been adduced by the committee, since certain White Citizen Council members were publicly boasting of their part in the campaign against me.

My condemnation of the report is impersonal. Many of the committee members were personal friends, and were probably hurrying through a distasteful task with a bit of rationalizing, "Brooks is not contesting the election." This prevented any tension between me and old friends, but it does not obliterate the House leadership's responsibility for condoning the travesty. The committee members were captives of a bipartisan decision to get out of the difficulty in the easiest way—blandly assuming that the certificate of election, bearing signatures of Arkansas officials, was valid on its face and should not be disturbed, although that certificate bore the stains of shocking irregularities.

Had I known that John Wells's complaint against those credentials would not be seriously considered in accordance wtih the promises made publicly by the committee to him and his lawyer, Marcus Hollabaugh, I might have felt conscience-bound to contest the election myself. The difference would have been as follows: A decision of election irregularity would simply have voided the election, and a vacancy would have been created. If I had contested the result, the committee would have had to decide which one of us received the greater number of legal votes. I had shown my preference for the former procedure. Unfortunately, the House actions seem to support the view that citizens protesting the denial of their right to be represented by the majority choice have less claim upon the congressional sense of pride in electoral integrity than a controversy between two aspirants for the office. This is regrettable.

As *finis* was being written on my congressional career, doors of opportunity for creative work were being opened at the Tennessee Valley Authority, the State Department, important universities, and at the White House. Adventure lay ahead as well as behind.

I am sometimes asked, "What happened to the doctor who defeated you?" He served two terms in the House, and then in 1962, after the redistricting placed him in the same district with Wilbur D. Mills, the powerful veteran, he decided to oppose Governor Faubus, who was running for a fifth term. Defeated in 1962, Alford decided in 1964 to support Faubus in his bid for a sixth term. He was moving from one side to the other just as he had on the Blossom plan. (The school board record indicates that as a board member he had voted for the integration plan.) Dr. Alford's final effort to regain political position came in 1966, when he made a second unsuccessful race for governor following Governor Faubus' announcement that he would not run for a seventh term. Some of the details of that campaign will be related in the next chapter.

Back to the events of the day following the 1958 election and my defeat for a ninth term. Buoyed by evidence that old friendships were firm and that in the inner circle there was near unanimity as to the correctness of my course, I returned from Lindsey's office to my office in the Federal Building. My faithful secretary, Kitty Johnson, was already sorting telegrams expressing regret over my defeat. Seventy-five had come in big batches before noon. A call from the Washington office reported that among the first scattered messages were wires from John Foster Dulles and John F. Kennedy. One of the finest letters I received following the 1958 defeat was from a former colleague, Richard M. Nixon, who was completing his sixth year as vice-president of the United States. He had obviously given more than a passing thought to my misfortune.

I had further proof of that in September, 1970, when President Nixon invited Walter Judd and me to conduct a Sunday morning service at the White House. We were serving as co-chairmen of Former Members of Congress and the president invited our entire membership, with spouses, to attend. I was reluctant to accept this invitation, since I believe these "private" services tend to encourage a civil religion. However, since it was for the Former Members organization, I felt constrained, as co-chairman, to accept.

In a conversation before the service, the president asked, "Brooks, do you remember my writing to you when you lost the 1958 election?" I said, "I do, Mr. President. I even remember that your letter appeared on the front page of the New York *Herald Tribune* on November 24, 1958." The text of this remarkable letter follows:

November 18, 1958

Dear Brooks:

When I learned upon arriving in Miami that you also were there, I tried to get in touch with you but, unfortunately, you had checked out of the hotel before we were able to make connections.

As a Republican who campaigned in twenty-five states, it goes without saying that the results on November 4 in many states and districts were disappointing to me.

But, writing to you not just as a personal friend but as one who has always admired your statesmanlike leadership in the House of Representatives, I can say without qualification that there was no more tragic result of this last election, from the standpoint of the nation, than your defeat in Arkansas. When statesmanship of the type you represent in such an exemplary way becomes the victim of demagoguery and prejudice, it is time for men of good will in both of our major parties in all sections of the country to exert more positive leadership in developing the public understanding on the issue of civil rights which is essential if America is to continue to be a nation of responsible laws rather than irresponsible men.

I use the term in all sections of the country advisedly. Having attended one of the south's great universities, I am aware of the acute difficulties this problem presents and I know of the enlightened leadership which you and other southerners have been and are providing for its solution.

And as one who has lived most of my life in the north and west I know this is not just a southern problem. Those in the north must not point the finger of accusation at the south without recognizing their own responsibility to put their own house in order.

I know too that our well-publicized failures in the field should and must not be allowed to obscure the record of success and progress which has been made in many areas.

But that is why it is all the more important for the responsible leaders of both our major parties to join together in helping to mobilize public opinion on the side of law and order and against the forces of prejudice and vandalism.

Only in this way can we make sure that both at home and abroad the strident voices of hatred and discord will not be mistaken for the voice of America.

In any event, as you leave Washington you can be proud of the fact that millions of Americans of both parties are deeply appreciative of the fine service you have rendered not only to the people of your district and state but to the nation in the fifteen years you served in the House.

Mrs. Nixon joins me in sending our very best wishes to you and Mrs. Hays.

Sincerely,
Richard Nixon

It is not an exaggeration to say that, partly because of the influence of this message, with its eloquent references to racial equality and democratic ideals, I had tender feelings completely unidentified with political considerations about the tragedy in Richard Nixon's life. On August 9, 1974, he ceased to be president, but he did not cease to be our fellow human being, so along with other well-wishers I hope to see him seek and find an authentic reconciliation with the human family.

From receipt of these messages until the issue was finally resolved by the House itself, the stream of sympathy flowed unimpeded. Daily, there was fresh evidence that the unusual circumstances of the defeat had tapped some strong sentiments in surprising depth. It could not be explained in terms of region, race, party, or religious faith. I had unintentionally become a momentary symbol of something that would bring pride and satisfaction to a far greater degree than continuation in office could have produced. I was sorry that Kitty and I could not have the two highly competent Washington staff members John McLees and Lurlene Wilbert with us to share our feelings.

Speaking engagements took me away from Little Rock within a few days. My term as president of the Southern Baptist Convention had eight months to run, and there were Baptist colleges and congregations expecting me to appear, if not with political credentials, at last as their titular "head." My realization of an emotional stirring from the defeat was when I made the first post-election appearance at Stetson University in Florida. When I walked quietly to the platform, I expected only the polite reception for a visiting speaker, but I had never, I believe, had such an ovation. It took me by complete surprise. Surely, I thought, these people have misread the returns! They must not know that I am the vanquished—not the victor. The next appearance was in Miami's Central Baptist Church. A packed house greeted me. However, it was marred by a bomb threat, and at the conclusion of the service the building was emptied quickly. I rather enjoyed the excitement, the Arkansas newspapers carrying the headlines, "Hays Speaks in Spite of Bomb Threat."

The symbolism of my part in the Little Rock episode was not one to draw applause in every group. In Atlanta, a few days later, for example, there was tension that I was not aware of until I was telling the chief of police good-bye on the following day. He had been in the welcoming party at the airport, and I thought he was merely adding dignity and ceremonial importance to the event, but he smilingly told me as I stepped on the plane that he was relaxing for the first time in twenty-four hours. "I have had plainclothesmen within a few feet of you every minute you have been out of the hotel room," he said. "You are not popular with everybody, you know," and, of course, I knew what he had reference to.

In Atlanta something did happen that stirred my own emotions. I went to the Atlanta *Constitution* to see my old friend Ralph McGill. He came to the reception room without his usual happy greeting. He started to speak but choked up and put his big arms around me, merely saying, "To think it had to happen like this."

Another great physical frame that shook with sadness belonged to my Republican friend, the lovable senator from Wisconsin, Alexander Wiley. He saw me in the Senate dining room a few days later—walked over to shake hands, but was speechless and turned away as he stifled his tears. "I'll tell you later," he managed to say. There were others. I refer to them, partly to confirm the truth of the quoted statement of Walter Hines Page, "The world is infinitely cruel; the world is infinitely kind." It has certainly been kind to me and my family in unusual degrees following the Little Rock incident. Another reaction that surprised me occurred in the office of Joseph Johnson of the Carnegie Foundation in New York City in December when I dropped by to say hello after a visit with Dag Hammarskjöld. After a very subdued greeting from my old friend Joe, I sat silently waiting for him to say something. Suddenly I saw big, I mean big tears, running down his cheeks. As he reached for his handkerchief, he said (and he seemed unembarrassed), "I have a very sensitive tear gland."

Finally, there is the story related by Congressman Henry Reuss of Wisconsin. He said, "Brooks, I noticed at the big dinner in your honor that you and Mrs. Hays didn't shed a tear."

"Of course not," I said, "It was a very happy evening."

"Well," the congressman added, "I sat at the same table with John Sherman Cooper and Kenneth Keating, and they both blubbered all evening." A year later I was with Senator Cooper and told him of the conversation, intending to evoke a smile. But no smile appeared. He quietly said, "But I was not weeping for you, Brooks; I was weeping for my country." Anyone who knows that fine Kentuckian knows that he was speaking out of his heart. He is not given to histrionics.

The event referred to by Congressman Reuss was the remarkable dinner that was held for Marion and me in the Willard Hotel on December 18. Over seven hundred friends gathered at $7.50 a plate, regarded as a bit high in those days, just to say they thought as much of us as ever, and to signify that, while there were differences on many issues, there was a feeling of unity growing out of what I had said and done to save my city from violence, and to put obedience to law above political considerations.

My former secretary, Claude Curlin, had worked hard, with a lot of volunteer help from John McLees of my staff and others, in setting up the testimonial. It was achieved without Madison Avenue methods. The cross-section character of the audience was marvelous to behold. The whole spectrum of political ideas was shown. Howard W. Smith sat near Senator Jacob Javits. Doris Fleeson, liberal columnist, and Bertha Atkins of the Republican National Committee were there. Also Ed Hébert, Louisiana conservative, and Senator John Kennedy joined in approving my stand. And next day one of the diners said, "My liquor dealer was there, and he thought Billy Graham's speech was great."

The broad support was reflected in the rest of the program. The chairman was the president of the University of Virginia, and the former governor, Colgate Darden, and speakers included Mary Pillsbury Lord, Senator Monroney of Oklahoma, and J. P. Richards, chairman of the House Foreign Affairs Committee, who drew loud laughter from the audience with references to "ole Brooks."

At the end I was given a beautiful embossed statement signed by the "Committee to Honor Brooks Hays," composed, I learned later, by Dr. Ernest S. Griffith, the scholarly and popular director of the Legislative Reference Service. It is not modesty which restrains me from reproducing the entire text here, but rather a consideration for those who read it at page x of the foreword of my book *Hotbed of Tranquility.* I stifle this concern enough to quote the following final words of the salute, since it supports my thesis that happiness and peace of mind are not dependent on election results: ". . . the day which some may count a day of defeat, but which to us is a day of victory.

"We salute you as a man of faith. We count this the greatest of all, because we know that it is to you of all things most precious. The love of others for you, as your love for them, knows no boundaries of creed in the consciousness of the common fatherhood of God."

Saying goodbye to the Congress brought a pang, of course, but with an outpouring of understanding and affection such as was evidenced in these events, there could be only buoyancy and hopefulness as I faced the future.

During the remaining years of his service as governor, Orval Faubus continued to advocate resistance to school integration, going so far (in a speech to Little Rock University students in April 1959) as to liken resistance to integration to the American Revolution. According to the *Arkansas Gazette,* he said, "Suppose it *is* the law of the land; that does not mean it has to be obeyed. The orders of George III were the law of the land for the colonies, but they didn't have to be obeyed."

His ties to the movement of moderation which, at the time of his first election as governor, seemed so firm were completely cut by 1959. Having heard his commitments to President Eisenhower at Newport on September 13, 1957, I experienced a personal sadness in his abandonment of the position as stated at Newport that "the Supreme Court decision in the school desegregation case of 1954 is the law of the land and must be obeyed."

In the spring of 1979 Orval Faubus appeared on an American Broadcasting Company program with Dr. Terrance Roberts, one of the nine black students who were turned away from the high school in 1957. During the exchange Mr. Faubus in defending his action in calling out the National Guard and blocking the enrollment of the black students said, "At that time it was not possible to make any other decision and assure the safety of everyone and survive politically in Arkansas."

Mr. Faubus' statement reminds me of a conversation between the governor and myself in one of our last meetings at the mansion before President Eisenhower's use of federal troops on September 23. At a crucial point in the negotiations between the governor and the president I had Sherman Adams' assurance that if the governor would agree to the admission of the black pupils and pledge the use of all his civil authority, meaning the state police and other functionaries, leaving the Guard out of such commitment to protect the nine black pupils, then the president would not intervene with federal military authority to enforce the court orders, and would avoid any overt federal action. Sherman and I had agreed in a phone conversation upon the appropriate language. When I showed the agreement to the governor in the mansion he was obviously leaning strongly toward that step as a resolving of the deepening conflict. As I recall, he said, "I think I can go along on this," or words to that effect. "I'll talk to the boys," he added and he fixed a time for me to return. When I did return I found him in a different mood. As in previous talks he did not seem unhappy with me. But my spirit slumped when he said, "I mustn't do it, Brooks, they say I'd be committing political suicide and I'm not going to do that."

Governor Faubus defended his actions on the basis of a working rule followed sometimes by public men, namely when an overwhelming majority of the people point in a certain direction, then follow that sentiment. My answer to that is that it depends on the nature of the issue— whether basic and eternal principles are involved. And protection of those nine black pupils in the exercise of their legal rights made the matter of personal political survival irrelevant. It has puzzled some observers of these conflicts that the governor and I wound up in diametrically opposed positions without an enduring bitterness toward each other. I do not have an explanation, except that just as soldiers of opposing armies may, when weapons are laid down, laugh and even weep together, so political adversaries may display the ordinary emotions of life.

Following my 1958 defeat the governor and I rarely saw each other. In December of 1960 when Mr. Kennedy announced that I would be appointed assistant secretary of state, the governor reacted with some ill-tempered language, but in the intervening years I have detected a mellowing of his attitude toward me and it has been easy for me to reciprocate. Regardless of our past differences, I think it is not a fanciful hope that Orval Faubus will enjoy, as I do, our state's steady march toward the goals that the Brown decision pictured.

Marion and Brooks Hays enjoying the evening, dedicated to them by friends, December 18, 1958. *Cowles Magazines, Inc.*

An audience with Pope John XXIII, in 1963. Also present was Monseigneur
Ligutti, an old friend of the Hayses.

With President John F. Kennedy, at Hays's swearing in ceremony as one of the special assistants to the president.

With Adlai Stevenson and Hugh Patterson, publisher of the *Arkansas Gazette*. Little Rock, 1965.   *Arkansas Gazette photo*

With President Lyndon B. Johnson.

'Stay Away — You're Exciting Our Cat!'

(1965)

Speaking at a meeting in the House of Burgesses Chamber in the Old Colonial Capitol, Williamsburg, Virginia. 1965. *Colonial Williamsburg photo*

Brooks and Marion walking with Vice President Hubert Humphrey, at Wake Forest University, April, 1968. The occasion was the inauguration of Dr. J. R. Scales as president of the university.

With President Gerald Ford, at a meeting of the Former Members of Congress, 1975.

President Jimmy Carter and Brooks Hays in an informal exchange of greeting in the White House, 1979. *Official photograph The White House*

Mr. and Mrs. Hays with three of their grandchildren, Little Rock, 1963.

With daughter Betty Brooks Bell (seated, at far right) and other members of her family.

Son Steele Hays and his daughter, daughter-in-law, and son.

Chapter 12 PEAKS AND VALLEYS
1959–1961

Meadows trim with daisies pied,
Shallow brooks and rivers wide.
Milton

WHEN my eighth and last term ended in January, 1959, it was difficult to plan my future. I did not want to leave public service. I was barely sixty years of age and in good health. The response to my defeat, due to the special circumstances, was heart-warming. We received letters from every state in the union, thousands of them. The reaction persisted, and I found even that many members of Congress who were aggravated by my action in the Little Rock situation had personal goodwill for me. Ties in the legislative service are not lightly broken.

One thing that brought distress was my father's deteriorating health. While mantaining my base in Washington, as I literally had to do, I was still able to be with him quite a bit. I made eight visits to Russellville between December, 1958, and June, 1959, when he died.

I renewed my activities in Washington, with a tentative interest in the law practice. I was admitted to the Washington bar, and my long-time friend and fellow Sigma Chi Richard S. Doyle gave me space in his office. Mrs. Lurlene Wilbert, who had been one of my top staff members during the last ten years of my service, was available to help me; and Marion was very helpful, too, although work of this kind was a new experience for her. Some additional honors that came to me from my church and related activities produced a new avalanche of letters, and once she exclaimed, "If my husband does anything else to make people congratulate him, I'm going into a nunnery."

However, we were able to keep current. In spite of my need for an income, I did not want a presidential appointment. Some Republican friends, knowing that the president's action in sending troops to Little Rock and my support of his course had been a factor in my defeat, wanted an appointment for me. Still the president knew that I acted as I did, not to curry favor with the administration, but because I felt that the president was right in his determination to put down violence and secure enforcement of the court orders. It had been an easy decision for me.

I was offered a position with a refugee agency, largely through the influence of Mary Pillsbury Lord, with whom I had worked as a member of the United Nations delegation in the General Assembly of 1955. I declined because I wanted to stay on this side of the Atlantic. Sherman Adams asked me if I would accept a place with the USIA, and this too I declined. Sherman also told me that I would be offered a federal judgeship. This was surprising. I remember saying, "Well, Sherman, do you think I would make a good judge?" And I was cheered by his extravagant response regarding my capabilities. It brought back recollections of earlier proposals of this kind which had been frustrated by Senator Hattie Caraway. Since I knew that Sherman had been talking with Attorney General Rogers that very day, I assumed that it was a firm decision by the administration, but nothing ever came of it. I never heard it referred to again, and I can only assume that there was resistance by Arkansas political interests, unidentified by me, to what President Eisenhower desired.

In 1959 there was a flurry of mild excitement among some of my friends over the possibility of my being considered for the vice-presidential nomination. It was stirred by a full-page article appearing in the *New Republic* and written by Gerald Johnson, who had been for many years top editorial writer for the Baltimore *Sun*. He assumed that the presidential nomination would go either to Stevenson or Kennedy, and built his arguments around the wisdom of picking a southerner to provide geographic balance and a Baptist for "theological" balance. "Why wouldn't it be helpful for a Boston Catholic to have a Southern Baptist on the ticket with him? And shouldn't an Illinois Unitarian be happy to have as running mate an Arkansan whose church credentials were good enough to win election as Baptist Convention president, having a constituency of ten million members?" If I had possessed a base and could have gone to the convention with the support of even a single state, a way might have been found to run Gerald Johnson's horse by the stands, but, to mix the metaphors, further talk would be chasing rainbows.

Some outstanding Democrats with real prestige, such as former governor Colgate Darden of Virginia, long-time friend, applauded the Johnson statement, but even he counseled our friends to forget it. Some of those friends did, however, carry the latent hope to the 1960 Los Angeles Convention that the nominee for president might be convinced that I had a good image, nationally, as a result of opposing Governor Faubus' efforts to preserve segregation, and would pick me as running mate. I had no illusions, and was not surprised to receive a phone call from Luther Holcomb of Dallas, who was with the Texas delegation in Los Angeles, informing me, "It will be Senator Johnson."

Years later, after Lyndon Johnson altered the Vietnam policies and withdrew from the 1968 race, one of my young friends said, "Well, we could dream, couldn't we?" "Yes" another young friend said, "but how different our nation's course would have been. No generation gap with Brooks as president."

In May of 1959 I had a telephone call from Charles Bartlett, a prominent news representative in Washington. He asked, "Are you going to accept the TVA appointment?"

I said, "Charley, this is the first I have heard of that."

"Oh, you didn't know that it's going to be tendered?"

I assured him that I did not. But in a few days I received a call from Gerald Morgan, one of the top assistants to President Eisenhower, asking me to come to the executive office. I went at once, and I had hardly taken my seat when he said, "The President wants to appoint you to the vacancy on the Tennessee Valley Authority Board. Will you accept it?"

I asked for a few days to think about it, although my reaction was definitely favorable. I only wanted to be sure that it was the thing to do, and that Marion would not be unhappy living in another city. I had been a supporter of TVA from its inception, and my enthusiasm for it had increased with the years as I observed the vast economic and social benefits of that great program. Within a few days I had resolved all doubts about it. Among the friends who called to urge me to accept was Helen Hill Miller, who had a special knowledge of the agency. I recall how excited she and Francis Pickens Miller, her husband, were about it. They, as few others did, knew of my long-time concern with the problems of southern life.

The appointment was announced while I was presiding over the 1959 Baptist Convention in Louisville, and there was a favorable reaction among my fellow Baptists. The Senate quickly confirmed it, but not until after some laudatory remarks by the majority leader, Senator Lyndon Johnson, and some friendly reference to me on the Republican side by two of my former House colleagues, Senators Case of New Jersey and Keating of New York. Another former House colleague, Senator Bartlett of Alaska, a Democrat, expressed his warm approval. I was touched by Senator Bartlett's remarks, since I had disappointed him by not voting for the admission of Alaska to statehood.

Some of my friends wondered why neither of the Arkansas senators spoke up for me. I could and did forgive them because the political situation at home was still explosive, and a defense of the appointment was unnecessary. Francis and Helen Miller, knowing that the two sitting members of the TVA Board, General H. D. Vogel and Mr. Arnold Jones, were in Washington when the Senate confirmed my appointment, quickly arranged for what would be called a cocktail party to introduce me to the two men with whom I would be associated. I had never met either of them, and they seemed to be a bit surprised that I would even show up at a cocktail party! I explained that while I had conformed generally to the views of my Baptist people, having in mind their historical position regarding the personal vices, smoking, drinking, etc., if I had declined even to attend Washington cocktail parties, I would be living the life of Peter, the hermit.

The Baptist image is something that I suppose I will never lose. One of the best illustrations was the statement appearing in a Mississippi newspaper. When I was appointed to the TVA Board, the editor had this to say: "We do not know how much Mr. Hays knows about navigation, flood control, or hydroelectric power production, but one thing for sure, the Baptists now have access to the largest baptismal pool in all the world."

My induction quickly followed confirmation, and it was a happy occasion. For the swearing-in ceremony in Knoxville I opened the Bible at the 46th Psalm and referred to the fourth verse, "There is a river, the streams whereof make glad the city of God." I added, "Whether a river is to be a demonic enemy or benevolent friend depends on how we treat it. I am thrilled to be part of an agency that reflects the concern and pride of the people in this mighty resource." That was about all I said—one of my shortest speeches.

Marion wore a pretty blue summer dress and a white broad-brimmed hat. Newsmen and photographers couldn't help noticing her. One Knoxville newspaper carried her picture on page one and quoted my comment in reply to a reporter's query, "Where did you two meet?"

"At the University of Arkansas, in our freshman year," I said. Then, factually, rather than sentimentally, "She is the only sweetheart I ever had." That line was beneath her picture and got more prominence than anything else I said. She did not scold me, but it's the kind of thing she does not like.

My colleagues were well established in their respective functions, General Vogel in engineering, and Mr. Jones in the fiscal phases. The human problems just naturally wound up in my area. However, we shared our specialties and operated as a unit. I was asked to do a lot of speaking, both in the Valley states and in other regions. I tried to restrain the use of florid language, seeing the wisdom of Walter Hines Page's words, "Next to fried food, the South has suffered most from oratory."

I had from boyhood recognized the value of religious traditions in southern life and the reverence of rural people for their forebears. I tried to adopt Mr. Lincoln's style in the use of Bible passages. I believe what I did was a proper response to Isaiah's bidding to "look unto the rock whence ye are hewn and to the hole of the pit whence ye are digged" (Isaiah 51:1).

Congressman Percy Priest, a native of the Valley, related an incident which bore out this quality. One of the residents of a remote section of the area to be flooded did not want to give up his "patches," the venacular for their little farms, and particularly objected to the government taking his cabin "where the fire of my fathers has always burned." The practice was to bank the fires when not needed, and later to activate the coals so that "the fathers' fire" could be said never to have expired. One of the TVA staff hit upon a plan that induced the patriarch to surrender. A great oil drum was brought in to hold the live coals, and two men were assigned to keep fanning the fire as the contents of the huge fireplace were transported to the new home that had been constructed for the family.

In northern states I was occasionally invited to discuss the TVA's vast operation in relation to the economy of other regions. Occasionally I encountered skepticism and even hostility. In Philadelphia, for example, one of the audience said, as we walked into the conference room, "I hope you will explain why I should be taxed to provide a good thing for the people who live in a valley that Pennsylvania is not a part of."

"I'll answer it right now," I said. "For the same reason *they* are taxed to pay for the control and development of *your* Delaware River, for which Congress just yesterday voted several million dollars." In my talk I gave impressive figures on the dollar amount of TVA purchases of electric equipment from Pennsylvania industries. He was convinced, he told me later, of TVA's national character and value.

Tennessee is "Baptist country," and one finds there some fascinating offshoots of the Baptist denomination. I recall making reference once to a small group of churches with the awesome name of "Two-Seed-in-the-Spirit-Predestinarian-Baptists." Shortly afterward a friend wrote me, "I was quite fascinated by your story of the 'Two-Seed-in-the-Spirit-Predestinarian-Baptists.' I am a 'one-seed in the spirit Roger Williams-Thomas Jefferson-Adlai Stevenson-Estes Kefauver-Brooks Hays unification Baptist." He was obviously mixing up religious and political ideas here, but since he included me in that distinguished group, I enjoyed passing it on to my friend Adlai Stevenson with a comment, "I'd like to know whether he is naming us in ascending or descending order of importance." This was below Adlai's standard of wit, but both of us tried to keep our correspondence lively and colloquial.

After a telephone conversation with him on the day that Khrushchev pounded his shoe on his desk at the U.N. General Assembly, Adlai called me on the phone to ask about something, and before the conversation ended, he said, "By the way, Brooks, what do you think of Khrushchev's performance today?" My reply was, "I think he overegged his puddin'." Adlai said, "What was that? Where did you get that expression?" I told him it was an old southern saying. That night, to my surprise, Harold Macmillan, who was then foreign minister and attending the General Assembly, said in a radio address, with his pronounced Oxford accent, "In the language of an old British saying, Mr. Khrushchev overegged his pudding." I pondered the question, "Did Adlai give him this, or was it in reality something Mr. Macmillan was quoting from English folklore?" I wrote Adlai, "Whatever the source of that comment by Mr. Macmillan, it only proves how the deep roots of Appalachian life are in Elizabethan culture."

I had not remained in Congress long enough to see the culmination of a controversy regarding TVA financing and the fixing of its boundaries, but I was one of the directors of TVA when the compromise bill was passed in 1959. It authorized the agency to issue bonds and limited its expansion to the area historically served, with some carefully prescribed additional territory. It was good legislation and brought relief to both friends and foes of TVA.

Before it was signed by the president, however, a hitch developed. President Eisenhower concluded that it carried what he called "an erosion of executive authority," and he summoned General Vogel, Mr. Jones, and me to the White House for an explanation of his views. Subscribing in principle to the bill, he was emphatic in the insistence that he could not approve it unless convinced that presidential powers were unimpaired. What followed our conference is a good illustration of the value of extra-official actions in promoting the legislative process. We, the directors, were agreeable to an interpretation of the language that reserved his authority, but the bill's language was, as he indicated, a bit fuzzy.

A veto would have necessitated starting all over again at the other end of Pennsylvania Avenue and would have canceled out the good work of our friends in Congress. We resolved the problem with this rather novel procedure. The president would approve the bill in the form submitted, provided we could secure passage of a simple resolution with clarifying language to meet his objections. This was easily and speedily done. I discussed it with Speaker Rayburn and the Senate Democrats, the other directors with Charley Halleck and his Senate counterparts. The technical requirements were quickly disposed of and the president signed the bill, completing a gentlemen's agreement that satisfied the president and the Congress.

While on a trip for the Tennessee Valley Authority to the World Power Conference in 1960, I contacted some of our embassy officials in Madrid who were familiar with the problem of securing a greater degree of freedom for our Baptist people in Spain. In a debate on the House floor I had made reference to the Spanish constitution and its special provisions granting full religious liberty, although, of course, in the same document there is the assertion that the Catholic religion is the official faith of Spain. I pointed out that the language extending individual rights of religious freedom is clear enough. My statement was challenged, however, by another member. Next day he told me that he had been mistaken, that he had the wrong impression about the Spanish constitution; but following my speech he had checked and found that I was right, that their constitution does indeed grant religious freedom. However, it is not strictly observed, and I appealed to our embassy officials in Madrid to try to induce Spanish officials to recognize Protestant rights of assembly and to publicize meetings under their constitution. I left Spain with some hope that, since I had elicited the interest of top staff men in the embassy, we might induce Spain's foreign office to act.

During our few days visit in Madrid my wife and I had gone with some American Baptists to the modest meeting place of the small congregation of Baptists in a residential section. It was an unmarked frame building on a side street with no signs or other identifying marks to indicate that it was a place of worship. The doors of the little room were flush with the sidewalk and were locked. Our Baptist guide knocked on the back door of the adjoining house and found that the family living there had the keys and they unlocked the doors to show us a small uninspiring room. It was obvious that the Spanish constitutional grant of religious freedom did not mean much in Madrid, else the Baptists would have been permitted to advertise their place and times for meeting. However, in Barcelona a few days later we saw a sign in Spanish above the entrance to a small meeting place of the Baptists, so perhaps the disapproval seen in Madrid had not prevailed in Barcelona.

When we returned to the United States, I prepared a memorandum setting forth what I thought was a proper policy toward non-Catholics by the Spanish government, under their own constitution, arguing that repression of the kind we had encountered in some places in Spain was inconsistent with their new constitution. I contended, too, that the cooperation of Protestants could be expected in maintaining the policy of the Spanish government of preserving their Catholic faith as a cultural heritage. I even suggested that the government might find the Baptists and others willing to limit their evangelizing activities to those in Spain who were not practicing Catholics. In other words, there would be no overt proselytizing, and the result would be a plus for national morality and international comity.

This was an informal personal suggestion that I hoped would get into conversations between Protestants and Catholics, because it was obvious that in Spain, as in other countries, there are many people who are only nominal church members and who might be interested in attending services of the other faiths. I submitted the memorandum through channels to our embassy in Spain.

The general secretary of the Baptist World Alliance at that time was Josef Nordenhaug. He told me later that my efforts bore fruit. It was his belief that the memorandum reached the top officer in foreign relations and conceivably—and he believed this to be true—it got to the desk of the Generalissimo himself. In any event, I had reason to feel that this expenditure of time and energy was justified. Mr. Nordenhaug's belief was confirmed in a conversation in 1974 with John Davis Lodge, my former colleague in Congress, who was our ambassador to Spain at the time.

The pleasant TVA service continued until February, 1961, when, after a long delay, I was sworn in as assistant secretary of state for congressional relations. In December I had learned that Mr. Kennedy wanted me in that position. This information came to me after Adlai Stevenson accepted the appointment as Ambassador to the United Nations, and I received a call from Adlai saying that he wanted to see me in New York. I flew from Knoxville to New York, thinking perhaps he wanted to talk to me about an appointment in the new administration, and this turned out to be the case. We had hardly sat down when he said, "I want you to be one of my two deputies here at the United Nations. It carries the rank of ambassador."

Knowing that I would be congenial with Adlai, and that it would be exciting, I gave him an enthusiastic affirmative answer. He walked to the door with me, and suddenly said, "By the way, you'd better stop in Washington and talk to Dean Rusk. He may have other plans for you."

We turned back then to do some telephoning, and wound up talking with Chester Bowles, the under secretary. It was agreed that I would see Chester when I got to Washington. However, I found that my good friend Mr. Rusk was already sending word that he wanted to see me, so I went at once to his office, and he lost no time in seeing me. He had not yet taken the oath, but the Eisenhower administration had arranged for him to have facilities at the State Department.

When I went in, he said, "Let's sit over here in the corner of the room on this comfortable couch." Then he said, "Brooks, I have just come from Mr. Kennedy's Georgetown headquarters, and he wants you to be assistant secretary of state for congressional relations." I was disappointed, of course, but I said, "Well, if that's what the president wants, then of course it will be that way. I did have something else in mind!" I did not tell Mr. Rusk what it was, because I was ready to conform to the president's wishes. Mr. Rusk seemed quite enthusiastic himself over the prospect of my serving as an assistant secretary. What I did not know then and do not know now is how Mr. Rusk and the president might have responded if I had put in a plea for the United Nations job, repeating Mr. Stevenson's request that I serve with him. I wish now that I had explored it with Mr. Rusk.

I went back to Knoxville and quietly adjusted affairs there, anticipating an early announcement that I would be in the State Department. That announcement did not come. Weeks went by. I knew that one of my sponsors was the publisher of the Washington *Post*, Philip Graham, who was very close to Mr. Kennedy. Finally, I called (it was late in December) to ask Phil if he knew the reason for the delay, and he was unable to enlighten me. Another call produced nothing—it was one of those mysteries that go with political transitions. Finally, in January, I flew to Washington to see what the difficulty was. I met Mr. Rusk in his office; he was not very communicative. Finally, when answers were obviously evasive and I pressed him for some explanation, he said, "I suspect it would be a good idea for you to talk to Mr. Rayburn." I assumed that he was supplying all the information that I needed. Obviously my Arkansas opposition had reached Mr. Rayburn and my nomination was being held up by the Speaker.

A heavy snow, the snow that had made the Kennedy inauguration so miserable, was on the ground. I could not get a cab, but I had called Speaker Rayburn's office and he indicated that he would see me that very afternoon. It was about five o'clock then, and the January darkness was descending. I started through the snow from the State Department and walked the mile and a half to Mr. Rayburn's office. I was exhausted, since in places the snow was deep.

Mr. Rayburn was not very cordial. He seemed like a different man from the warm personality I had known for sixteen years in the congressional service. I had resolved, however, to present my position vigorously, and I think the Speaker realized early in our conversation that I was not going to give "them," meaning him and the Faubus organization, an easy out. I told him without mentioning my source, that I was amazed to find that there was opposition from the House side to my appointment.

I told him that I knew my opposition in Arkansas was hostile, but that I would fight for the appointment and that I intended to explore it fully, if for no other reason because of my pride in my national Democratic status. He said, "But you see, Brooks, you're out, and they are in." Frankness was one of Mr. Rayburn's virtues. He added that, yes, he had offered his protest to the appointment. He indicated that he was sympathetic with that resistance because the "ins" are entitled to prevail over the "outs," and I was an "out."

I knew that Mr. Rayburn was aware of the sacrifices I had made to help in the civil rights struggles and to hold the national party together. As reported in a previous chapter, I had been a member of the preconvention platform committee for both the 1952 and the 1956 conventions, and I had accepted that assignment at the request of Mr. Rayburn and John McCormack, then the majority leader. They knew that there were just three or four of us from the South (few having been as sympathetic with civil rights legislation as I had been) who were capable of interpreting each side to the other. I was surprised when Mr. Rayburn told me that Alford in asking him to oppose me had invoked my refusal to help in his campaign for a second term. Mr. Rayburn said, "You wrote letters to your district opposing his nomination." I did not want to make anything of the fact that I had certainly *not* conducted a mail campaign against him. I did remember making a modest contribution to his opponent, Robert Hays Williams, who had been a law partner of my father. I said, "Well, Mr. Speaker, he surely couldn't expect me to write any letters *for* him." And I added, "It seems to me that he has no basis for opposing my appointment to a position that he would have no interest in, since he is not a member of the Foreign Affairs Committee. It is clearly an act of vengeance, and frankly I am surprised that the leadership would entertain it for a moment." I spoke feelingly, "Mr. Speaker, you know better than anyone else how hard I have fought to hold the party together, and the sacrifices I made because, when you asked me to put myself in the middle of the platform discussions in Chicago in two conventions, even abandoning my own campaign for a few days in 1956 to do my part, I did it. You know better than anybody that taking this position did not help me in the emotion-charged politics of Arkansas."

He looked very grave when I hammered at this. He said something then that I thought was revealing, "Well, Wilbur Mills has tried to talk Alford out of it." I wanted to say, "Why didn't *you* talk Alford out of it?

Why should Wilbur Mills be depended on for convincing Alford of any-thing?" He should have said "No" to Alford. This was rather infuriating to me because Mills had been my colleague for sixteen years, and I had never crossed him—I had acknowledged him as a strong political arm of the delegation. But obviously Mills was trapped by the scheme to prevent my confirmation. I doubt that this was very pleasant for him, because he knew that I still had friends in Arkansas and in the Congress, and he had no reason to participate in a vendetta. But he, too, believed in working with the "ins" and depending upon the "outs" to accept what he would call "the rule of politics."

I didn't see it that way, and told Mr. Rayburn so. Finally, with a voice indicating how strongly I felt, I said, "Mr. Rayburn, after my defeat I was appointed by a Republican president to a nine-year term on the Tennessee Valley Authority. In 1955 I was appointed by the Republican administration to membership on the delegation to the United Nations General Assembly. These are honors I've had from our opposition. *I have never received any comparable national honors from my own party.* If this Democratic administration yields to this kind of pressure and commits an affront which would grieve me deeply, I think I have a right to feel that my party—which I've served faithfully—has let me down. And Mr. Rayburn, you are the key to this, because you know what I have sacrificed and what I have done to be a good soldier. I cannot believe that you will leave the record like that, that you will permit the record to stand that I have referred to, that I go out of public life honored at the national level only by the Republican party and receiving a rebuff from the party that I have served so long."

I let it stand at that. I waited for his answer. He looked rather grave. After a moment he stood up and said, "Brooks, it will go through. Don't you worry." My little talk had been effective. As we walked toward the door, he said, "Tell them to send the nomination out, but tell them not to do it until the resolution to raise the Democratic membership on the Rules Committee is acted on next week." I knew that he meant it, and I think I left him happier than when I came. I carried the message to Dean Rusk, and within a few days I was nominated and confirmed.

News that the official appointment had been made was given me by one of my favorite bellmen at the Andrew Johnson Hotel in Knoxville. It was our home during the almost two years that I served on the board, and the entire hotel personnel had become our friends. I was especially interested in this young man named Leon, a student in Knoxville College (a Presbyterian college with a large black enrollment). He was working at odd hours at the hotel to pay his college expenses.

I had been away for several days on a TVA mission. When I returned that morning in January, Leon met me at the door, took my bag, and exclaimed, "Mr. Hays, have you seen the morning paper? You're on the front page!"

"I haven't seen the paper."

"Well, Mr. Kennedy has appointed you assistant secretary of state for congressional relations!"

I confessed that I was pleased. As we rode in the elevator, Leon said, "We'll miss you here, Mr. Hays, but I'm happy for you, and I am not surprised. You see, I don't agree with Plato that the mechanisms of democracy seldom raise the best men to the top."

I said, "Leon, you're full of surprises this morning. Did Plato say that?"

"Yes, he did, Mr. Hays." And then he added a little diffidently, "Sometime when you have a few minutes to spare, I'd like to argue with you about something you said in your book."

It was my turn to grab the initiative. "You'll have to be more specific—I've produced two books." Then I told him about my father's comment after the second book, published by the University of North Carolina Press, appeared. A neighbor had asked, "Mr. Hays, have you read Brooks's last book?" My father would never overlook an opportunity like that. "I hope so!" he said.

When we got to the little suite, Leon deposited my bag and said good-bye. In a few moments, when I was alone, the full significance of the recent turn of events that had closed my congressional career appeared to me with great clarity. What loss I had sustained as one individual was nothing in comparison to the potential loss of opportunity to black Americans. If ten years later this brilliant young man were to still have to carry bags to make a living, the American dream would not have been fulfilled. I am grateful to be able to say that much has changed.

Chapter 13 TENTS OF THE MIGHTY 1961-1963

*If we fulfill the world's hope, it
will be by fulfilling our own faith.*
John F. Kennedy

WHEN I took the oath as assistant
secretary of state on February 1,
1961, I was promptly installed in
a beautiful office in the same corridor with Averell Harriman, Chester
Bowles, and George McGhee, and very close to the suite occupied by
Secretary Rusk.

I found the daily meetings of the staff one of the most exciting things
about my new employment. They were always opened with a statement
from the secretary, after which the experts took over. There was a daily
briefing on the conflicts in Southeast Asia, and then, as we went around
the table, everyone would have something to say about significant happenings affecting his office. I found that the staff came to expect me, in
rendering my report on congressional activities, to spice it up. This I was
glad to do because it was a new audience for the Arkansas folklore that
had come to have a secure place in my thinking and speaking.

I am indebted to my friend Dean Francis B. Sayre of the National
Cathedral in Washington for an interesting characterization. In March,
1975, he was one of the speakers at the annual meeting of the Presbyterian Ministers Fund, the oldest legal reserve company in the United
States. I had served eleven years on the board and was planning to retire.
(The company insures ministers of all faiths.) Dean Sayre said, "Brooks
comes from the Ozark hill country whose people he loves, and he learned
from them that the profoundest ideas are the least pretentious and are

222

best conveyed by the little chariots of anecdote and gentle humor." I hope I can live up to that reference, for humor should never carry a barb, and "one should never dilute the oil of anecdote with the vinegar of fact." (Louis Brownlow's injunction.)

One morning the secretary turned to me and said, "Brooks I want you to see Senator Fulbright today about this matter," and then he detailed the assignment. I sensed the fact that it required his personal attention, and expressed my opinion that this was something he could not delegate to any staff member. I cited biblical authority for this: "You will find that the Bible says, 'Jacob, leaning on his staff, died.' " I don't think that any effort I made that year to entertain the staff was ever more successful than that one. Soon I had a phone call from James Reston of the New York *Times* asking me where that passage was located in the Bible. Fortunately, I was able to tell him he would find it in the eleventh chapter of Hebrews.

During this time I met a large number of speaking engagements. A firm State Department policy, which I helped the legal office work out, prevailed as to honorariums. Among other factors it was agreed that total honorariums should not exceed five thousand dollars in a single year. Special situations grew out of the numerous requests from congressmen for me to speak in their home districts. Some were obviously in the line of official duty and, of course, I accepted no honorariums in such cases.

Senator Styles Bridges, a leading Republican, once asked me to substitute for him at (of all things!) a meeting of the Republican Women of his home state of New Hampshire. He detected a bit of partisan glee in my acceptance but he said, "I trust you." It was not difficult to speak of a bipartisan foreign policy under those circumstances.

On the other hand there were some urgent requests from former colleagues and others that I give some talks of a humorous and philosophical nature to constituents' groups wholly unrelated to foreign affairs, and modest honorariums could therefore be accepted. The five-thousand-dollar limit for honorariums disarmed any critics who might suggest that financial considerations were diverting me. I viewed this limited extracurricular activity as having a public-relations value since congressional goodwill was involved.

The State Department's experience in the period I am covering here would be helpful in the recently stimulated studies of political ethics. The prodding of conscience in such matters, in both public and private sectors, is wholesome. Washington newsmen enjoyed the cynical comment of Groucho Marx on one politician's performance: "He thinks ethics is an old automobile, and scruples is a new Italian dish."

Secretary Rusk maintained high standards regarding gifts and honorariums. Also, he was extremely careful not to accept invitations to address segregated audiences. I followed the same course. I recall that the secretary refused to speak at a convention of his college fraternity because of this policy. A Georgia member of Congress once asked me to find out if the secretary would allow friends in his boyhood home town to present him with a suit manufactured in a new plant there when he spoke at a homecoming. There was a courteous "No" with thanks. Both were transmitted through me as his congressional liaison officer.

In 1961 I received an invitation to address the annual meeting of the Alabama Bar Association. I was pleased, of course, because while I had had some important speaking engagements in Alabama prior to the Little Rock school desegregation crisis, I realized that I was not popular in the state, for it was politically dominated by the segregationists. I wanted to accept but I thought I should seek the advice of my old colleague, Albert Rains, one of the leaders of the Alabama House delegation. Telling him about the invitation, I said, "Al, what should I do?" He replied, "First, you better check it out to make sure it's authentic. It's hard for me to believe you've been invited to speak in Alabama. You know, mothers used to quiet their children at night by frightening them with your name."

I knew, of course, that this was a gentle taunt and was an exaggeration, yet there was enough truth in it to give a concern—but I did accept. However, when the usual request was made of the two houses of the state legislature (then in session) at that time for adjournment to hear my speech, there was objection to the unanimous consent request by one member who said, "I object. I can conceive of nothing that Arkansas integrationist might say that would be of interest to the sound-thinking segregationists of Alabama." It captured big headlines in the Alabama papers and helped swell my audience, one of the largest in the history of the association. They were standing around the walls of the ballroom of the Tutweiler Hotel in Birmingham when I was introduced.

I had prepared a manuscript for clearance with the Public Affairs Office of the State Department in which Carl Rowan, a distinguished black journalist from Minnesota, later our ambassador to Finland, was director. He returned the manuscript with the comment, "This is cleared. It is consistent with the department's policy but it is pretty strong and may get you into trouble in the deep South. If you do get in trouble, I will send help; I will not come myself!"

It produced no trouble whatever, perhaps because while confronting some of the racial aspects of our foreign policy problems, and the relationship to domestic issues having to do with racial justice, I presented my views in my customary style of drawing upon the folklore of the southern mountains. So I was talking to people who had no difficulty with my accent, and appreciated my love of the rural South of which they too were a part. At the end of my talk, I received a tremendous ovation, which naturally moved me deeply since I had had considerable buffetings after my defense of the use of federal troops in the Little Rock crisis.

Following the meeting, I joined my host, Robert Garrison, a Birmingham attorney, to go to the airport. We were three or four floors above the ballroom but already one of the audience had reached that floor and, approaching us as we waited for the elevator, he said to Mr. Garrison, "Did you hear Brooks Hays a while ago?" Mr. Garrison nodded and said, "Yes." He turned to me and said, "Did you hear him?" I said, "Yes, I heard him." He said, "Well, Sir, I don't see how they defeated that bastard." The conversation ended with laughter when I quickly identified myself. He said, "Well, I'll have to stand on that proposition. I don't see how they did." Such public relations assignments were enjoyable, and apparently the president approved of my work in that field.

One of my first visitors was Sargent Shriver, who came to ask my advice about the proposed Peace Corps legislation. I was visited by a few ambassadors and foreign officials of lesser rank, courtesy calls. I believe that at least a fourth of my time was spent on the telephone, discussing matters with representatives and senators. I did not regard these as trivial, but they constituted the kind of requests that I could refer to my able staff. One staff member was my long-time associate Warren Cikins, who had come from Harvard to my congressional office in 1956 as an intern, having been recommended by another intern, H. Bradford Westerfield, later a distinguished professor of political science at Yale University. Warren lived up to the high recommendations; we had a sort of father-son relationship, because of his youth and his ability to sense my viewpoint, my ideas, and assumptions in political life even before I could phrase them. He had brought to the congressional office good intellectual equipment, having graduated at the Littauer School of Government at Harvard, and having completed practically all of his work for a doctor's degree. When I was defeated, I helped him find other employment on Capitol Hill. Senator Clair Engle of California was delighted to procure his services, and in the Engle office he displayed rare talents in the field of power legislation. He visited me a few times in the Knoxville TVA office, and later his transfer to my staff in the State Department was arranged.

He could see something of my difficulties growing out of the White House staff's making decisions that I believed should be made in the State Department. This was without personal ill will. I had a pleasant relationship with Larry O'Brien and his staff, but I found no way to make my feelings known about the need for a more precise recognition of the authority of the department. On one occasion Secretary Rusk called me to say that a committee was being set up by the White House to go to Capitol Hill for some conferences with legislative leaders, and that the White House thought perhaps I should not go since they did not want the Executive Department group to be too large. He asked what I thought. I was ready with an answer. I said, "Mr. Secretary, you're about to lose control of your legislative program. This would signify that you may have already lost control, because they're telling you whom to take and not to take. While I will, of course, abide by your decision, I do not think it's good from the standpoint of your leadership that you acquiesce in this suggestion." He said, "I see what you mean." And he asked me to go with him.

The first signal I had that members of the White House staff were quietly invading the prerogatives of the State Department came with the appearance on the scene of a brilliant New York lawyer, a young man named Ted Tannenwald, later a member of the Tax Court of the United States and eventually a good personal friend. We had no tensions at any time, but I felt that I should have been consulted before the appointment was made, and certainly should have had some authority in connection with his activity because we were constantly, by the very nature of things, working at cross-purposes. I tried in every way to avoid any conflicts and in this I was fairly successful.

But this was only the beginning. There were other indications that the authority of the department was being eroded, and all of this in the interest of what was regarded as White House efficiency and overall control. From the standpoint of legislative results I could see no basis for a White House complaint regarding our performance. For example, the foreign aid appropriation request went through Congress without a dollar being cut from it, the first and perhaps the only time this has occurred. The difference in White House philosophy and mine was that I was trying to win over the House sub-committee chairman, Otto Passman of Louisiana, and the White House staff was trying to circumvent him. My plan worked. Larry O'Brien was heard to say when he found that Congressman Passman was supporting the emergency request for $500 million for Latin America, "Great goodness! I wonder who in the world did that trick?"

Well, I did that trick. It was a personal conference, a long talk with Otto, my friend in the Congress. Mr. Passman was chairman of the Appropriations Sub-Committee on Latin America, a Louisiana congressman of pronounced conservative temperament, but my personal relations with him were very warm. He was a fellow Baptist and apparently appreciated my church position and responded to the interpretation I gave to international relations in terms of brotherhood and humanitarianism. Although he was at the other end of the spectrum ideologically, he listened attentively and I was as surprised as O'Brien to find that I had made a sale, that Otto was ready to defend this full emergency appropriation because of the potential results for American goodwill in Latin America.

But relations did not improve. I remember that one Sunday night when my daughter and her husband, William E. Bell, were in our home for the night, the phone rang at 1:30 A.M. It was Larry O'Brien wanting to talk with me. My son-in-law said, "But Mr. O'Brien, Mr. Hays is asleep. You don't want me to wake him at this hour, do you?" To which Larry said, "Yes, indeed, I do. Get him to the phone." When I reached the phone, Larry said, "Brooks, I understand you're to see Otto Passman tomorrow to talk about some legislation." And I said, "Yes, I do have an appointment with him at nine o'clock in the morning." Larry said, "Don't fill it. I have reasons for not wanting you to talk with Otto Passman."

In the light of the results of previous talks with him, I felt that I should argue that out with him, so I insisted that Larry was making a mistake in instructing me not to go. But he held his ground, and consequently I canceled the appointment the next morning. I never learned the reason for Larry's decision regarding that engagement. I unhappily record the fact that this evidenced a worsening of the relationship, but again it was impersonal. My relationship with Larry and others of the White House inner circle remained cordial. This has continued to the present. I recognize Larry's masterful handling of political matters and his personal charm. The reason for sticky relations during my year at the State Department still puzzles me.

One of my favorites at the department was a new friend, Roger Jones, an exceptionally competent administrator who had been transferred from the Budget Bureau to the State Department to improve the procedures in our sprawling department. He did a good job, but along with Chester Bowles, competent former congressman and a Kennedy team member, and myself, found that the difficulties occasioned by the White House staff interference I have described were too severe, and so in late November of the same year we three were transferred out of the department. Mr. Bowles became ambassador to India, Mr. Jones returned to the Bureau of the Budget, and I went to the White House as one of the special assistants to the president.

I left with a sense of pride in my part in the legislative innovations such as the establishment of a disarmament agency, the Peace Corps, the Alliance for Progress, and the foreign aid program that took a new turn under President Kennedy.

The news that a change in the department was desired reached me in a phone call from Mr. Rusk. I was in Chicago in late November, 1961, to address the National 4H Club convention. I was told by Mr. Rusk that I could have an appointment as an ambassador in one of the Geneva international offices. Without hesitation I told him, "No, I do not want to leave the country and would not be interested in an ambassadorship." (My good friend Roger Tubby was later given this appointment.) Mr. Rusk asked, "What would you like?" I said, "I'd like to go to the White House and serve on Mr. Kennedy's staff and I know that there is work for me to do there." After my talk with Dean Rusk, I let Philip Graham know about it. It was Philip Graham, with the help of McGeorge Bundy, who arranged for my appointment as one of the special assistants to the president.

The newsmen were justified in speculating that there were differences between me and some of the White House staff, though not with the president—he would hardly retain one on the White House staff who was persona non grata. I never at any time talked with the president himself about the shift, and the only information I had about his continuing warm feelings of friendship for me came from my close friend, Philip Graham. When the public announcement was made, arrangements were completed for my taking the oath of office as special assistant in the president's reception room. It was a great event for the Hayses. Kenny O'Donnell, a close associate of Larry O'Brien and of the president, handled details. The president himself presented me. The oath was administered by my former roommate in George Washington Law School and former law partner in Little Rock, Judge Bolon B. Turner of the Tax Court of the United States.

When the certificate of appointment was handed to me by the president and I was invited by him to make some comments, I thanked him and then said, "Mr. President, you will let me refer to the fact that my wife's mother, ninety-five years of age, is here. And you're familiar with the old saying that back of every achievement is a proud wife and a surprised mother-in-law. She is surprised; she thought I would be the president." The president threw his head back with a typical Kennedy laugh at that effort.

One disappointment about the ceremony was a result of the fact that neither the president nor I knew that standing in the background was a very important figure, Vice President Lyndon B. Johnson. He came up to shake hands with me. It was obvious from the president's expression that he was disappointed that he did not know the vice president was there. He said, "Oh, Lyndon, I didn't know you were here. I would have wanted you to say something." The vice president acknowledged that with an expressionless countenance, so I don't know what he was thinking, but the president's sensitivity bore out my fears that there was some strain between the two, a strain that went back to the preconvention campaign in Los Angeles for the nomination.

I settled down to a wide variety of duties. Lee White, one of my favorites at the big round luncheon table, said, "Brooks, what is the new assignment?" I said, "Well, it has to do with relations: Congressional relations, international relations, federal-state relations, and church-state relations, which I don't mention officially." Lee said, "Everything but poor relations. After the New Deal, you didn't have any poor relations down in Arkansas, did you?" I confirmed it and added, "But during the twenties there were some Hayses struggling with poverty, including me."

A large amount of my time was given to activities with the Commission on Intergovernmental Relations. Warren Cikins, whose monumental services I have alluded to, joined me at the White House as executive assistant on January 1, and that happy relationship was maintained.

I was asked many times by the president and his inner office assistants—O'Brien, Sorensen, O'Donnell, Dungan, and others—to make speeches for the administration. This included some rather important conferences such as the mayors' national meetings and those in which an authentic statement of White House policy was needed. They knew, too, that I had a style for luncheon and dinner meetings that meant emancipation from a manuscript, and at the same time, my experience in Congress had helped develop a technique that would avoid conflicts with Congress.

Surprisingly, my activity in the field of intergovernmental relations was exciting, and I also enjoyed the special assignments from the president's office in church-state relations and even in congressional relations, since in 1962 the reciprocal trade authority would be expiring, and as usual, it required considerable effort to get this important legislation extended. I made a number of speeches across the country for the measure. This came easy because of my enthusiasm (going back to the 1930s when I worked with the Southern Policy Committee) for the elimination of tariff barriers which had worked so tragically against southern agriculture. I had been a Cordell Hull fan from the start. I not only extolled the reciprocal trade idea, but did some footwork on the Hill, carefully coordinating my work with Larry O'Brien's office, which was responsible for congressional relations at the White House level.

One of the most interesting activities during the two years in the White House with Mr. Kennedy had to do with conferences with governors and mayors who were becoming vocal in protesting the domination by members of Congress of "grants in aid" programs. Governor Grant Sawyer of Nevada was chairman of the Planning Subcommittee of the Conference of Governors, and I worked with him to get something of a practical nature done at the highest level to correct the situation. At my request, the president sent a memorandum to all the cabinet members directing them to keep in touch with the governors and the mayors and to supply current information that theretofore had not been given them until after the members of Congress had released the information.

This practice of discriminating against state officials had been damaging to relations between federal and state governments, and it was a topic often discussed in meetings of the Commission on Intergovernmental Relations, of which an old-time friend of mine, Frank Bane, was chairman and William G. Colman the executive director. We worked closely with that commission and had a fine relationship with its staff.

Other groups that were exceedingly helpful in getting better coordination of federal and state functions were the offices of the national organizations of mayors, county officials, and governors. Again, career men were in top positions and I had continuing contacts with them. I refer to Brevard Crihfield of the Council of State Governments, John Gunther of the Conference of Mayors, Bernard Hillenbrand of the County Officers Organization, and Oren Nolting of the International City Managers Association.

Among the friendships growing out of my 1955 service at the United Nations was that of Virginia's former governor, Colgate W. Darden, Jr., who was at that time president of the University of Virginia. In 1963 he suggested that I could be helpful in straightening out situations in some of the English-speaking nations of West Africa where there were educational and welfare programs involving our government. These countries —I refer to Sierra Leone, Liberia, and Nigeria—had all come to appreciate the value of medical and educational aspects of the foreign mission programs of the various churches of the United States. I had personal knowledge, as a former Baptist official, of our great programs in Nigeria, for example, where perhaps half of the total Baptist expenditure for foreign missions was made. The educational leaders of Nigeria were loud in their praise of the mission schools all over that important African nation. With President Kennedy's warm approval, I went to Africa in April, 1963, my wife accompanying me, for about a month, spending a little more than a week in each of the two smaller countries—Sierra Leone and Liberia—and better than a week in Lagos, the Nigerian capital, with side trips into the interior. Marion and I were guests during the entire time in the home of our career ambassador Joseph Palmer, and our friendship with him and his wife, Margaret, began with that visit. Ambassador Palmer arranged for me to meet many of the leading figures in the Nigerian government including the outstanding Prime Minister Balewa, who was later assassinated. I had a good visit with him in his office, and when I made my report to the president, almost the first question he asked was, "Did you see Balewa?" The picture of that distinguished Nigerian statesman hung on the wall of the oval office.

We began our mission at Freetown, capital of Sierra Leone, where my former colleague on the House Foreign Affairs Committee, Albert Sidney J. Carnahan, served as ambassador. Carney, as he was generally known, enjoyed his ambassadorship tremendously and was a very effective representative of our government. Again, he was helpful in arranging conferences with the leading officials of the young republic. I found in Sierra Leone a profound influence of mission work by a relatively small Protestant church—the United Brethren. Mission schools all over Sierra Leone bore evidence that good foundation work for modern education had been done by these dedicated missionaries from the United Brethren Church, one branch of which later consolidated with the Methodists, and they are today a part of the United Methodist Church. Most of the officials of the three republics I have mentioned attended colleges in the United States, and I enjoyed talking about educational problems with them. I did not get to see the prime minister of Northern Nigeria, one of the three areas in the Nigerian Federation whom I had met in Knoxville when I was a member of the TVA Board. I refer to Prime Minister Bello, who was also assassinated at the time that Prime Minister Balewa was killed. However, Prime Minister Bello during a tour of the TVA area had indicated in a press conference in Knoxville that he knew of my interest in race relations and gave a rather surprising answer to one question when a newsman said, 'Have you found anything in America that you could not endorse, or that you could criticize?' (He had expressed warm appreciation for many aspects of American life and praised the TVA). "Yes," he said, "I would say that the failure of the people of Little Rock, for example, to make a good demonstration of how school integration would be accomplished is something that my people deplore." Then the newsman, seeing the prime minister cast a glance in my direction, said, "But Mr. Hays also deplored it, didn't he?" "Of course," said the prime minister, "that's the reason he is here in Knoxville."

If anyone doubts that the black leaders of Africa are well informed regarding the problems of our nation, he should reexamine the situation. In all three nations we made trips into the interior, going as far as two hundred miles to an agricultural high school in Liberia in the province of Zor Zor. I had the privilege of being made an "honorary paramount chief of the tribe of Zor Zor," and enjoyed the ceremony in which robes were ritualistically put on both my wife and myself. We stayed all night at the home of the principal of the agricultural institute, Mr. Queen— graduate of Tuskegee Institute. I remember asking him what part of the

United States he was born in. He said, "I was born in a little town in Arkansas you never heard of." I pressed him for details because, I said, "I've heard of nearly all of them, having made two races for governor." He said, "The town of Atkins in Pope County." I said, "Well, isn't it interesting that the two of us didn't meet until we converged in the heart of Liberia! Because that's where I spent the first five years of *my* life."

I spoke to the students at his school, about fifty young ambitious agricultural students, who were preparing themselves to engage in farm pursuits. I had a litttle difficulty establishing contact, so I decided to resort to an anecdote for the purpose of revealing my concern with the rural problems of the area. It was the old trick, "I'm a country boy myself." I told a story, fictitious, of course, of the Arkansas farmer who went by bus to Memphis to visit his relatives. He found himself in the company of a city man, a salesman (we would refer to him as a "city slicker," a phrase which fortunately has passed out of circulation). The city man said, "Would you like to make some money playing quiz games?"—to which the old gentleman said, "I don't know nothing about them. What are they?" The city man said, "If you can answer questions, you can make money. If I ask you a question that you can't answer, you give me a dollar. But I'll give you a dollar for any questions you ask me that I can't answer." Well, the farmer was too smart for that. He said, "No, I wouldn't be interested. I'm not educated and I can see you are."

To this city man said, "Well, perhaps you'd be entitled to a little advantage. We'll just make it fifty cents for anything I ask you that you can't answer, but you get a dollar if I can't answer your question."

The farmer said, "All right, let's just play the game."

The city passenger said, "You start."

The farmer's question was, "What is it that's got two heads, six wings, two tails and it can't fly a foot?"

The city man pondered the question awhile and finally gave up. He said, "I don't know. Here's your dollar. What is it?"

The old man said, "Well, I don't know either. Here's your fifty cents."

The wild response of these students convinced me that humor, even mediocre humor, has a universal appeal, and with that good start I had no problem holding their attention. I talked about the deep desire of the American people to help build strong economic and educational foundations for their continent.

On our return we stopped in Rome, on October 23, 1963, just a month before the president was assassinated, for the historic visit with the great man that I admired so much, Pope John XXIII. I gave Mr. Kennedy an account of my audience with the head of his church and he chuckled over some of the things that I related. I told him, for example, that we know from the Pope's first words that we were in the presence of a warm-hearted fellow Christian. He said, "Mr. Hays, I know you are a Baptist, and Baptists and Catholics haven't always loved each other as good Christians should, but I am Baptist too, I am John."

He asked about our family and I told him about our son, Steele, a Little Rock lawyer, and Betty (Mrs. William E. Bell), secretary for the Bethesda, Maryland, Baptist Church and informed him that it was her birthday. He asked about my wife's given name and I was about to say "Marion" when the interpreter gave it in Italian, 'Maria," which pleased us, since it is so revered by Catholics. As we were leaving, he said, "It is my practice in my rosary prayers to pray for others by name and I shall pray for you and your family today particularly your daughter on her birthday." His parting statement was, "We are brothers in Christ." I regard that as historic, since he knew of my Baptist roots and certainly knew that his great church had, for centuries, held that "there is no salvation outside the church." It is conceivable that I was the first Baptist to have heard such an encircling declaration by the Church's highest authority, at least one so directly personal.

Later I read that there was deep concern over Pope John's failing health. On that day I walked from our home on Second Street, S.E., across the street to a quiet corner of St. Peter's Cathedral and prayed for him. I prayed, first, that he might be spared and, second, that the redemptive and humanizing influence which had been released by this loving spirit might make an impact upon the world's life. The first petition was not answered in the way I desired, for he died soon after that, but it seems to me that the answer to the other part of the prayer and the prayers of millions was visible in the drawing together of Christian forces and the strengthening of the bonds of understanding and goodwill between all faiths.

There was scarcely a meeting of church leaders who visited Washington through the two years that I was on the president's staff that I was not asked to participate with him and others or represent him in Washington sessions. I also answered some of the mail having to do with church-state relations.

I remember on one occasion that I was asked by Ted Sorensen to help with the text of the talk to be made by President Kennedy at the annual prayer breakfast. In some strange way the signals had been confused, and I did not know until seven o'clock on the proceeding evening, when Miss Evelyn Lincoln called to ask me for the manuscript, that I was expected to work on his talk. I exclaimed in horror that there was no manuscript, that this was the first news I had of it.

I rushed down to the White House and worked until eleven o'clock on the statement for the president. I left it on Mr. Sorensen's desk close to midnight and I know that it reached him because, whereas the talk as actually delivered by President Kennedy was quite different, there were a few phrases he had lifted from my manuscript. His failure to use the exact text was not disappointing. On the contrary, I would have been disappointed if he had followed in exact detail what I had written, since I took pride in his ability to come up with eloquent and original statements of his own on almost any subject.

He was speaking to an ecumenical group, of course. The theological interests of that gathering covered the entire spectrum of religious life, and I was proud that this Catholic president was devoted to the American concept of religious freedom and was so appreciative of the religious foundations for our political life that he could deliver an eloquent statement on that occasion.

He had asked me once, "What kind of Baptist are you, Brooks?" When I told him, "An ecumenical Baptist," he looked quizzical, and I said, "Just say a catholic Baptist, Mr. President, but spell it with a little c. Later I wished I had added, "And I hope that you are a protestant Catholic, spelling it with a little p."

On one of my speaking trips late in 1963 I received a phone call from officials of the National Conference of Christians and Jews asked me to serve as national chairman of the 1964 Brotherhood Program. I immediately called the White House and reached Evelyn Lincoln. I said, "Miss Evelyn, please get word to the president that I am being asked to serve as brotherhood chairman, and will accept if he approves." She promptly replied, "You tell him yourself, Mr. Hays. He's in a cabinet meeting, but there's a phone at his elbow. I know he will want to talk to you." In a split second I heard him say, "Brooks where are you?" I caught the implication. I replied, "In Fayetteville, Arkansas, Mr. President," and I then asked if he approved my accepting. The chairmanship rotates between Republicans and Democrats, and I would succeed Governor Nelson Rockefeller. The president said, "I certainly do approve, and you're the one to do it." Not much else was said, and I record this minor detail in a day's work partly to indicate that President Kennedy was accessible to his staff. Further, to say that it was the last time that I ever talked with him.

In the early fall of 1963, Dr. John O. Gross, of the Board of Education of the Methodist Church, came to my White House office to invite me to speak on Methodist College campuses across the country, suggesting that I ask a month's leave of absence without pay for this purpose. The Methodists would replace my salary. The president thought well of the idea. In his best kidding style, he said, "Brooks, you've already got the Baptists. Are you trying to take over the Methodists, too?" I said, "Mr. President, no one ever had the Baptists, and I find the Methodists are just as difficult." The board trusted me to speak without partisanship, and to help students appreciate and respond to the great outlets in the political vocation for religious idealism. I was scheduled to give lectures on fifteen campuses stretching from Randolph-Macon in Ashland, Virginia, to California Wesleyan in San Diego. The itinerary included several colleges that were predominantly black.

I had only two engagements to fill when President Kennedy was assassinated. Marion and I were in Lakeland, Florida, for a series of lectures at Florida Southern University on that fateful November 22. I had just completed a talk to the local Kiwanis Club on the theme of national unity when the tragic news reached me. We hurriedly terminated all engagements and flew back to Washington.

Early the next day I went to my office across the hall from Dr. Arthur Schlesinger, for whom I had developed a great admiration and a special congeniality. Our reaction to the deep malaise of 1963 was emotional. We were quickly notified that the staff were to serve as honorary pallbearers and to please appear in formal attire. I had to borrow a frock coat and the accessories.

In the rotunda services I stood with Arthur, and a few feet from Mrs. Kennedy and Caroline and John. In the long wait for the ceremony to begin, I whispered to Arthur, "Will you stay on?" He said, "I don't know that the president will want me to." For the first time, the mystic words *the president* had a strange new connotation. It was an eerie feeling. Ted Sorensen just in front turned to say to Arthur, "Yes, he told me he wanted you to remain." A few days later Bill Moyers told me that I, too, would be asked to stay.

That period was a harrowing one for those who loved and admired Jack Kennedy. Only Marion knew how crushed with grief I was over the tragedy. One emerges from a trauma of this kind with few clear recollections of events. I do remember the poignant experience of meeting Ed Murrow on the stairs as we were taking turns for a few brief moments beside the flag-covered casket in the East Room. He was conscious of the fact that he was dying of cancer. His momentary grasp of my forearm conveyed a sadness I have seldom experienced. It symbolized the fact that the world of politics, my world for sixty-five years, would never again be the same.

While I continued to carry the title special assistant to the president, my contacts with the Oval Office were less frequent and were generally through Bill Moyers. Bill had once been referred to by President Johnson as "my protégé," and Bill promptly interjected, "Yours and Brooks's." I clearly recall the beginning of the relationship which sparked Bill's comment to the president. I was the commencement speaker in 1958 at the Baptist Seminary in Fort Worth, and Bill was one of the graduates. He introduced himself after the ceremony and asked if he could drive Marion and me to the airport. I accepted, and during that brief ride together he sought my advice. "I have an important decision to make," he said. "Senator Johnson has asked me to join his staff in Washington—it would involve use of my experience in journalism which has been my sideline. Please help me decide. Should I give up plans for a career as a Christian minister, or do you think the opportunities for leadership in the public service are comparable, or even greater perhaps, than the church role I have planned?"

I gave him a sketchy review of my idea that public or political life can be, if accompanied by dedication, just as significant in a religious sense as a pastoral service. He took the job and has always credited me with aiding him in a tough decision. He carried heavy responsibilities in the Johnson administration and became one of this period's best interpreters of Christian ideals applied to politics.

I appreciated President Johnson's good qualities. He had a dynamic personality and an interest in disadvantaged people of all races, and his position on social and political issues would provide a congenial base for my continued activity. But it did not seem possible for me to continue with the same enthusiasm that I had had with Mr. Kennedy, and although I had detected differences between the new president and myself they were mostly matters of style. As his policies unfolded, however, one difference appeared to be more substantial.

The idea of my becoming Arthur Vanderbilt Professor of Public Affairs at the Eagleton Institute of Rutgers University originated with Donald G. Herzberg, director of the institute and Willard Heckel, dean of the Rutgers Law College. They came to my White House office in February following President Kennedy's assassination and renewed the invitation to accept the professorship. I had declined it in the spring of 1959 following my 1958 defeat, but after Mr. Kennedy's death I was prepared to change jobs.

I found the work at Rutgers University exciting. It was there that I was able, with my wife's help, to complete the book that was published finally by Macmillan in 1968, *Hotbed of Tranquility.*

The Eagleton Institute had been financed by a remarkable couple, Dr. and Mrs. William Eagleton, and was a product of their feeling that the physical sciences had been favored over the social sciences in the current philanthropies. Their fortune, or at least part of it, had been derived from the medical profession, and thus their sponsorship was unique. The one-year course for a limited number of twenty fellows led to a master's degree; and one requirement, assuming their undergraduate grades were acceptable, was that they would commit themselves either to run for elective office or devote a certain period of time following completion of the course to service in the office of a member of Congress or some other elected official. The course was designed to improve the quality of service by elected officials and to prepare young men and women for careers of this kind. Consequently, it did prove, as I had hoped from the outset, to be a very fine adventure in teaching.

I became acquainted with the New Jersey Democratic political leaders, notably Dave Wilentz of South Amboy, who suggested that in due time I seek one of the New Jersey congressional seats if there should be an opening. It never came.

Marion enjoyed it too. She had a happy and informal way of conversing with students and politicians from both parties who visited Eagleton.

When a press conference was conducted to introduce me to the New Jersey press she surprised me with an interjection in answer to one of the first questions: "Mr. Hays, it appears from the university blurb that you are a lawyer, a politician, an author, a churchman, and now you're becoming a professor. If we asked the real Brooks Hays to stand, who would rise?" Before I could give them the honest answer—"the politician"—she confused them further by chirping up, "Just an Arkansas social worker." I was interested in her comment because I had realized that in my law practice at Russellville after we married she had seen me often diverting my energies from the law practice to work for improved agricultural conditions, or in the field of health and education. She never complained about it, and perhaps her comment indicated she was pleased with that part of my history. Another question was, "Mr. Hays, how many brothers and sisters do you have?" And when I replied, "None, but I have forty-three cousins and I love every one of them," she again interjected a comment. "Yes, he even searched out some of mine that I never heard of, and he loves them too."

Early in 1966 about the time I completed my assignment at Rutgers, I received a phone call from Bascom D. Tally of Bogalusa, Louisiana. He was at that time president of the Louisiana State Bar Association and an outstanding civic leader. He informed me that he, with five other citizens of Bogalusa, had concluded that one way to relieve racial tensions in their city was to invoke the aid of the church people of that community. Joined with Mr. Tally were Paul Gillespie and Jerry Chance, Baptist ministers, Bruce Shepherd, an Episcopal minister, Ralph Blumberg, the owner and manager of a radio station, and Louis Major, the publisher of the Bogalusa *Daily News*. Mr. Tally was the spokesman for the group. They wanted me to come as a former president of the Southern Baptist Convention and one who favored the moderate approach to racial problems to counsel with the leaders of the various churches.

Bogalusa was being plagued by the same type of threatened violence that overwhelmed the cities of Little Rock and Selma. They felt there was an appeal in my position as a former member of Congress and a responsible Baptist official that would be helpful. I accepted at once. But no sooner had the announcement been made than the Ku Klux Klan became active. The mimeograph machines were busy turning out diatribes against me, and the Klan issued the kind of threat that ordinarily would have resulted in some arrests, since the appeal to violence was very clear. The bulletins, among other things said, "Mr. Hays is a known intergrationist [sic] and anyone going to hear him will be delt [sic] with accordingly." This action created new tensions and I could understand why the committee decided to take a second look at their plans. While they were debating the question as to whether the invitation should be withdrawn or not, Governor McKeithen got into the picture and issued a statement saying that "Mr. Hays should not come to Louisiana," that they needed no help from "an outsider." He also tried to make capital out of the fact that other states including the one which I represented in Congress had troubles that should be engaging me, and that Louisiana should not be "picked on." He was asked about this in a press conference by a newsman. "Governor, do you mean that Mr. Hays, a former congressman and president of a great religious organization, would not be welcome in Louisiana?" "Oh, no," he said—and here, of course, he was in an ambivalent position—"Mr. Hays would be welcome in our state." But the import of his first statement was clear. The committee, fearing violence, withdrew the invitation and, naturally, at all stages I followed their feelings sympathetically.

A year later in the city of Williamsburg, Virginia, at an assembly of students from southern colleges, at the end of the keynote speech which I had been asked to deliver, a student rose and asked the privilege of the platform, identifying himself as a representative from Louisiana State University. In an appealing speech he presented a certificate to me signed by the governor of Louisiana, John J. McKeithen, the same governor who had told me not to come into Louisiana. It confirmed honorary citizenship in that great state. The response of the students was heartwarming. I have no explanation of the governor's apparent change of attitude.

During the two-year tour at Rutgers I was able to enjoy more frequent contacts with the officials of the National Conference of Christians and Jews in New York City. Among them was the late Mr. Samuel Leidesdorf who was a well-known, self-educated civic and business leader in New York. He once told Marion and me about Dr. Albert Einstein's coming to Princeton Institute of Higher Learning, on whose board he served. He asked one of his staff to go to London to talk to Dr. Einstein, with authority to finance a trip to New York to discuss terms of a professorship. The great man agreed, and he came to New York with the aide. Mr. Leidesdorf told Dr. Einstein that his mere presence on the campus would be a valuable addition to the institute, and he would have only such duties as he would impose upon himself.

Mr. Leidesdorf described this greatest scientist of the century as follows. His coat and trousers (not matched) were patched at the elbows and knees, and his shoes apparently had never had a shine. What followed revealed something of the reason for his shabby attire. In response to "We will pay you $15,000 a year," Einstein asked, "Mr. Leidesdorf, vat vould I do vid all dat money?" This renowned mathematician and physicist could not even keep his expense accounts and personal records in understandable form. When Mr. Leidesdorf examined his schedules and in order to help him with investments asked about certain entries, Dr. Einstein inquired, "Vats de matter, Mr. Leidesdorf, did I do something wrong?" He could crack the mystery of nuclear power but he could not keep his accounts straight. The brainiest scientists in the world could not always understand him, but they were awed by his presence. His sponsor did us a great service bringing him to our country and establishing him in the modest home on the edge of the rolling grounds of Princeton.

Shortly after a new House committee on ethics began its work in 1967, the committee under the chairmanship of Melvin Price of Illinois asked me to serve as a consultant. The creation of the committee grew out of congressional recognition of the widespread public demand for action in this area. A bipartisan approach was agreed upon with an equal number of committee members from each side of the aisle. A seasoned legislative expert, John Swanner, was chosen staff director and won the confidence of the committee. He and the members worked on guidelines for standards of official conduct. It was a pioneering work, testing the skill of both the committee and staff. My contribution was a modest one and was made chiefly through the director's office, although I did have a part in the preparation of the final report.

There was obviously a need for consensus at that stage in meeting demands for high standards. The question of disclosing certain fiscal matters that might relate to conflict of interest proved to be difficult. The final decision reflected a proper balancing of two factors: (1) the public's right to know and (2) the rights of privacy. If, however, conflict of interest appears, rights of privacy have to give way. As a result of the committee's labors there is now a requirement for full disclosure to the committee where conflicts of interest are involved and limited disclosure to the public. As experience and equity point the way improvements can be made in the elimination of conflicts of interest. The outstanding results of the committee's work was the establishment of a permanent House committee with an appropriate name, "Committee on standards of Official Conduct." In unprecedented action the committee has exposed irregularities, and recommended to the House censure or reprimands for a half dozen or more members.

Remaining for comprehensive legislative attention are the problems of election procedures and lobbying practices. The House gave to the House Administration Committee jurisdiction over campaign practices rather than conferring that authority upon its new and permanent ethics committee. The Administration Committee had an able chairman, Frank Thompson of New Jersey who succeeded Wayne Hays of Ohio.

I suppose that a "public person"—and after a half century of politics I can claim to be "public"—never turns completely loose from his legislative concerns. There was a lift of spirit each time when a House or Senate committee in my "retirement" period indicated that my testimony on pending legislation would be welcome.

I recall at least four occasions when I did occupy the witness chair: (1) addressing the House Agriculture Committee in support of liberalization of the food stamp program, stressing the hardships of the low-income groups; (2) sharing White House experiences as an advisor in federal-state relations with a joint committee studying these problems (presided over by Senator Edmund Muskie); (3) offering suggestions to a Senate committee regarding the tightening up of legislation affecting tax-exempt foundations, this a result of my service on a House Select Committee's survey of the problems; (4) suggesting certain amendments to Senator Sam Ervin's bill to limit the president's power to impound appropriated funds (some of which were embraced by the committee).

The audience at such hearings may regard the kind and gracious words of sitting members that are extended toward a former colleague who occupies the witness chair as "ointment," but we old teammates derive great satisfaction from this display of the fraternity spirit.

Chapter 14 HOMING PIGEON 1966

Two chief concerns of every person, even in the later years, are peace of mind and creative work.
Grove Patterson

MY work at the Eagleton Institute ended in the spring of 1966, but I was still serving as a consultant for President Johnson with occasional trips to Washington. I also accepted an assignment from the National Council of Churches to be chairman of a special study of what was called the "Delta Mission"—an effort to improve poverty conditions in the black communities of Mississippi.

We were in the midst of one of these studies in Jackson when I received a call from an old friend, Bill Penix, an attorney of Jonesboro, who told me that he thought the time was right for me to make another race for governor of Arkansas. I agreed to think about it, and that's all it took to get a front-page story in the *Arkansas Gazette*. I was on my way then to making an important decision regarding further activities in the Arkansas political arena. I was inspired partly by the feeling that the mood of the Arkansas electorate had changed considerably since 1958, and that the forces of moderation might prevail. It appeared that the extremists were in disarray, and that the better influences in the racial area were prevailing. Further, I suppose that I had never entirely given up the ambition to be govenor of the state where I had been so deeply involved. They never go back to Pocatello, but they never quit dreaming that someday they *will* go back.

I made a trip to Little Rock to talk to some of the local leaders, par-

243

ticularly Marlin Hawkins, whose leadership as sheriff of Conway County was impregnable, and whose influence outside that county was well recognized. He told me of a conversation he had had a few days before with Governor Faubus. They were sitting in the Capitol restaurant when the governor said, "Marlin, who could beat Winthrop Rockefeller?" Marlin said, "Well, I have one name to suggest, and don't throw this glass of water in my face when I tell you who it is." He smilingly put it that way because he had not forgotten, of course, and he knew the governor had not forgotten, the circumstances of my 1958 defeat. Marlin said, "Brooks Hays."

"Well," the Governor said, "I won't throw water on you, and I may surprise you by saying I have no animosity toward him. But Brooks ought to talk to us. Why don't you tell him to come to see me?"

This, of course, called for meditation and consultation. To become beholden to Governor Faubus would make me a surrogate candidate, a status I would never consider. I talked to Steele, as well as to Marlin Hawkins and several friends whose judgment I trusted, not only in practical politics but in the moral aspects of such strategy. We came up with this conclusion: Governor Faubus was the titular head of the Democratic party; and since I would run as a Democrat, I would not be involving myself in his personal politics to meet with him to tell him what I had in mind.

I did call him a few days later. He said, "I'll meet with you at the mansion," and within a few minutes, I was with him again in the room that had become very familiar during the conversations when I was working out the conditions for his meeting with President Eisenhower at Newport in September, 1957. The maid, who brought a cup of coffee to me before the governor came in, recognized me, and she seemed pleased to have a glimpse of me again, which indicated, though she said nothing that the governor would have been offended by, that this black employee of the governor appreciated my position in that unhappy episode of 1957.

The governor was not effusive, but his old charm was evident as he gave me a friendly handshake and sat down. I got to the point pretty quickly, but not until he had told me about his recent well-publicized appearance with President Kennedy at the dedication of the Greers Ferry Dam. He said that he had not been as kind to the president as the president had been to him, and there were some implications in the same vein with reference to his relationship with me. I got the idea without his being overt about it that he felt some faint remorse in letting Claude Carpenter and others launch the Alford campaign against me.

The substance of my comments to him was, "I think I will make the race for governor this year. It will not be a pro-Faubus campaign and it will not be an anti-Faubus campaign. I do have ideas about the state, some of which you would disagree with; but if the Democratic party is to merit the confidence of the people, there are some things to be done that I believe I can do. At any rate, I am ready to make the effort."

He said, "Well, I intend to stay out of it, of course, except I could not support Jim Johnson for the nomination." And we talked about that. Jim Johnson had lost much of the old-line support by reason of his extremism in racial matters. That was about the only enlightenment I had on personal preferences from the governor. He was interviewed later by a newsman, and what he said publicly was quite consistent with what he had said to me at the mansion that day. The headlines were, "Faubus says, without committing himself, that Hays is the strongest candidate."

Before I made a final decision, we arranged for John Kraft, a professional poll taker, to conduct a poll, and he came up with the answer that there was considerable name recognition in my case, and that while there was also considerable strength for Johnson, it appeared that I could defeat Winthrop Rockefeller and Johnson could not. Still, it was not an easy decision. I knew it would involve hardships for many of my friends, particularly for my son who had a law practice that took all of his time, and this would be diversionary and would, of course, be felt in terms of a lower income from his practice. He was inclined to think that I should do it, that I owed it to those who had ambitions for me, including many people in other southern states and elsewhere. They would receive, in his words, "a big lift" from a victory for me in Arkansas.

One thing that distressed me, however, was the possible effect on my personal relationship with Rockefeller. We were friends, and I had at every opportunity expressed appreciation of what he had done for the state's industrial development. I recognized his concern for Arkansas progress and his ambition to be governor. I would not enjoy defeating Winthrop Rockefeller, but I was thinking in terms of getting the Democratic party in Arkansas on a better base, a more democratic base, and with complete elimination of the racial feelings which had done so much to cloud the political mood and thwart the advancement of disadvantaged people of Arkansas.

After my decision was made, one of the first things I did was to call Winthrop. I located him in Texas on a cattle-buying tour, and I broke the news to him very quickly. I said, "Win, I'm calling to give you some information that you should have, and you're almost the first friend outside my immediate circle to get this news. I have decided to run for the Democratic nomination for governor."

He did not say anything for a long moment. Then he said, "I think you're making a mistake," and I said, "Well, I would expect that to be your reaction and I'm glad, because I would assume that you had the same feeling of friendship for me that I certainly entertain for you. But," I added, "I am trying to do for my party what you have done for yours, that is, give it a better base, a more reliable and a better moral tone. If I am the Democratic nominee, as you, of course, are bound to be for the Republicans, we can conduct an old-fashioned, friendly, and impersonal campaign and not allow it to mar our friendship."

I think I took time to refer to the Taylor brothers of Tennessee, the gubernatorial campaign at the turn of the century between Alf Taylor, the Republican nominee, and Bob Taylor, the Democratic nominee. The Taylors went through the campaign together touring the state, presenting different views on public policy, and giving a demonstration of what can be done when men of good will work together, even with conflicting political ambitions. Later, I told Winthrop about the incident in a Tennessee town where Bob Taylor said, "Now my friends, I hope all of you know how much I love my brother, Alf. It's just his party that I oppose. When I think of the difference between the party he represents—the Republican party—and the party I represent—the Democratic party—I think of an eagle typifying the Democrats: the eagle soars above us piercing the clouds and flying into the blue ether high above the earth, its mighty wings sustaining it, compared with a little English sparrow resting on the lowest rail of a worm fence. That's the Republican party."

When they got home that night, Alf started to pack his valise. Bob said, "What's the matter, Alf?" His brother responded, "Well, I promised Mama when we left home that if you made a fool of yourself, and I got mad, I'd come straight home. And that's what I'm doing." Bob apologized. Alf said, "Okay, I'll stay, but don't you ever call me a sparrow again."

I had the usual press conference arrangement for making the announcement, which received good publicity, and there seemed to be a lot of interest in my decision to make this final drive for a place in the political sun. It had been thirty-six years since I had made a state-wide race, and I presume it is worth a footnote in political history that this is unique —I doubt if any other person in the fifty states ever made two early races, and then waited thirty-six years before a third race for the governorship, although I have known of men being elected governor on third and even fourth campaigns. (LaFollette of Wisconsin and Richards of South Carolina were elected on their fourth tries.)

I remained in Little Rock, laying the basis for an active campaign. On the following Sunday when I was alone at the Sam Peck Hotel, I had a visit from my old friend Bill Penix, who had influenced me in making the decision to run. He was bearing bad news. He said he had just come from the home of Frank Holt, associate justice and former attorney general of the state, and a very popular person. Frank had told him he had decided to make the race for governor himself. This was disconcerting because it meant that Holt would take some of the moderate vote from me, although he had not identified himself with the minority groups aspiring to civil rights that had been denied them under Faubus. He was known to be friendly with some of the political leaders who had been active in Faubus' campaigns. The information we later got about the pressures on Justice Holt indicated that five leaders representing such special interests as bonds, liquor, and printing urged him to enter the race. Evidently, those interests knew that they had little influence with me, and they had not been attracted by my type of leadership. At the same time, being reluctant to give up the advantages they had in the Faubus administration, these particular individuals influenced Justice Holt to try to fulfill his long-held aspiration to be governor. There were probably no overt agreements regarding advantages to be acquired by any of the five under his administration if elected, but he was the type who would certainly not be crusading in any of the areas that affected them. From their point of view Holt would be almost an ideal candidate, considering his wide acquaintances and his long friendship with the Faubus intimates. Justice Holt and I had been on good terms, and he had told me in one of the election years while I was congressman that he decided not to oppose me, primarily because he did not want to run against someone he respected as much as he did me. So, we entered the campaign with friendly attitudes, and perhaps each of us was conscious of the fact that if one were eliminated in the preferential primary, the other would wind up supporting him, in view of the fact that the other strong candidate was Justice Jim Johnson, whose racist views were intolerable.

The weekend was a dreary one. It rained all day Saturday and Sunday. I was away from Marion, who had remained in Washington to arrange things in our home there so she could be with me in Arkansas for the campaign. Robert Hays Williams of Russellville (no relative), my father's law partner for many years, and Marlin Hawkins came to see me that Sunday afternoon and we explored the situation. We were shaken by the Holt announcement, and at one stage I remember suggesting that with that turn of events, having lost the opportunity to be the only challenger of Johnson and to be the reconciling force leading to a united Democratic party, perhaps I should withdraw from the race. They promptly squelched this idea; of course, having announced, I should not show the white feather—unless this was in accordance with the views of those who had to carry the burden of the campaign.

So we went into the campaign with a handicap; but I felt encouraged when I found that many young people were responding to my appeal, and that I had considerable popular following throughout the state, the remnants of previous races including my seven years' service on the Democratic National Committee. The tone of my campaign was about what it had been in previous state races, except that this time there was no incumbent to oppose. It was a wide-open race.

Other candidates appearing after the Johnson, Holt, and Hays announcements were: Raymond Rebsamen, a Little Rock businessman, and Dale Alford, who had defeated me in 1958. Another candidate was Kenneth Sulcer. When he was asked if he were not running himself, which of his opponents he would like to see win, he promptly said, "Mr. Hays."

One whose candidacy seemed to lack logic was Sam Boyce, who had made an unsuccessful race for attorney general, but his campaign was damaging to me because for some strange reason certain reporters on the *Arkansas Gazette* staff favored Boyce. However, the *Gazette*, as expected, did give my candidacy favorable editorial notice.

My campaign style in the preferential primary was quite different from the one I would have adopted had I been able to make the runoff, with Jim Johnson, because of the wide differences in our views on the race question. I conducted a quiet campaign, stressing my experience in the Congress and as an assistant attorney general in earlier days, and my identification with reform movements of the past. I talked about the state's need for a more progressive Democratic party, but everyone recognized that my appeal was somewhat muted because I was holding my fire until the runoff when we would have only two candidates for the nomination. I was under the onus of avoiding fragmenting the party, and at the same time not repudiating my political past. Justice Holt followed pretty much the same path, and I presumed that his organization had reached the conclusion that the decisive period of the campaign would be the runoff.

I had at the outset of the campaign the advantage of outspoken public support from such highly respected leaders as the lieutenant governor of the state, Nathan Gordon, who agreed to manage my campaign. Others were old-time friends who had helped me win the Congress race in 1942 and who had confidence in my ability to provide a new direction for the state. One who identified himself with me for the first time was E. Grainger Williams, who had supported Mr. Terry in the campaign for Congress in 1933, but who believed in my philosophy and who seemed happy to "atone" for the opposition he had given me in the first race for Congress. I have mentioned Marlin Hawkins: He attracted to the campaign many of the county judges and sheriffs whose confidence he had won in his long service in Conway County. He had a very good sales talk. He was known as "an organization man," but he had never represented to his political friends that I would be a vehicle for any group interest. He said that there would be "no bosses" if I were elected.

Another one of my active supporters was Lewis J. Johnson, better known as "Red" Johnson, who headed the Farmers' Union for many years, and he was particularly effective among the county officers and rural leaders. He knew of my interest in the farm cooperatives and rural electrification projects and all matters affecting the welfare of rural people. I am sure he was aware that his support had the approval of the union's national president, my greatly admired friend, Jim Patton.

Another active worker was a young priest, Father J. Bruce Streett, Jr., of Camden, whose father had been one of my warm supporters in the earlier races for the governorship. Father Streett probably acted on his own without any permisison from the Catholic officials, but in any event, there was no interference by the hierarchy. This is understandable, in view of my ecumenical commitment and my concern for the Catholic minority's rights, beginning with the Ku Klux Klan days.

Steele spent most of his time in headquarters, directing the activities of volunteers, many of whom were college and high school students—a few blacks among them. He was an assistant to Mrs. Irene Samuel, who had been drafted as overseer of the campaign. She was ideal for this job, ably assisted by Sarah Murphy.

One morning I went into headquarters merely to let them know that I would be in town a few hours, as most of my time, of course, was spent campaigning. Father Streett and Steele were alone at headquarters, beginning the day's chores. I greeted them, "Good morning, Father, good morning, Son." With that, the priest looked up and said, "Good morning, Holy Ghost." This was typical of the young Catholic leader, who felt, I presume, that we were all members of the larger religious community that made differences between Southern Baptists and Arkansas Catholics inconsequential. He boasted to fellow Catholics that I had had the privilege of private audiences in the Vatican with both Pope John and Pope Paul, the only Protestant layman to have had that privilege.

Among my active supporters, a man who had considerable imagination in charting the campaign was a law partner of former governor Sidney McMath–Henry Woods. Henry worked out a plan for bringing to the state the facilities of Charles Guggenheim, the film expert, to produce a film for our use. It was an expensive film, but we decided the cost was justified. Mr. Guggenheim was enthusiastic over my campaign, and he gave us a bargain rate for the film. He sent his crew to Arkansas, and they spent two or three weeks in the preparation of it. It covered the story of my early life in Pope County, with scenes from the Arkansas River Valley which had commanded so much of my interest.

Before concluding this account of the preferential primary, which ended so disappointingly in my placing third, I must make reference to my talk with President Johnson. I had advised him of my decision to go back to Arkansas to make the campaign for governor. He asked the White House photographer to take a picture of our farewell handshake, but about all he said was, "Now, Brooks, don't involve me in your campaign." Still, I believe that he would have been happy to have his old staff member elected governor. At least, we had followed very much the same philosophy and concern for the disadvantaged, being particularly congenial in the struggle of the racial minorities for civil rights. He had made public reference to my contribution to this cause. However, I have reason to believe that when the Faubus forces determined to place Justice Holt in the race, they got word to the Johnson administration, perhaps to

President Johnson himself, that there must be no help of any kind coming from the White House to my campaign.

I was not perturbed by this development, since I did not want to be regarded as a national administration candidate. In fact, I had concluded by then that escalating the Vietnam War was wrong, and while the issue was not involved in the race for governor, it was a matter that I was beginning to feel strongly about. What I did regret were the apparent signals given to some friends in Texas who were within the circle of the Johnson influence that personal contributions should not be made to my campaign. This was ironic, since in almost every speech that Jim Johnson made in his virulent attack upon me, he was saying, "Hays is Lyndon's boy." This was to Jim Johnson's advantage and he knew that I was helpless, for I certainly did not propose to disavow President Johnson, regardless of the conflicts to which I have alluded. Jim Johnson's worst reference to me, however, involved my position in the Central High School desegregation events. He termed me "that old Quisling."

I found it surprisingly easy to accept the frustration of a third defeat for governor. I knew from the outset that it was a risky undertaking; but one thing that had motivated me was that if I could reestablish myself politically in this fashion, it would open additional doors of opportunity for my kind of leadership in the South which had commanded so much of my energies for two generations.

One of the most gratifying aspects of the campaign was to witness for the first time in my Arkansas experiences enthusiastic and substantial political leadership supplied by the black community. I had often pointed to the fact that in my 1942 race for Congress, when I was first elected, I did not receive help from the black community. For years my student audiences seemed shocked at my words: "Not a single Negro voted for me!" But I would add, "Not a single Negro voted, period!" This was before the Supreme Court banned the white primary.

I was elected to Congress (in the Democratic primary, which in those days was decisive) with only 16,000 votes. My opponent received 12,500 votes so the total cast was only 28,500. In the election of 1958, in which I I was unseated, 61,000 votes were cast. This tremendous increase was due largely to repeal of the poll tax, and to the admission of black Democrats to participation in the primary. It was an extremely wholesome development in which I took great delight.

I recall with much pleasure visiting many black communities in 1966, speaking in church buildings, in school houses, and sometimes out in the open. Speaking one night in a church house in Desha County with the usual enthusiastic response from my black supporters, I observed the chairman and the ushers handing everyone palm leaf fans, and before presenting me, the chairman mentioned something that I had already observed, namely, the presence of mosquitoes. He said, "We have a lot of welcome admirers for our candidate for governor, and we also have some unwelcome visitors which I hope he'll be able to fight off while he speaks." This ability to smile at their adversities that most black people have was observed by me with mixed feelings because this should not have been taking place in a nation that had moved upward so rapidly in personal incomes. I realized that the new prosperity was not getting down to all of the rural communities.

During the campaign the pastor of the First Baptist Church of Pine Bluff, the largest city in the plantation country, Dr. John McClanahan, called to say he was inviting all of the candidates for governor to appear in the assembly room, not the sanctuary, of his church for a question and answer period. He hoped I would come. I did go, and two of the other six candidates appeared. It was in this session that I was asked about the guidelines for integration issued by the Department of Health, Education, and Welfare—an explosive topic. The questioner bristled and made a comment to the effect that the federal government ought to keep its hands off Arkansas schools. I dropped any inhibitions that I might have exhibited at first, and said, "Regardless of how one feels on this subject, it seems to me that the course of justice and common sense is to cease our dallying, and get down to the business of making sure that educational advantages are fully equalized, and that the injustices of the past are corrected, and corrected promptly. We will feel better about it if we will stop carping about any technical mistakes that the departments in Washington make, and just busy ourselves as fair-minded people should, for I know that the people of my state are a fair-minded people."

My outburst (and such spontaneous things do happen occasionally in political meetings) drew applause from a community that had considerable race consciousness since it lies in the heart of what is called the "black belt" of Arkansas. Moreover, after the campaign was over, I had the satisfaction of having the spokesman for one of the other candidates identify himself, and say, "Mr. Hays, I had never met you, and I had the usual feelings about the federal government, but I admired your answer very much and I wish you would run for governor once more so I could vote for you."

I carried Pine Bluff, but by a narrow vote. It did enable me, however, to say that I have never lost that city, although I never carried the county in which it is located in a governorship race. My plurality in one race was one vote.

It was evident as the primary approached that Jim Johnson had pulled ahead with his "divide and conquer" tactics, and that Judge Holt had probably edged ahead of me. I knew when I went home near midnight of the election that I would not be in the runoff. I had my usual eight hours' sleep and got down to the headquarters around nine o'clock the next morning. Mrs. Samuel said, "We haven't forgotten that you asked us not to be unhappy, so we're taking it in stride. All of us, that is, except the young people. Some of them are weeping, and I just wonder if there is anything you can say that will make them feel better. They aren't as hardened as we old-timers are." I said, "Well, perhaps I can help. Let me meet with them at two o'clock."

They were college and high school students working for me during the vacation period, generally without compensation, although there was a small expense allowance for a few. Young men and women, black and white, sat around me. I think I can recall substantially what I said to them, after warm thanks for their work: "I understand why you feel as you do about our defeat. You wanted to see me ride in the big car at the head of the parade. You wanted to hear the band play in my honor. You wanted to hear people call me 'Governor Hays.' You wanted to come to the mansion to greet me as chief executive and to see me not only enjoy these honors but to have a chance to do some things for Arkansas that you thought I could do. It will never be. I will never be governor. But these are baubles! The important thing is that we see politics as a great adventure in human service. That whether as officeholders or as citizen-voters, as doorbell ringers, participants at the precinct level, or higher, all of us will be doing what we can for an incorruptible government, for a dynamic and useful government that concerns itself with healing wounds, and with attending to the needs of people, particularly of disadvantaged people. From this activity can come real inner peace and happiness. I covet that for all of you. Now I would like to think in this group are future mayors and legislators, congressmen, and conceivably a president of the United States. It would be a lot of fun to greet one of you in the White House some day as 'Madame President.' Who knows?"

And I added this (it was prior to Martin Luther King's famous speech in Memphis about "the promised land")—"I will never run for governor again, but I have had the privilege of standing on a high place and looking over into the promised land. I cannot possess it, but I'm quite sure that whether you fully possess it or not, you will live long enough to penetrate it. You will realize many of the hopes that I have painted. You will be able to accomplish some of the things that I had hoped to accomplish. So there is joy enough for me in viewing the promised land, in holding to the fervent and positive hope that you will possess it."

One final footnote for that 1966 campaign. There were six counties in the congressional district that I represented at the time of my defeat in 1958 by Dale Alford; and in this 1966 campaign in which we both were candidates, I ran ahead of him in every one of those six counties. In the state as a whole, I ran 11,000 ahead of him. It was clear that the mood of the people was changing.

Chapter 15 PLEASANT INTERLUDE 1967

I know no South, no North, no East, no West. The Union, Sir, is my country.
Henry Clay

SOON after the 1966 Democratic primary, which led to the nomination of Arkansas' most outspoken racist, Jim Johnson, virtually assuring Winthrop Rockefeller's election as governor, I was tendered an appointment as visiting professor of government at the University of Massachusetts. The appointment was recommended by a distinguished political scientist, Dr. William C. Havard, graduate of Louisiana State University and head of the University of Massachusetts' government department. This "invader" from the South made it easy for me to establish rapport with the yankees.

In Amherst, Marion and I resided in the faculty club building, said to be the oldest structure in western Massachusetts. We loved the tone of college life in that area. Everything about it seemed appealing, even though the second-floor apartment that we occupied had a low ceiling and slanting beams on which I bumped my head several times a day until I learned how to dodge them. The house was erected in 1724 and had frame work of hand-hewn timbers of tremendous size. The original building probably looked very primitive but I accepted the story that the 1966 building stood on the same foundations and was framed by those same powerful timbers.

In Amherst and nearby Northampton areas people liked to point out the homes of Emily Dickinson, Robert Frost, Chief Justice Harlan Stone, Henry Steele Commager, Calvin Coolidge, and a score of other important

255

figures in literary, academic, and political life. As immigrants from the hinterland, we reveled in it.

The interesting year went by too rapidly. I was hired first for a semester under a Ford Foundation grant to provide "practical" instruction in politics for a special group of students under a plan of rotation which kept a balance of Republicans and Democrats. My immediate predecessor was the former Republican governor of Kansas, John Anderson, and he followed Neil Staebler, a Michigan Democrat who had served in Congress. I was the final lecturer in the series, and Dr. Havard scraped up enough money from his austerity budget to carry me an extra semester.

Two projects grew out of the discussion of contemporary political situations. I provoked the first by asking if the class might discover from our collective studies some method to utilize an untapped resource, "the experience and capabilities of former Senators and House Members." Encouraged by the students, upon my return to Washington I assembled several of my former colleagues to explore the possibilities of establishing a formal organization of that type, and today Former Members of Congress, Inc., is a going concern; it has more than five hundred members and regular meetings, one of which is held annually in the House Chamber with sitting congressmen as hosts and the proceedings carried in the *Congressional Record* as a tribute to "the old timers." I served as first president and was succeeded by Walter H. Judd, Minnesota Republican. We are officially regarded as cofounders of the organization, since the blueprint was designed by the two of us.

A grant from the Lilly Foundation enabled us to establish a Washington headquarters and employ former congressman Jed Johnson, Jr., of Oklahoma as executive. Under his competent and energetic direction our activities have been stepped up. The group is arranging for oral histories by all former congressmen, and participating in programs designed to acquaint the people with congressional procedures and problems.

The other project grew out of a discussion of the 1968 presidential campaign, just a year away. It was related to the candidacy of Governor George Romney of Michigan. I regarded him as one of the progressive Republicans who could be counted on to maintain the momentum for civil rights legislation. His interest in improving housing conditions and economic opportunities for the black minority were among the qualities that seemed to make him an acceptable Republican candidate for the presidency in 1968. However, there was one factor in his background that would be viewed skeptically and was a potential source of religious tension. I refer to the attitude of the Mormon Church (of which he is a prominent member) toward all members of the Negro race. His Church interpreted Bible passages as putting blacks under certain penalties and did not permit them to serve as priests, although admitting them to membership. By divine edict they were regarded as confined to a secondary role in society.

In classroom talks I mentioned the cleavages growing out of the 1928 campaign in which Governor Al Smith's Catholic faith was made an issue and pointed out that damage to our electoral processes would again result unless the double problem of race and religion could be disposed of in advance. Ordinarily, it would not be proper for a Democrat to concern himself with the problems thus posed for Governor Romney, but I justified my interest on the basis of the urgency of campaigns being free of racial and religious prejudice. We should do advance thinking to help prevent it. I feared that unless Governor Romney himself were aware of the potential dangers he would find himself a target just as Al Smith had been in 1928. We owed it to him to help in avoiding such a divisive issue.

I composed a carefully considered statement addressed to him, offering, as an admirer in the ranks of "the opposition party," to work within my party to allay unfounded fears and to join with fellow Democrats in disclaiming such appeals to racial and religious prejudice. I pointed out in the letter, however, that his own disclaimer would have to come first, and I invited him to draft a statement indicating that what was regarded as his own church's policy toward the black race was not his personal view, and to harmonize, if possible, his own liberal position and his church's pronouncements. I tried hard to avoid an affront to his church, and explained that I wrote with a sense of urgency regarding religious and racial prejudice, having gone over the text carefully with my students. Only one of my fifty students in the two classes questioned the wisdom of writing to the governor in this vein.

The letter was mailed late in the spring of 1967. Weeks went by without an acknowledgment. In July I was in Colorado for a series of lectures, and at Greeley our hosts at the state college gave my wife and me a sight-seeing tour. As we returned to the campus, one of the president's aides ran to the car to say, "Mr. Hays, Governor Romney is on the phone." My wife said, "Maybe he wants you for a running mate!" It developed, though, that it was not the governor but a top assistant, and he was calling to apologize for the long delay in replying. I said, "I do hope the governor recognized that I was trying to be helpful in a delicate political problem." "Have no concern on that score," he said, "Goodwill breathes from every word."

But when a letter from the governor himself finally reached me it added little to this expression of gratitude. I presume it was too much to expect that he would question, even by indirection, the teachings of his church. It was obvious that the governor deplored the suggestion that he might not be fully committed to the ideals of racial equality, and that he felt secure in his impressive record of accomplishments for minority groups. These accomplishments would be his buttress. Maybe so, but if he had become his party's nominee for president in 1968 I believe he would have found it necessary to reexamine his posture and devise a discreet and honest disclaimer. In the meantime, his Democratic critics would be exposed to the charge of bigotry. I like to think my letter might have been useful, and that the consequences, in terms of Democratic gains or losses, would not be nearly so important as carving out of the issues an extraneous and disturbing factor in a presidential race.

I fully expected that the great Mormon Church would, in its own way, relieve its members of this onus, and my hopes were fulfilled in 1977 when the elders proclaimed that a new revelation had lifted the obstruction to blacks being admitted to the priesthood.

One of the church's finest lay women, a prominent national leader, Esther Peterson, had previously sought my advice, knowing that I had been subjected to a somewhat similar situation in the fifties when several Deep South congregations of my own Baptist faith condemned my position in the Little Rock school crisis. "Can I afford to stay in the church and thus imply that I embrace the doctrine of castes in our Christian family?" she asked. I advised her to stay and to work within her church community for change. How much my advice influenced her I do not know but I was glad that she remained in her church to exert her influence there.

In January of 1968, Dr. James Ralph Scales, the new president of Wake Forest University, a prestigious Baptist institution in Winston-Salem, North Carolina, came to see me in Washington. His purpose was to invite me to come to Wake Forest to inaugurate what he termed the first Baptist Ecumenical Institute in the world. I was fascinated by the idea. It was to be primarily an academic institution, not affiliated with any Baptist convention, but was designed to symbolize the aspirations of many Baptists (though unfortunately we are perhaps still a minority among Southern Baptists) for closer relations with other church bodies. I gladly accepted, so in February Marion and I were established in a modest two-room apartment in the Alumni Building, which had been the home of one of the R. J. Reynolds family and given by them to the university.

I spent at least half of my time working on this exciting adventure. At one stage when there appeared to be a bit of criticism on the part of a few ultraconservative Southern Baptists, President Scales raised the question: Should the name be changed to something like the one used by the Baptist World Alliance, "The Commission on Cooperative Christianity?" I contended that the name should not be changed, that we needed a symbol in Baptist life of our determination to break through the old isolation barriers and become a part of the total Christian community. He quickly agreed, and I am happy to record this, since I feel that if we had allowed criticisms to force a retreat at that time it would have deprived not only the university but Southern Baptists as well of something that has come to be a very fine influence in Baptist life.

I continue to be a consultant although I am no longer the director, having passed these duties on to a dedicated instructor in religion, Dr. J. W. Angell, who in turn was succeeded by Dr. Claude U. Broach, longtime popular pastor of Charlotte's St. John's Baptist Church. And in 1974 Belmont Abbey College, operated by Benedictine brothers, joined Wake Forest University as sponsor of the institute, inaugurating a historic venture in Baptist-Catholic joint endeavors.

A number of conferences which I deem significant have been held with Catholic leaders, with other Protestants, with Jewish leaders, and with black Baptists. Invariably these conferences have been well received by students of religious movements. I am glad to add that we found our conference with Jewish rabbis and laymen highly productive in promoting an understanding between the two religious bodies that have great differences—they are important and profound—but the great contribution of an institute of this kind is through the dialogue, with honest confrontations of our differences. Thus we can promote goodwill and brotherhood.

In February, 1970, Governor Robert Scott appointed me chairman of the state's Human Relations Commission, and I was continued in that assignment by his successor, Governor James Holshauser, for more than two years. I thus became an active Tarheel. It was easy for me to establish rapport with North Carolina audiences. I had been making speeches in that state for about forty years, all the way "from Murphy to Manteo," and was personally acquainted with many political, church, and educational leaders. The similarity between my native state and my adopted state was striking.

Although there has been something of an erosion of North Carolina's progressive tradition since the days of Governor Charles Aycock, who at the turn of the century, launched a bold program in support of public education for both blacks and whites, there is a great tradition in that state and it has seen many worthy leaders. In later years we had such outstanding sociologists and public figures as Howard Odum and Rupert Vance, also Dr. Frank Porter Graham, president of the university at Chapel Hill, who served under an appointment by Governor Kerr Scott for about two years in the United States Senate; Clarence Poe, a great agricultural leader and editor of the *Progressive Farmer*; Hugh Bennett, who launched the soil conservation program in the Franklin Roosevelt administration, and many others. In the field of religion I want to mention William L. Poteat—president for many years of Wake Forest College. His career had significance for political scientists as well as churchmen. When the antievolution laws were being proposed throughout the southern states, this Baptist stood on the platform of a Baptist Convention and denounced it as an impairment of freedom and against the Baptist tradition. At that time there were more than a score of graduates of Wake Forest College in the North Carolina legislature—the highest representation of any North Carolina college or university—and practically all of these graduates followed their revered president in opposing the antievolution bill, a courageous course which was highly influential in its defeat.

Chapter 16 CAROLINA IN THE EVENING 1968–1974

It is only religion, reaching the ultimate solitude of the soul (for which our pleasing amiabilities are but husks), that can create the unpurchasable man, and it is only man unpurchasable by any society, that can create the sound society.
W. E. Hocking

I had assumed that the 1966 race for governor of Arkansas would be the last of my political ventures, but after only two years residence in North Carolina, some of the Democratic party leaders called on me to see if I would consider accepting the nomination for Congress in 1970. I declined.

One year after I went to North Carolina on a half-time basis to direct the affairs of Wake Forest's Ecumenical Institute (and it would have been a full-time assignment except for the institute's budgetary problems), Marion and I had registered as voters in Forsyth County. We made North Carolina our legal residence, not because I had political plans but primarily because there was so much activity in that state, and with North Carolina providing employment for me, I felt it was only right that we vote and pay taxes there. This also included joining the Wake Forest University Baptist Church, resulting in a rather unique posture for us as church members. The pastor, Warren Carr, a fine liberal leader, felt that membership in his congregation should not necessitate our severance of membership in the Calvary Baptist Church in Washington. So we were members of both for about six years. This dual membership made it possible for me to become a vice president of the National Council of Churches in 1969 (since the Calvary Church not only maintains ties to the Southern Baptist Convention, but it is also associated with the American Baptist Churches, affiliated with the National Council).

261

I greatly enjoyed my work on the Wake Forest campus, appearing occasionally in some of the classrooms for lectures on politics and related subjects.

In 1972 the request that I run for Congress, opposing the Republican incumbent Wilmer (Vinegar Bend) Mizell was renewed. I responded first by saying I would not be willing to go through two campaigns, the primary and the general election. This was disposed of easily because it was felt by these leaders that if I was willing to make the race against the popular incumbent, others would defer to me. While Mr. Mizell continued at peak popularity, I felt that I had, with a four-year residence, established a basis for a campaign, although my age (I became 74 in August of that year), would be a disadvantage. Democratic leaders encouraged me. I said to Senator Sam Ervin, "I am receiving some gentle pressure to be the Democratic nominee for Congress in this district." His reply was, "Well, let me apply some pressure that I would not term gentle. I am enthusiastic over your running and I hope you will do so."

This indicated that I had respectable support from the state leaders as well as from local Democrats. Actually, however, many of the Democrat leaders were rather passive that year because, as it turned out, it was a Republican year in North Carolina as elsewhere. It was decidedly a Nixon-Holshauser-Helms year—Holshauser being the successful Republican candidate for governor and Helms the Republican candidate for senator to succeed Senator Everett Jordan.

The mood of the electorate was fairly well summed up in a little story that was circulated about this time. It was said that when I spoke at one of the Rotary Clubs in the Piedmont area, a poll was taken and it produced 131 for Nixon and 8 for McGovern. The chairman announced, "This is Brooks and the seven waiters."

Sam Ervin and I were among the half dozen, and I cannot think of any others except Terry Sanford of statewide prominence, who publicly endorsed McGovern's candidacy. I was the only candidate in our district —except for a few local candidates—who endorsed the national ticket. It helped with only one group, and even in this case it was far from a perfect score. I refer to the young voters. Young people generally, at least those most active in politics, responded fairly enthusiastically to the McGovern candidacy and they were particularly grateful to me for showing up at the McGovern rallies and saying exactly what I believed about him. I remember in 1973 when I happened to run into George, my old colleague in Congress and fellow staff member in the Kennedy days at the White House, he thanked me and I told him something that I had said in a speech that he seemed to appreciate. "George, I said about you, 'Some of the true Methodist piety,' and I distinguished true piety from the false piety that sometimes gets into political rhetoric, 'of that little Methodist parsonage out in South Dakota comes shining through in his passion for peace and his deep concern for the poor.' "

A group of my young friends in Washington had decided to organize for solicitation of funds for my campaign and to help with research for speech material. One of Senator Henry Jackson's staff, Robert O. Sailer, was chairman and he rendered yeoman service in the Washington office. Just as in the case of the 1966 governor's race when perhaps half of all of my campaign funds came as a result of mail solicitation, chiefly from outside the state, so in the 1972 campaign for Congress the friendships across the country provided a great buttress in the financial struggles.

We decided that one way to counteract the impression that at seventy-four I might be past the age for Congress would be for me to walk across the district. This was not original, of course, since that ploy had been successfully used by the new senator from Florida, Lawton M. Chiles, Jr., and by others. The people of North Carolina knew little of these other experiences so I was given undeserved credit for an innovation. I began the trek at West Jefferson, at the west end of the district in Allegheny County near the highest peak of the Blue Ridge Mountains. One comment at the time was, "The Republicans will laugh you out of the race for walking downhill." My response was (and this was the last time the objection was heard), "Any candidate who is stupid enough to walk uphill when he could walk downhill is too stupid to go to Congress." Actually, in the 154 miles from West Jefferson to the county seat of the southernmost county, Lexington, there are up and down stretches, so one does not walk downhill merely because the end of the walk is 3,500 feet below the starting point.

It was a delightful experience; I was not exhausted on a single day. In fact, I remember only on one occasion, on one of the hot days, that I felt a warm soaking for my feet would be helpful. I wore out a good pair of shoes and in a fund-raising auction near the end of the campaign this old pair of shoes brought $45. I understand that the purchaser gave them to our mutual friend, Lawrence Davis, whom he wanted to become congressman later on.

I had an opportunity in these walks, which were from four to seven miles a day and in all kinds of weather (I walked seven miles on the hottest day of summer), to talk to people in stores, on the highways, at the crossroads post offices, and even sometimes to residents on their porches. I talked about any number of issues. While I could not reach very many voters with this plan, I nevertheless created some conversations in the various townships.

The Charlotte *Observer* sent a reporter, Brad Martin, to walk with me one day. He carried a notebook and scribbled my comments as we walked. He was curious about my political posture. "Mr. Hays," he said, "you are known as a liberal. Is that a correct description of your political philosophy?" *Liberal* was a fighting word not only in North Carolina but throughout the South in the 1970s, and while I did not want to dissemble, particularly on something as vital as a political philosophy, I had to do something besides provide a yes or no answer. I said, "I presume that an accurate designation would be *moderate* because I have advocated the spirit of moderation, particularly in racial conflicts and in the struggle for full civil rights, but I also have some pronounced conservative elements in my background." He inquired at once, "What are they?" In effect I said, "My faith in the institutions of America, and I mean the institutions of government, of education, and of religion. Moreover, hardly anyone is consistently either liberal or conservative." Remembering this principle from the late congressman Pettengill of Indiana, I said, "This dog, old Fergus here, that goes with me every day is a liberal when he's sniffing through the bushes looking for a rabbit, but a conservative when he buries a bone."

During the last week before the election Senator Ervin spent a full day campaigning for me. He walked through part of Winston-Salem with me, stopping at filling stations and stores to identify himself and to put in a good word for "his long-time dear friend, Brooks Hays." He made references that brought back recollections of President Harry Truman's first speech to the joint session of Congress the day after he was sworn in to succeed Mr. Roosevelt. President Truman said in that famous speech at the conclusion, "I pray as Solomon did for an understanding heart and that I may be a good and faithful servant of my people." Sam Ervin was kind enough to say that I had "an understanding heart." As I reflect on the favorable things that were said that year, I believe that I cherish this more than anything else, for I was indeed trying to understand the problems of the people of rural North Carolina. I studied urban problems as well, although I shall continue to think of North Carolina as basically rural, for the culture of the rural counties was carried into the cities as people pulled up their roots, seeking jobs and homes and opportunities in urban areas.

The climax of Senator Ervin's day with me came in an evening in one of the community houses of Winston-Salem. The room was filled to overflowing. The chairman and sponsors of the meeting concluded that the best strategy would be for Senator Ervin and me to avoid orating and entertain the people in what they called a "story swapping session." So for about an hour we swapped yarns, I being expected to tell Arkansas stories and Senator Ervin to indulge in North Carolina folklore. He started by saying, "Brooks, tell me an Arkansas story." He may not know until this day that what I gave him was a western North Carolina story. Confusion about the origin of stories in the rural South illustrates how folklore moves from one area to another. This was the story: A lawyer was talking to his client, a widow charged with killing her husband, and said, "Do you remember your husband's last words?" "Why shore," she said. "He wuz talking to me. He said, 'Go ahead and shoot. You couldn't hit the side of a barn.'"

I accompanied this with an authentic Arkansas story I had recently gotten from a friend in Washington. "Seth," said one of the mountain men to his neighbor, "I understand you and Nancy ain't been getting along so good." "No, we ain't. It's a case of plain old cuss fighting. She made me so mad not long ago that I hauled off and hit her. I never seen that woman for three days, but the fourth day, this right eye began to open up a little." "Yes," his friend said, "I know what you mean. Myrtle and I have had our troubles too. I got mad at her and hit her a hard blow. She give me the silent treatment. She never spoke to me for four hours, but she finally broke her silence." Seth asked, "What did she say?" "She said, 'Come out from under the bed and fight like a man.'"

Senator Ervin's stories were a bit more sophisticated and brought howls of laughter from our audience. He said that in his county—and I believe it was in the county seat, Morganton—a young lawyer fresh out of law school was having a hard time making a living. There was virtually no business for the young man. He was "starving." He dropped in at a church service one Sunday evening and the minister, knowing of his difficulties and hoping to help him, identified him as a lawyer and called on him to pray. The prayer went like this, "Oh, Lord, stir up much strife among these, Thy people, lest this, Thy servant, perish."

The friend from Washington in senatorial circles who was most active in my campaign was Senator Ervin's competent staff member Rufus Edmisten (currently North Carolina's attorney general), whose handsome face became familiar to American viewers of the Watergate hearings. It was about this time that a minister in North Carolina preaching on the fifth chapter of Matthew said, "As our Lord said in the Sermon on the Mount, and Senator Sam Ervin says he was right . . . ."

I was thoroughly prepared for a Republican victory in my campaign, although I was a bit surprised that I received only 35 percent of the vote. My friends said that my effectiveness could hardly be charted statistically, that I had given heart to the other nominees, and had helped to hold the party together in the "summer of its discontent." I ran far ahead of the national ticket, and in comparison with many of the county candidates made a good showing. I led the ticket, strangely enough, in all the black precincts—and I say "strangely" because there were a half dozen outstanding black candidates and they were vying with each other after the election insisting, "Next to Mr. Hays, I ran best among my own people." This was a gracious thing for the black candidates to say as a gesture of good will for me since they knew that I had made quite a sacrifice to accept the nomination and it was something that I cherished. When one of the very popular black candidates commented later that he was "prouder than anything" that he was second only to me, I said, "Well it's just as interesting to me that you got a bigger vote in many of the white precincts than I did."

I can insist on the basis of close observations of the 1972 campaign that the day is not far off when people will not think primarily of color in connection with candidates. The fact that the city of Raleigh elected a black mayor, Honorable Clarence Lightner, in 1974 indicates that old patterns were being discarded.

Congressman Mizell declined to meet me in joint debate. A forum sponsored by the Intercom Corporation was at a luncheon meeting and I represented the Democrats. Candidate Jesse Helms, the nominee for the Senate, represented the Republicans. An announcement was made by the Republican chairman that their fund-raising dinner would be held that very evening and that all were invited to come upon payment of the fee.

When my time came to speak, I feigned hurt feelings. I said, "It was very disappointing to me that I was not asked to preside at the meeting, since the Democrats used me as chairman last evening for their banquet, and I thought it would be so nice if the Republicans would do likewise." Helms replied in the same spirit and carried his end of the contest very well indeed when he said that what he hoped to do was to have me and Mizell as joint chairmen. With that pair in charge, he believed "we could have the biggest crowd since Notre Dame played SMU in the Cotton Bowl."

One interesting feature of the campaign was a result of the decision by one of the networks to have, as a preliminary to the All-Star baseball game, an appearance by Vinegar Bend and myself for comments. Marion and I were having our vacation in London when this occurred. We had received a trans-Atlantic call to see if I would be willing to participate in a pregame statement about the value of baseball and to say anything I wanted to say about the campaign against one of baseball's heroes, my Republican opponent. Of course I consented, and I thought that a good spirit of sportsmanship was maintained in our brief comments. I spoke in a friendly way of having been a fan of the St. Louis Cardinals which boasted of Vinegar Bend's prowess as a pitcher, and he spoke warmly of me as a personal friend.

The campaign was free of any sour notes except toward the end. It was said by the Mizell headquarters that my service on a fund-raising committee for Democratic senatorial candidates in 1970, which included Senator Frank Moss of Utah who had supported the anti-cigarette legislation, meant that I was "anti-tobacco." This posed a problem for me because I had determined not to appear in any false light on a matter so serious as health legislation. I had concluded when the campaign was young that I would not discuss the tobacco issue at all, except to say that in a transition period if processors and producers of tobacco should have to convert to other commodities they would have my very sympathetic support, and that I would work vigorously to supply government help for them. All we did to meet this rather explosive charge (the Fifth District of North Carolina is heavily dependent upon tobacco and, of course, cigarette manufacturing is basic in the city of Winston-Salem) was to point out that tobacco had nothing to do with my support of Senator Moss, that his opponent was just as "anti-tobacco" as Senator Moss. In fact, all Mormons—and both were Mormons—are bound by their church affiliation to oppose tobacco.

There was, however, one other thing in the Mizell candidacy that I vigorously disapproved of, and I publicly attacked the practice. The privilege of Congressmen of circulating material by congressional frank was abused by the Mizell committee. In the final phases of the campaign, the district was saturated with campaign folders mailed under the franking privilege from Washington, although, of course, an effort was made to give it the appearance of a nonpolitical document; they represented that it was "a report on legislation," but an examination of the content proved otherwise.

The redistricting action of the North Carolina Assembly had changed the district lines so that for the first time two counties of our district were new territory slated to become part of the fifth district in 1973. In other words, the residents of those counties would become constituents of the winner but he was not entitled to use of the frank since they were still in the district served by Congressman Jonas. However, the same plan of distributing these circulars, which carried full summaries of congressman Mizell's position on issues was distributed just as in the case of counties which he was then representing. This was obviously, then, not a service of constituents since they were not constituents. The franking privilege (which does have value in constituent service) can be purged of the objectionable features if Congress will only take a good long look at the excesses. Congressman Hechler of West Virginia and others were attempting to do this.

One issue that I did not elaborate on in 1972 was the busing question. My opponent had taken a categorical position and was vehement in denouncing court orders that required busing to carry out the Supreme Court decision of 1954. In Thomasville in Davidson County, at a small Democratic rally, I answered questions, but this issue did not come up. At the end of the meeting, however, a reporter asked my position on busing, and in an effort to avoid hedging, I said, "Let me begin by saying that some busing is absolutely necessary, not only to carry out the school integration decision but to equalize opportunities for rural and urban pupils." I said some other things about it, but my opening statement produced the headline. I said in the interview, "I oppose busing children inordinate distances, and in any event, we should not put our faith altogether for avoiding injustices in the Congress which cannot prescribe a national policy that takes all local variations into account. The local character of most conflicts of this kind makes it unwise for Congress to attempt a rigid nationwide policy." The headline in the newspaper was picked up in advertisements by my opponent—it went something like this, "Hays Favors Busing." I had no complaint, really.

I passed up an opportunity to use one issue, namely, Mr. Mizell's vote against granting congressional permission to the friends of Mrs. Mary McLeod Bethune, a distinguished black leader, to erect a statue in her honor in Lincoln Park in Washington. I had known Mrs. Bethune for a number of years, having served with her in the thirties on the Rosenwald-financed Commission on Interracial Cooperation. She was a noble woman and entitled to the respect of both races, as indeed, she had it in places where she was known. There were close to a hundred votes, however, in the House of Representatives against the erection of the statue. I did not use it because I did not need to press my advantage with the black community, and it was the kind of emotion-filled issue that would have tended to sharpen the cleavage between the two groups; but I make reference to it here because, as a friend of Mrs. Bethune, I want to register my strong feelings about the mistake of those who voted against honoring a great southern woman.

One of the Republican candidates for governor of North Carolina, Jim Gardner, declared during the 1972 primary campaign, "In politics, the only thing that counts is winning." I felt a powerful obligation to the young people in my own organization to take vigorous issue with this point of view, an all too prevalent sentiment. Not expecting any political returns for my position, I took his shocking statement as a text for more than one speech. I felt an urge to speak out on something so basic. Following my defeat, I looked back on the speeches with satisfaction. As an illustration of my contention that defeated candidates may contribute a great deal, I cited the legislative history of the proposed New River dams.

The question of constructing hydroelectric power dams on the New River appeared to be an issue early in the campaign, but it tended to dissolve when my opponent clarified his position by agreeing with me that the dams should *not* be built. Still, I continued my vigorous argument that thousands of acres of good farm land in two North Carolina counties should not be inundated.

Congressman Mizell's later pronouncements against the dams sharpened what I felt was a vague position during his four years as representative, and left me free to contend that he was impressed by the sentiment opposing the dams which I had built up. Further, I influenced Senator B. Everett Jordan to introduce a bill classifying the New River, second oldest river in the World, as a "wild and scenic river," the first of such proposals to go into the legislative hopper.

Two of the warm friendships that developed during the campaign were with Linda Carter, editor of the Wake Forest University magazine, and Lloyd Brinson, Duke University graduate and newsman, who took over the management of the campaign and in the early part of my trek across the district walked with me.

Not in politics alone, but in life generally, one needs a conditioning of mind and soul for defeats. This is illustrated by an incident in the life of Robert E. Lee. It was recorded in W. E. Woodward's biography of the general that, after the war, while president of Washington College in Lexington, Virginia, he cautioned a student about his grades and warned him against "failure." According to Mr. Woodward's story, "The student, with the brashness that only a sophomore can exhibit, said, 'But General Lee, you failed.' The great man quietly replied, 'But I want you to do better.' " Being a "loser" did not rob the general of the qualities that make for inner peace.

It was during these North Carolina years that the Chappaquiddick incidents took place. Marion and I were in London in the summer of 1969 for a short vacation trip. As a long-time friend and associate of Jack Kennedy and his brother Bob, and with a sentimental tie to the whole family, I was deeply concerned over the tragedy. We were too far away to get enlightenment on the details, although for two solid weeks the stories designed to clear up the mystery (some, I fear, obfuscated it) were on page one of the London dailies.

I was primarily interested in Ted's recovery from the trauma of the experience—the political impact was secondary. I was interested, not in the career of Edward M. Kennedy, a senator from Massachusetts, but in the recovery of morale for the brother of two dear friends, and for the welfare of an individual who was entitled to the support and counsel of friends who appreciated him. I wondered what I could do to help. Suddenly, I thought that perhaps my close and greatly admired friend, Arthur M. Schlesinger, Jr., one of the family's trusted confidants, might be interested in my impressions regarding Ted's decisions and future course. I wrote a longhand note to Arthur at once, with a firm feeling that I should present a point of view that might not otherwise get through the screening.

A letter from Arthur was in my mail when we reached Washington a week later. He said, "Your letter is marvelous. I have sent it to Ted." Soon afterwards, I had a fine letter of thanks from the senator, and within a few weeks an invitation to have lunch with him—just the two of us— in his office. Chappaquiddick was not mentioned in our conversation. Only a single topic was discussed—one of the consuming interests of my own political life—the future of the movements for justice and a better order of living for the South's neglected poor, black and white, rural and urban. Talk of political strategy for advancing these causes was muted. Content of programs, not maneuvering for advantages, engaged us.

My letter to Dr. Schlesinger was as follows:

> Dear Arthur:
> Marion and I were enjoying our vacation in Britain till Ted's misfortune occurred. With myriad friends we are deeply grieved. Since you are my bridge to the family I want, as an old teammate, to give you some impressions even though they may never meet any eyes except your own.
> Right now, we should be thinking only of Ted's morale. His right to a gratifying and happy life must be made secure. His future as a person of influence (no matter what transpires, much of it will be undamaged) is very important. In forgetting, at least for the time being, our hopes as political partisans, we can concentrate on helping a lovable human being endure the pain of a terrible experience.
> Cardinal Cushing is no more devoted to the concept of intercessory prayer than we Baptists are. I am not an orthodox Baptist but I do have a faltering faith in intercession and certainly a strong confidence in Tennyson's appraisal of prayer in this world's life so I shall continue to pray for Ted.
> A page out of my own history comes to mind. In 1933 my first election to Congress was blatantly stolen from me. It was confirmed by the state supreme court and I prayed hard for myself; but at the last stage, not for anything but a grip on myself. In substance, it was, "If I am not hurt inside, I cannot be hurt at all." This is true of Ted (even if there were actions that he might not be proud of). If he is not hurt inside he will not be hurt at all. He will always be important and always a symbol for something precious in American politics.
> Incidentally, my prayer in 1933 was answered. The theft of that

election swept away hope of being governor or U.S. senator or more, but it is not immodest for me to say that in saving myself I saved a modicum of the power which God gives each of us for his times.

This letter is already long enough. I may write more later on. I want to see you when we get back to the United States.

Marion wants to be remembered. We talk about you and the olden golden days quite a bit.

Chapter 17 DREAMS AND VISIONS

Your old men shall dream dreams;
your young men shall see visions.
Joel 2:28

A constituent once said to me, "Brooks, I was eighty years old yesterday; I am an octogeranium now." I have become that kind of flower myself and I want to savor every hour of every day remaining in my allotted years. I hope I can always have the two things that my friend Grove Patterson, editor of the *Toledo Blade*, said are the principal interests of life at this stage—"peace of mind and creative work."

Among the blessings that accompany old age are the enjoyment of memories of the lengthening past and the dreams of future achievements, plus some activities denied to us when making a living took so much time. Not until my recent slow-down have I had much time for the enjoyment of my mountain of memories. One of my fellow professors says that the human brain has ten thousand times the memory capacity of the world's finest computer. Most of my memories are pleasant. The most painful ones are those of situations in which I was not perfectly just to another person, but even the painful recollection of failures to act justly has value, however, since it seems to sharpen one's determination not to let the list of injustices grow. Mrs. Eleanor Roosevelt once said in an informal talk with Department of Agriculture employees when I was present that a man in his nineties told her that his chief concern was not in always being right but in always being kind.

I find pleasure in the memory of some insignificant happenings, such as the expression on my Grandmother Hays's face as she looked over her gold-rimmed glasses at me from our front porch the hot July day when, wearing my khaki uniform, I returned from Fort Sheridan during World War I. This ability to recall one's past exists, I presume, because a loving Providence intends that family and friends shall be happy influences until the end of life.

I remember buying watermelons sometimes for five and ten cents a piece. Recently when I paid seventy-five cents for a piece of pie in a San Francisco cafeteria, I recalled longingly the good five-cent slices of cherry pie at Bob Gholson's lunch room at the university in 1916.

I remember, not so pleasantly, my baptism in the little church at Russellville when I was twelve. It was in February and they had not heated the water in the big zinc baptistry, and when I stepped into the water my body turned blue; it almost made me want to be a Methodist!

Among the memories of congressional life I recall the visits to my office of some noted people, including General Coxey of "Coxey's Army" fame, and some from across the seas: Crown Prince Otto, last of the Hapsburgs, Martin Niemoeller, a victim of the Hitler persecutions, and the Reverend Tanimoto, pastor of the Hiroshima Methodist Church, who survived the nuclear bomb.

The creative work mentioned by Grove Patterson as a benefaction need not be abandoned with retirement, though there is wisdom in the statement of Dr. Henry Hill, long-time president of George Peabody College for Teachers: "One should not retire at sixty-five, but rather transfer to another activity which at that age he can do more competently."

And if physical incapacity makes work difficult or impossible there is consolation in the fact that creative thought, when conveyed to others, *is* creative work. My attention was recently called to a study of four hundred public achievements which indicated in this limited survey that 25 percent of these outstanding achievements were by persons over seventy, and 10 percent by persons over eighty.

As to the buttress of individual faith in old age, I can say that my thoughts about death are not more frequent than in earlier periods, but they are less agitating. I am not afraid to contemplate the experience, though sadness always comes with the realization that either Marion or I will, in all likelihood, some day be left without the companionship that has been the source of so much happiness, and that there will be separation from other loved ones.

I hope I will be as well prepared for the inevitable as an Arkansas judge, J. S. Maples, father-in-law of my colleague Congressman Jim Trimble. Jim described the scene to me. The judge had been sick a few weeks but was not thought to be near death. One morning he called for all of the family to come into his sick room. He told them that he had hoped to recover, but that he was convinced he would not get well, and he wanted them to know his feelings and to be as well conditioned as possible for his going. Jim said that it was a beautiful valedictory. When he finished acquainting them with his mental attitude, his wife, who always called him "Mr. Joe," a quaint southern practice still persisting in places, said, "Well, you're not afraid to die, are you, Mr. Joe?" He quickly responded in a clear, crisp voice, "Not a bit!" And fell back on his pillow in sudden and painless death.

Public men are often exceptionally sensitive to this concern for the other world, and their meditations on the subject may be as comforting as the words of a minister. For example, John Adams, aware that the end of his life was approaching, wrote to Thomas Jefferson to inquire if his old friend might strengthen his hope of an afterlife. He was not disappointed by the reply that came from Monticello. "Yes," wrote Jefferson, assuring him that there is a basis for such hopes. Happily, the estrangement of these two great men had ended at an earlier date. Jefferson's first inaugural address contained a reference to "God's desire for man's happiness *here* and his greater happiness *hereafter*," indicating that twenty-five years earlier Jefferson had such hopes. Jefferson's profound interest in the practical application of Christian principles was responsible for his assembling the sayings of Jesus in the familiar booklet "Jefferson's Bible."

The role of religion as comforter is universally accepted, but its equally vital role—the judgmental function—is often challenged, particularly, by public men, sometimes because individuals want to be free from moral judgments, and sometimes because believers in the status quo fear that critical moral judgments of the social order will produce changes that they do not want. But both the comforting and judgmental functions are essential. They are not competitive and both have history's confirmation.

Being free from the responsibilities of political office, I have in the retirement period enjoyed indulging my role in religion to a much greater extent than in the middle years. And it is delightful to be free from the suspicions by some of my opposition that I exploited religion for political gains. I like to think that this was not ever a substantial matter, but I suppose that all churchmen in public life encounter it to a greater or lesser degree. There are instances, of course, of dubious religious values being exhibited by members of our profession, but eventually the public learns how to apply the tests of authenticity in these situations. Exploitation may be subtle. It showed up in an off-election year talk by a southern office-holder that I listened to. He said to a group of clergymen, "I have never tasted an alcoholic beverage, the stain of tobacco has never been on my lips, and I have never uttered an oath." A few years later he was in prison for embezzling several thousand dollars.

When my name was first suggested for the Baptist Convention presidency, one minister said to another, "We don't want a politician for our president do we?" His friend replied, "Well, Brooks ain't enough of a one to count." One concern of my adult years has been to find ways of relating these two areas of life, religion and politics, without violating the American doctrine of separation of church and state. I believe with Thomas Carlyle that "a man's religion or his no-religion is the most considerable part of him," and that he should not suppress a normal and wholesome expression of faith nor stifle impulses to apply religious principles to human problems, merely because he carries political responsibilities.

This is not a sectarian approach—sensitive religious leaders of all faiths recognize that our Christian principles have governmental implications. This fact inspired my friend Rabbi Julian Feibelman of New Orleans to make the following response to a young Baptist's question, "Do you have any message from a rabbi for a Baptist youth conference in Oslo?"

"Yes," said this Jewish leader, "tell your friends to go home to work hard for a Christian world. If the world in which Hitler came to power had been in reality and not just in name a Christian world, six million of my people would not have been done to death."

My work with students and my other activities in the educational world during retirement have given me a new understanding of education's reassessment of *its* role in modern life. As a member of two college boards, I shared the feelings of most trustees that student life during the sixties was about to become decadent. This was an illusion. The rebelliousness of that period finally passed, and it might have passed sooner if we, the trustees and the administrators, had been able to harness the idealism and serious-mindedness that many student leaders possessed. It was largely a result of their work which finally sealed off the violence and irresponsibility of the few who threatened the entire structure.

My experiences as visiting professor at three state universities, and assembly speaker and seminar director at 282 other institutions, has given me confidence in the moral solvency of American student life. Every area of society will reflect this quality in the next generation, and politics will be one of the major beneficiaries. The teaching profession, therefore, continues to lure me.

When Sir Thomas More advised Richard Rich to be a teacher instead of a politician, Rich protested, "But who will know about me?" Sir Thomas: "Your pupils, your friends, God. Not a bad public, that."

It will be a great day for the world when religion, education, and politics recognize that the three constitute a tripartite responsibility for the redemptive and humanizing forces in this earthly existence. Politicians will be expected to avoid cant and pretension, and not many will fail to do it. Religious leaders must bring enlightenment on the valid claims that the poor and disadvantaged have upon us, and if able to do it competently, link Church life to the government's legitimate and essential activity in housing, food, and child care. The educator must accept a part in the legislative processes. The educator and minister, with the media, are really forerunners of law and public policy, a concept well stated by Sir Henry Maine: "Social opinion must be in advance of the law, and the greater or less happiness of the people depends upon the narrowness of the gulf between them."

All must recognize that power resides in the people, and that the destiny of popular government depends upon popular education and popular devotion to justice and equality. There are occasional lapses in our national standards and it compounds our problem of putting down cynicism (described by Henry L. Stimson as "the only deadly sin"). And if Oscar Ameringer were still living perhaps he would say to the skeptics, "I didn't intend for you to take it all as literal truth when I said, 'Politics is the art by which politicians get money from the rich and votes from the poor under the pretext of protecting each against the other.' " The democratic ideal is not served by the class appeals, explicit or implied. The demeaning of the intellectuals or of the poor or of any group for purposes of building a power coalition of affluent and favored elements in society is not only against the Judeo-Christian faith but also against the American governmental traditions. Moreover, if American democracy remains healthy those appeals will bring only temporary advantages to the tough recalcitrants who are now flexing their muscles.

There are many hopes for our country and the world that I will not see fulfilled, but young people around us will see many such hopes realized. I have this confidence, not because I believe God will intervene to save us from folly, but because of my faith in our avoiding folly and pursuing a philosophy to hold the human family together. Many thoughtful Americans expect that a number of privileges and advantages of favored groups will be yielded in the interest of stability and justice and in a wider sharing of our affluence. Access to resources and equality of opportunity are the imperatives. Idealism of an authentic and historic character must displace materialism and political expediency. These may eventually be posed as political issues just as in the situations in which the evils of slavery and segregation required clear mandates in the past.

The two-party system as now operated will not automatically produce such options. We should, as legatees of a powerful religious faith, resolve to move in whatever direction that faith leads even if it should produce painful changes. Tennyson left us words to ponder:

> Our little systems have their day.
> They have their day and cease to be.
> They are but broken lights of Thee,
> And Thou, O God, art more than they.

American philosophers have thought in the same vein. Emily Douglas, wife of Senator Paul Douglas and daughter of Loredo Taft and former member of Congress from Illinois, has echoed this idea. I like these somber words attributed to her father, the famous sculptor: "The time will come when it will be regarded as wrong for some to possess so much more than they need, when there are so many who possess so much less than they need." I asked Emily if this was correctly quoted, and she replied as follows: "I know exactly the quotation you are speaking of, and my father certainly used it. I have a list of some of the quotations he used and it runs like the one you quote. Unfortunately, he does not note an author, which could or could not mean it was his own, but I always associated it with Teddy Roosevelt. He also used two other quotes along the same lines. One was Spinoza who said, 'For myself, I am certain that the good of human life cannot lie in the possession of those things which for one to possess is for the rest to lose, but rather in things which all can possess alike, and where one man's wealth promotes his neighbor's'; and another attributed to Ratcliff, which was, 'Not money, but the life which a community provides is its real wealth.' "

In crisis periods such as the Great Depression of the thirties the words of Aristotle have more than ordinary significance: "Politics is the chief of sciences, since it alone has the power to allocate the always scarce resources of any society to the various elements of that society." But there is much to buoy our hopes. America's leadership role in the world places special obligations upon us, but we must not regard the air we breathe or the soil we live upon as having a chemistry that produces supermen and women. We will be able to make no contribution to the redemptive forces in an unstable world unless we demonstrate a deep concern for the whole human family. We may cherish the distinctive qualities in our national character and history without being chauvinistic, but national humility requires us to acknowledge that other cultures have had a big part in producing American ideals and aspirations.

In 1955 Walter Lippmann wrote eloquently in the *Atlantic Monthly* of the Western World's need of "a public philosophy" to hold society together. He pointed out that freedom of religion and thought was assured by denying to both state and church a monopoly in the field of religion, philosophy, morals, science, learning, opinion, and conscience. He added, however, that those who produced this condition were adherents of a public philosophy! "They knew the world could not get along without it," Lippmann added.

There is an affinity between law and theology that appears in our public literature. It was beautifully documented by Cicero, who, speaking of the same problems centuries before they were treated by Lippmann, compressed it into these words: "True law is right reason, everlasting and unchanging. It does not differ for Rome or Athens, or for the past, present or future, but one unchanging law shall be for all peoples and all times. That law cannot be repealed by any legislature nor can we be relieved by any statute of the obligations which it imposes, and we need not look outside ourselves for the true expounder of it." I like to believe that if Jesus had been in Cicero's company when it was uttered, he might have said, "Blessed art thou, Cicero, for flesh and blood have not revealed it unto you, but our Father who is in Heaven."

Thus, the spiritual and moral basis for a free society is found in the universal forces of justice and liberty and love. The great adventure of politics is merely to bring man's laws into alignment with the divine or natural law. It is that simple. If sacrifice and suffering are to be experienced let them be accepted without rebelliousness and with the inner satisfactions that an identification with humanity's yearnings and hopes supply.

In my own adjustment I am helped by recalling the contents of a telegram from Bill Bolton, a member of our New Orleans Baptist Seminary faculty at the time of my 1958 defeat, growing out of the Little Rock integration crisis. I looked at the orchid-bordered message on a congratulatory form, and thought, "This poor fellow has misread the returns; he thinks I was reelected." But he had not misread the news. The wire read: "Jesus constantly made the point that we gain by giving, we win by losing, and we live by dying. Congratulations on your victory."

Those are not hard lines to live by. They are the guidelines of happiness and peace and the hope of this world under whatever name they be proclaimed. In the belief that my defeat was a partial atonement for all of my mistaken judgments and acts of weakness, I am among the happiest of defeated candidates. And with what I believe is a rational interpretation of the telegraphed words, I will try to think in terms of gaining, winning, and living, and will carry with me to the end the words of my father, who at age eighty-five said, "A man's dreams should not die till he dies."

THREE POEMS
BY BROOKS HAYS

TO A PATIENT WIFE

Pain and remorse o'ertake me now
   As I recall our marriage vow
And think of things I did not do
   That might have lessened toil for you.

For routine chores I'd no desire.
   I was loath to build a warming fire,
To fix the roof or hang a door,
   To sharpen knives or sweep the floor.

Your food delights I never earned.
   The kitchen tasks I neatly spurned.
Too busy often screens to mend;
   Instead poor rhymes and prose I penned.

The babies' shoes I seldom tied.
   I only shared with you the pride
In things they did I'd never taught.
   Unearned, the happiness they brought.

Grandchildren now are growing fast—
   They'll ask you to appraise my past.
Be tender, dear, my faults conceal.
   Please make my phony virtues real.

I could have learned, had I not known
   One art, for which I'm famed alone:
You can be sure that loving you
   I never learned, I always knew.

1956

PRAYER FOR A WIFE ON A TRANSATLANTIC FLIGHT

O Thou who guides the angels' flight
    And watches thunderstorms above
Look for the flying ship tonight
    Whose wings sustain the one I love.

Please, Lord, her timid heart assure
    That faith in laws of sea and sky
Which built the vessel will endure,
    And thus keep clear the pilot's eye.

Should adverse winds the structure strain,
    She would not weaken faith in law
By asking Thee to intervene
    While I would pray, "God mend the flaw."

Yet in another mood I pray
    Not for Thy hand beneath the wing;
But for Thy presence on her way,
    Full confidence and Peace to bring.

London, England
1963

TO A BLIND COUSIN

Should angels gently touch your eyes
To dispel with mystic power
The darkness that surrounds you,
And I should have my wish to be
Among the first to meet your gaze,
You would not see me;
You would only look upon
The simple structure where I live.
Had you been curious about the contours of my face,
Your sensitive fingers might have traced them,
But this would not be me, me you had already seen.

Your sighted friends speak to each other
Of the beauty of your countenance.
They also recognize the profounder beauty
That finds expression in your gift of music
Your power of love and understanding
Your joy in elemental things,
Warmth of the sun,
The fragrance of the lilac bush.
But clearest proof is the revelation
Of an uncomplaining, unrebellious soul.

So, dear Alice, my fretfulness
That you are sightless shrinks
In contemplating things you see
And love and revel in.
My hopes mount up that greater powers of vision
Than either you or I have ever known
Will some day create breathtaking
Scenes of grandeur,
Not registered on retina or lens,
But by the powers of comprehension
Only God can give.
I crave meanwhile to have

286

Your gift of gentle speech
And the kindness which your unconscious gestures
Do each day reveal.

6/2/69

Index